STONE COLD

LEN OPIE IN VIETNAM

ANDREW FAULKNER

STONE COLD

The extraordinary true story of LEN OPIE

AUSTRALIA'S DEADLIEST SOLDIER

ALLEN&UNWIN

SYDNEY·MELBOURNE·AUCKLAND·LONDON

First published in 2016

Copyright © Andrew Faulkner 2016

Allen & Unwin
83 Alexander Street
Crows Nest NSW 2065
Australia
Phone: (61 2) 8425 0100
Email: info@allenandunwin.com
Web: www.allenandunwin.com

Cataloguing-in-Publication details are available
from the National Library of Australia
www.trove.nla.gov.au

ISBN 978 1 74237 378 2

All maps by Keith Mitchell, except Map 9 (by Fred Fairhead)
Index by Puddingburn
Set in 12/17 pt Minion Pro by Newgen Knowledge Works, India
Printed and bound in Australia by SOS Print + Media

20 19 18 17 16 15 14 13 12 11

*With acknowledgement of the Len Opie diaries,
faithfully transcribed by Len's comrade-at-arms
Vic Pennington.*

CONTENTS

LIST OF MAPS

LIST OF ABBREVIATIONS

3RAR—3rd Battalion, Royal Australian Regiment
AATTV—Australian Army Training Team Vietnam
AIF—Australian Imperial Force
BCOF—British Commonwealth Occupation Force
CFL—Cease Fire Line
CGS—Chief of the General Staff
CHQ—Company Headquarters
CMF—Citizen Military Forces
CO—Commanding Officer
CORDS—Civil Operations and Revolutionary Development Support
CSD—Combined Studies Division
CSM—Company Sergeant Major
DCM—Distinguished Conduct Medal
DSO—Distinguished Service Order
ICEX—Intelligence Coordination and Exploitation Program
KOSB—King's Own Scottish Borderers
KPA—Korean People's Army
KSLI—King's Shropshire Light Infantry
LCI—Landing Craft, Infantry
LVT—Landing Vehicle, Tracked
MATT—Mobile Advisory Training Team
MC—Military Cross
MM—Military Medal
NCO—Non-Commissioned Officer
NKA—North Korean Army

NPFF—National Police Field Force

NVA—North Vietnamese Army

OC—Officer Commanding

OIC—Officer in Command

PIAT—Projector, Infantry, Anti-Tank

POW—Prisoner of War

PRU—Provincial Reconnaissance Unit

PTSD—post-traumatic stress disorder

RF—Regional Force

RNF—Royal Northumberland Fusiliers

ROK—Republic of Korea

RSL—Returned and Services League

RSM—Regimental Sergeant Major

UNMOGIP—United Nations Military Observer Group India and
   Pakistan

VC—Victoria Cross

VC—Vietcong

WO—Warrant Officer

INTRODUCTION

A soldier cast in the image of Anzac, and revered in the post-World War II military as a peerless fighter, Len Opie stands alone in the Australian army pantheon. But he was also a paradox. Opie was a cold-eyed killer but drank nothing stronger than weak tea, never smoked and seldom swore. He killed people with his bare hands, a sharpened shovel and piano wire, but in civilian life he liked nothing better than a well put together model railway. Killing humans didn't bother him, but beware anyone who mistreated a prisoner or hurt an animal in his presence. He had loner tendencies and never married, but loved the company of women. He was a larrikin, yet went by the book—unless he decided the book was wrong. He set his own bar high and expected others to do the same. Those who crossed him risked the Opie evil eye, the pointed bone of his hex. Kill or be killed was Opie's mantra; he did a lot of killing and died of natural causes as an old man.

This, the first Opie biography, is based on his diary, a diary in which he revealed the army's many faults. His story is populated with as many fiascos and fools as it is bronzed heroes of Anzac. As such, Opie demolishes myths and demonises false worship. In this we see his unstinting devotion to the truth.

Born in Snowtown, South Australia, in 1923, Opie was an unremarkable student who revelled in the cadets and went train-watching when he should have been doing his homework. Through three wars, the quiet kid with the train set grew into one of the most decorated soldiers in the nation's history. He enlisted as soon as he was of age, and fought the Japanese in New Guinea and Borneo. But he wanted more, so he then signed up for Korea. Here he emerged from the ranks to almost singlehandedly seize a fortified hill, excel in the epic Battle of Kapyong, and, as a company sergeant major, play a key role at the Battle of Maryang San—which some call the Australian infantry's finest hour. He became the king of no man's land and master of the solo patrol. Opie was the digger at peak evolution—a brigadier said he was Australia's finest soldier in Korea.

As a member of the highly decorated Australian Army Training Team Vietnam, Opie was seconded by the CIA as it lurched towards Watergate. He shared barracks with Bay of Pigs veterans as together they trained South Vietnamese locals in the messy art of war. Opie's strict methods were not always popular with the South Vietnamese officers, especially the one who tried to kill him.

After training a Montagnard force formed especially to fight on the Ho Chi Minh trail, Opie was transferred to the CIA's black ops program—Phoenix. As the program's head of training, Opie was at the heart of the American counterinsurgency war in Vietnam. Some believe his CIA association continued after the Vietnam War.

Today, Opie is highly regarded by the generals he trained, and respected by the martinets he tackled. When he was finally discharged, to Opie's great disappointment, he had nineteen medals, a stack of friends in high places and a pining for the army that lasted the rest of his life. He was forever pleading to be let loose on the Russians or Iraqis or the Taliban.

When he died, in September 2008, the front-line diggers named an Afghanistan observation post after their mighty warrior. They called it the Major Opie OP.

They called him a Man of Sparta.

CHAPTER 1

A WARRIOR IN TRAINING

'It's easy to kill people but it's hard to teach people
to kill people.'
Len Opie

The list of Len Opie's medals reads like an infant has been let loose on a keyboard. Yet one of Australia's most decorated soldiers almost failed his first medical. The chest that one day bore nineteen medals was deemed too small for his height so he was classified A2 (Fit for Sedentary Duties Only) and banished to the orderly room to shuffle paper alongside a conscientious objector. Welcome to the army, Private Opie.

Leonard Murray Opie was born on 23 December 1923 alongside the railway tracks that carried South Australia's wheat to the world. The state—not yet 100 years old—relied on grain for its wealth and Snowtown thrived on its rail crossroads tucked just inside Goyder's Line of reliable rainfall. Len was a son for Glenn and Gertrude to go with daughters Molly and Patricia. Snowtown sowed in Len a lifelong love of the railways; he was forever at the station and by the age of five had a Hornby engine whirring around a four-foot circle of track. In 1928 his father's six-year term at the bank branch ended, so the family swapped Snowtown's wheat country for Minlaton, the self-proclaimed 'barley capital of the world' on South Australia's Yorke Peninsula.

No one remembers Snowtown's rail boom in the roaring twenties. They do know about the eight bodies found dissolving in acid in barrels in 1999. No one knows much about Len's passion for the railways either. Like his birthplace, Len is mostly associated with death and killing. But nothing is ever precisely as it appears. Seven of the eight so-called Snowtown murders were committed elsewhere, before the bodies were hidden in the town's bank vault. And there was much more to Len than the stories spread by diggers of his proficiency for garrotting enemy soldiers with piano wire. Here was an animal lover, a loyal friend and a gentleman—who just happened to be especially good at soldiering.

The country life suited young Len, who loved the outdoors and was so fond of animals he excused himself from the usual spotlighting hunts. An image of a shot rabbit in its death throes stayed with him for the rest of his life. 'The sight of that rabbit still haunts me,' he said years later. 'I've never shot anything other than people. But killing people never really worried me.'

Len was nine when his father was transferred to Adelaide, South Australia's capital, to take charge of a bank at the seaside in the working-class suburb of Semaphore. Len was different to the other kids, although not because he was a well-off boy sharing a classroom with children of wharf workers and labourers. 'He was the most unusual person of that age that I ever met,' his school friend Jack Cox said. 'He commanded respect from everybody. And he didn't know he was doing it. He didn't really make friends with anyone else in the class but they respected him. They respected him but they were a bit wary of him. He was extremely well mannered. It was always "Hello Mrs Cox" when he came to our house. He was brought up to be well mannered but it was just a very natural well mannered. He was like an adult but he was only a young person.'

Len progressed to St Peter's College, Adelaide's most prestigious Church of England school. There the boys observed Anzac and Remembrance days in the school's Memorial Hall, a grand auditorium commissioned as World War I still raged but not completed until 1929. It was built to honour the 172 old boys killed of the 1114 who'd enlisted. It was only natural then that the school invested time and effort into its cadets; and there was not a more enthusiastic cadet than Len Opie.

The cadets at St Peter's College could not have had better leaders. Their instructors were mostly World War I veterans, who passed on their experiences learned on the field of battle rather than the parade ground. Some were also regular army, professional soldiers who had remained in uniform after the war. Len said a Boer War and World War I veteran taught the cadets 'more about strategy and tactics than we were to learn in the army'. One officer, a 'dour unsmiling character', taught Len one of his most important lessons. 'His specialty was a lecture on withdrawal, and with a lot of shouting and waving of arms he preached: Get up and GET OUT! At all costs avoid a RUNNING FIGHT!'

His love of the railways continued to thrive alongside the burgeoning allure of the military; Len and his best mate, Adrian Thomas, father of the astronaut Andy (who is Len's godson), rode their bikes to North Adelaide to watch the trains crossing the Torrens into the Parklands. Soon the martial seemed to be edging ahead of the gunzel (as train enthusiasts are sometimes called). 'My father told me of one time running into Len in the school tuckshop, and Len proudly pulled corporal stripes out of his pocket to show my father,' Andy Thomas said. 'This was his first promotion and he was apparently very excited by it.'

After war was declared in September 1939, Len devoured newspaper reports of the fighting in Poland, then Norway, the Low Countries and France. He drew up battlefield maps dotted with pins of the opposing armies. It filled in the time until he was old enough to join up (a sergeant gave him short shrift when he presented at a recruiting depot at age seventeen). After Japan attacked Pearl Harbor and Malaya, Len volunteered to help prepare defences along the South Australian coastline. Forget Singapore harbour, the Japanese were apparently eyeing off Adelaide's Henley Beach! The army subsequently sent Cadet

Lieutenant Opie a letter of appreciation for his diligent toil digging
trenches and rolling out barbed wire. Ever the student of military
tactics, Len was unimpressed with the fortifications. 'As we pointed out
at the time, there wasn't much point in digging trenches on the beach
without any way to get into them from the landward side.'

After completing school Len found work as a clerk with the respected
old Adelaide transport firm the Adelaide Steamship Company. Now
growing into manhood and earning a good wage, Len showed no
interest in late nights or boozing or girls. As he later said, 'All I wanted
to do was get to the war. I didn't worry about girls. I've got two loves in
my life, war and railways. So if I'm not with the railways I liked to be
in a war.'

At eighteen, Len was old enough to serve in the Australian
Militia—the force of conscripts allowed only to defend Australia or
fight in its territories—but not the all-volunteer 2nd Australian Imperial
Force (AIF) that had fought so gloriously in the Middle East and so
gamely against the steamrolling Japanese. So after enlisting in January
1942, he had to bide his time in the militia until he could transfer to the
AIF once he'd turned nineteen.

Initially Len and the army seemed like oil and water. Yes, he had
excelled as a cadet, but before he was called up by the militia he had
applied to the Royal Military College, Duntroon, in Canberra. He
was rejected after apparently failing the entrance exam. It was a blow
that he believed became a blessing over time. 'The best thing that ever
happened to me was that I didn't get in,' Len said in later life. 'My
impression of Duntroon [was that] they take a lad and teach him to
be an infant, [and] a lot of them don't need much instruction so I was
never sorry that I didn't go to Duntroon.'

Throughout his army life Len railed against martinets and parade-
ground heroes. Before he was even sworn in he encountered a World
War I sergeant who ordered Len and his fellow recruits to march from
their tram into the Showgrounds. 'We were civilians, you know, we
could have told him to go and chase himself.' A pattern had been set.

Len and his fellow recruits were first sent to a camp on the outskirts of Gawler, 45 kilometres north of Adelaide. Len felt the camp, Sandy Creek, was aptly named—he described it as 'just a big sandpit'. The soldiers slept eight to a tent. 'With a hurricane lamp and eight sweaty bodies on the ground amongst all our belongings, equipment and weapons it was hardly conducive to gracious living.'

His A2 medical classification consigned him to the orderly room, where he befriended a conscientious objector who was 'treated like dirt' by another World War I sergeant. 'He wouldn't carry weapons but he'd do anything else and of course they gave him every dirty job and he was a very nice fellow really.'

After a month or so the army decided to shut Sandy Creek; the recruits would march 30 kilometres through the Adelaide Hills to the main army training camp at Woodside. Len's A2 rating meant he was considered too frail to march so he was sent to the mess to scrub grease from pots and pans. One glance at the fatty sludge made up his mind—he fronted the commanding officer (CO) who gave him permission to at least try the march. 'We started at midnight on a Saturday, marching for the usual 50 minutes in the hour and before we had gone more than a couple of miles people started to drop out,' Len wrote. 'We were marching in marching order, pack on the back, haversack on the side, full water bottles, all weighing about 50 pounds and it was a hard slog. As the weaker (and smarter) ones fell out, they were collected in trucks and ferried to the Chain of Ponds oval where the remainder arrived about 0600 next morning for breakfast and a rest. "Breakfast" was my initiation to bully [beef] and biscuits. One third of a tin of bully and three dog biscuits was the standard army ration throughout the war. The bully had an abiding taste with gobs and strips of fat mingled with the meat and the rock hard biscuits, completely tasteless. To drink, we had water. After breakfast we settled down for a couple of hours rest and it was decided that because of the high casualty rate, we would all be trucked to Woodside where we arrived about mid-morning.'

Those who did not drop out were rewarded with a 'guided tour' of their new camp; that is, another route march. The shirkers had their turn the following day. But Woodside was considered a palace after Sandy Creek. The men of 3 Infantry Training Battalion lived in huts with electric lights, although palliasses—sacks stuffed with straw—remained the army's bedding of choice. It was cold—the showers went out of action when the water froze in the pipes—but the camp was a comfortable place for the men to begin their training in earnest, although equipment shortages were an issue. Thompson submachine guns (SMG), colloquially called Tommy Guns, were produced but only a select few were allowed to fire them, and then only two rounds. Len thrived in an unarmed combat course taken by a 'hard and fit' sergeant who had earned a Military Medal (MM) at Gallipoli. The pair became friends; the friendship even survived a willing training bout that left Len hobbling for three days afterwards. Hard lessons were being learned that were to have grave consequences for future enemies.

Len soon talked his way into the Intelligence Section, where he set to work hanging and labelling aircraft recognition silhouettes in the lecture room—right up his alley given he was not only interested in trains, but also loved making models of planes, bridges, buildings . . . anything at all really. 'Len, he used to be keen,' fellow recruit Merv Fox said. 'He was keen right from the word go. If there was any job to be doing he'd get stuck right into it.'

Any job but boozing. Len never drank or smoked. Neither did Merv. Unsurprisingly they became friends and were amused when their mates staged a minor riot on one occasion after the canteen barman was caught serving the troops the slops mopped from the bar floor. '[The barman was] presumably counting on the fact that the customers would be too far gone to realise what they were drinking,' Len said. 'They weren't and they took appropriate action.' It was also no surprise that the recruits used their regular leave to go drinking in Adelaide. Len caught the train with them on Saturday afternoons and spent the night with his family before returning on Sunday night.

After two months at Woodside some of the men, including Len, learned they were to be sent to Victoria to continue their training. It was now summer, and an important task had to be fulfilled before they boarded the train for their journey across the border. 'Half-a-dozen chaps armed themselves with brooms and led one of our grubbier members . . . who had never been known to take a trip into the showers,' Len said. 'It was rather like the old bear-baiting days. The cold shower was turned full on and he was kept under for quite a while, at least going through the motions of getting clean.'

Len's new posting was 23 Infantry Training Battalion at Watsonia Military Camp—the present-day Simpson Army Barracks—on Melbourne's outskirts. His new company sergeant major (CSM) specialised in opening beer bottles with his teeth and the commanding officer excelled in censoring letters with a razor blade. 'Dear family' and 'Your son Len' was almost all that survived in one letter home.

One hot Saturday Len was ill—he probably had heat exhaustion after route march that morning—when he was ordered to take a soldier from the camp lock-up to the Melbourne Gaol. Never mind that he was technically on leave, let alone quite ill. The prisoner was handcuffed to a spindly tree, which he proceeded to climb in an attempt to escape his guards. He forgot that the tree forked into branches. 'All the way into Melbourne he kept up a stream of abuse at us,' Len wrote, 'by calling us "Provost bastards" and attempting to get away with resultant violence, which did nothing to help my sick headache. He kept this up all the way in to Melbourne, calming down only when the desk sergeant took his particulars but still muttering to him about the way we had treated him on the way in.'

Presently soldiers appeared at Watsonia wearing green uniforms that stood out against the rest of the troops' khaki. 'These apparitions in green, to become known as "grasshoppers", were a race apart,' Len wrote in his diary. 'Certainly they acted like veterans but they kept very much to themselves until one day we were issued the same outfit.' Soon the truth was revealed. The grasshoppers had been sent back to Watsonia after failing the jungle training course in Queensland. 'Anyone who failed the course was back-squadded into a special group and kept going until, in sheer desperation, they finally did pass.'

The move to the jungle training camp came soon after the new uniforms arrived. Len was in a draft of several hundred troops marched to Watsonia railway station and promptly marched back again because the army had fouled up the embarkation date. Never one to miss documenting an army stuff-up, Len noted the date—1 April. Once back in camp the men spent the rest of the day on an emu parade, 'a ritual clearing of the area performed by troops when those in authority can't think of anything else for them to do'.

They left the next day, and much as Len loved trains he did not enjoy being crammed into carriages with not enough seats for the complement of soldiers. Two-and-a-half days later they arrived at a Queensland railway siding, where they were directed to a 'congealed mass of fried eggs' and cold porridge left by unseen cooks four hours earlier. Finally they arrived in Canungra, 90 kilometres south of Brisbane, where they were directed to the standard eight-man tents and palliasses—without straw on this occasion.

Opened in November 1942, Canungra was supposed to churn out soldiers conditioned to the privations of the jungle battlefield. Training was 'tough and realistic in the extreme', the official historian recorded. Accordingly there were no ablution blocks; the Nerang River made do in place of showers. 'Amenities at [the] Jungle Training Camp were nil,' Len said. 'No YMCA hut, no canteen, no leave. Anyone making his way to the Canungra Village pub was quickly grabbed by the MPs.'

By early 1943 the tide in the Pacific War had turned. In New Guinea, the Japanese had been pushed back along the Kokoda Track to the north coast where they fought to the death at the cost of many Australian lives. The Japanese remained in strength at New Guinea bases such as Lae and Salamaua, but with US and Australian planes ruling the skies, attempts to properly supply or reinforce them were fraught. In March a convoy taking 7000 Japanese troops to New Guinea was wiped out by the Allied air forces. Every transport was sunk and at least 3000 Japanese soldiers perished.

Yet an enemy on the back foot is not an enemy brought to heel. Troops were needed to prise the Japanese out of New Guinea and then drive them back through the islands to their homeland. Canungra was a key cog in the supply chain. By May 1943, 500 troops were rolling off the production line each week.

Life at Canungra was hard. The commandant, Lieutenant Colonel Alex 'Bandy' MacDonald, was an uncompromising character whose edict to his instructors was, 'If you were in the firing line and needed a reinforcement, would you have him?' Len reviled a 'particularly obnoxious' sergeant who 'regarded anyone attending sick parades as malingerers'. He also apparently had little time for two instructors on loan from the commandos, Lieutenants Albert Westendorf and Reg Hallion. Westendorf was in the habit of ostentatiously wearing a 30-centimetre-long German Mauser machine-pistol strapped to his thigh, a spectacle that provided Len with much mirth.

During their exercises Len and his mates were set against an imaginary enemy and the very real foes of the jungle vegetation. 'Wait-a-while' bush was aptly named—any soldier caught by its barbs tended to hold up the column. Gympie bush, Len wrote, had flying hairs that dug into the skin, 'causing excruciating pain which can last for months—it has been known to kill horses and is known sometimes as the horse stinging tree'. There was an unconfirmed camp rumour that two soldiers died after falling into clumps of gympie. Then there was the lantana, sweet smelling and rampant; it stretched for miles at Canungra—'as thick as hairs on a cat's back and hundreds of acres of it', recalled Merv Fox. Len took a particular dislike to lantana, attacking it with unparalleled ferocity when the trainees were shown how to cut a jungle path with a machete. 'Len waited his turn to have a go,' Fox said. 'Then he'd walk up to the front to have another go. He was that keen.' According to Fox, Canungra was where Len 'really came to the fore'. It was where the others noticed his determination.

There was little tactical or weapons training, other than firing the .303 rifle; rather, the troops were relentlessly marched and drilled twelve hours a day, six days a week. Len nearly drowned during a river crossing that held portents for the men's looming New Guinea campaign. 'Fortunately there were several lifesavers at camp,' he wrote, 'and after I had gone down for what I thought was the last time—I remember hearing the music which drowning people are traditionally reputed to hear—I was dragged up on the bank and someone jumped on my back and proceeded to pump me dry. Each time I tried to turn and point out that I should be facing down instead of up the slope, I was pounded again until eventually I was allowed up.'

The course climaxed with a six-day bush bash on field rations. The 'obnoxious' sergeant tagged along but the platoon was so fit he ended up being the one on sick parade. 'We covered about 20 miles the first day and he pulled up so sore with blistered feet that we didn't see him again.' Those who emerged from the six-day trek passed the course, the rest were sent back to Watsonia as grasshoppers. Len passed, but an administrative error meant their next posting was delayed—the graduates had to do the four-week course all over again to fill in the time. Len's squad started with 48 men and finished with 24. One had shot himself and the chap who had been press-ganged into the showers with a broom back at Woodside was hospitalised after falling from a flying fox.

Meanwhile, the 7th Division, AIF, was recuperating in the Atherton Tableland in North Queensland after a rough time in New Guinea. Its infantry had inflicted Japan's first defeat of the war on land, at Milne Bay on the eastern tip of New Guinea. Later it had checked the thrust at Port Moresby in the Owen Stanley Ranges before joining the 6th Division in driving the overstretched enemy back through Kokoda to the sea. Here, both divisions lost heavily in eliminating Japanese resistance on the north Papuan coast. They arrived on the Tablelands victorious but also malnourished, suffering from malaria and in mourning for their dead mates. Their ranks were in sore need of replenishment; and a tea-drinking, shallow-chested, train-loving son of an Adelaide bank manager was on his way to join them.

■ ■ ■

Steel helmet cocked back and firing his Bren gun from the hip, Private Bruce Kingsbury strode to death, glory and a form of immortality on the Kokoda Track. For his gallantry in leading a charge against the Japanese swarming into Isurava, the 24-year-old real estate agent was posthumously awarded the Victoria Cross (VC) and mythologised by many as the man who stopped the Japanese strolling into Port Moresby.

Kingsbury and ten comrades comprised what is claimed to be the most decorated section in Australian army history. As well as Kingsbury's VC, its members collectively received a Distinguished Conduct Medal (DCM) and four Military Medals. Their 2/14th Battalion's fighting rearguard in August–September 1942 is at the heart of the Kokoda story. If Kokoda veneration is Australia's national religion, the 2/14th battle flag hangs in its greatest cathedral and Kingsbury is the order's most exalted saint. The 2/14th payed a high price for its glory. It lost 358 men killed or wounded in New Guinea after its 106 casualties in Syria the year before.

Never mind the 2/14th's glorious record, Len was singularly unimpressed with his posting. State allegiances were strong, and Len railed against being in a Victorian unit. He wanted to join the 2/14th's sister battalion, the South Australian 2/27th. 'In the usual army fashion we were shipped off to the 2/14th with the somewhat weak explanation that all the units had so many reinforcements after the Owen Stanleys and Buna/Gona campaigns that State units no longer existed, so we made the most of it,' Len said. After three weeks with the 2/14th, Len was given the choice of transferring to the 2/27th, but, trusting the army explanation that the units were 'all mixed up' anyway, he opted to stay put. He regretted this decision for the rest of his life. He and Merv Fox were bullied by their comrades in the battalion's C Company.

'Len and I were the only two South Australians to go to the 2/14th,' Fox said. 'I really copped it. Just because I was South Australian. "Bloody South Australians. How did we get lumped with you?" I was only a kid. To have that said to you. It affected me.' Fox applied for a transfer to the 2/27th but it was rejected. 'The mongrel company commander, as soon as he saw [the transfer form] he just tore it up. The bastard. I thought I was never going to get out of the show.'

Len wanted out too. Such was his dislike for his new platoon commander, the decorated hero of Gona, Lieutenant Hugh Dalby MC, he—and according to Len, the whole platoon—applied for a transfer to the commandos. 'It was obvious that Hughie was not very popular—not that it worried him,' Len said. The men were 'very smartly told to do what you're told'. Request denied.

The men were persecuted for their States of birth and also their faith, or lack thereof. Sunday church parades were compulsory. Before the service the Catholics were ordered to fall out for their own service. Then the Protestants were marched to the parade ground where the rest—anyone who declared to be neither Catholic nor Protestant—was lined up on the fringe and ordered to silently listen to the padre conduct his service. One man was made to produce his paybook for evidence of his claimed Muslim faith. There was none so he was made to attend the services. Len clashed with Dalby over the compulsory church parades; he felt the men should be allowed to attend church when and if they chose, not compelled to do so by the army.

Bullying by their platoon-mates strengthened the bond between Len and Fox, as, no doubt, did Fox's decision to quit smoking because of squabbles within the unit over cigarettes. Len had a different and slightly more charitable explanation for the bullying than Fox. 'The officers and NCOs [non-commissioned officers] treated us all right, but the people who didn't really were the reinforcements who'd arrived just a bit before . . . because we didn't know how long they'd been there. As far as we were concerned they were all heroes of the Kokoda Trail and in actual fact they'd only arrived a few months before we did. After Gona the unit was decimated and there was hardly anybody left, so they got a lot of reinforcements from northern New South Wales and southern Queensland. Everybody was mixed up.'

Len said he made only one close friend in the battalion. He was friendly with Fox, but his best mate was Lou Francis, a burly, bespectacled 'company runner cum medical orderly' who, scarred by a childhood abscess, answered to 'Scarface'. 'I never really mixed with anybody,' Len said. 'We were still eight in a tent and I was never friendly with any of those eight. We just lived together and that was it, but not as a compact group. We were all in the same section but we had nothing in common with each other.' Len's loner status was more down to his personality than a drill sergeant's advice that they not make any friends because their mates would soon be killed in battle.

The absence of any great camaraderie did not dim Len's enthusiasm for training, which continued to focus on river crossings and swimming. Hard lessons learned in Australia's early campaigns meant the battalion exercised in concert with aircraft, artillery and tanks— practices that also illustrated the Allies' growing matériel strength. The battalion was far better prepared for jungle fighting than it had been on the Kokoda Track. Khaki uniforms made way for jungle greens, steel helmets for slouch hats, and shorts for trousers tied off with US-style gaiters.

A plethora of games—Australian Rules, rugby and boxing, for example—were arranged to build morale and strength, further marginalising the sports-shy Len. An exercise with a US parachute battalion was followed by a rodeo and a race meeting, where the 7th Division commander, Major General George Vasey, adjudicated on the meeting's winners. The division so loved its leader it adopted the sobriquet 'Vasey's Cutthroats'.

The battalion welcomed a new commanding officer at Canungra, Lieutenant Colonel Ralph Honner, who was among the most experienced, brave and respected soldiers in the AIF, having fought with the 6th Division in Libya, Greece and Crete, where he escaped in a submarine three months after the German invasion. He emerged from the Kokoda campaign a hero, after rallying the 39th Battalion at Isurava then leading its fighting withdrawal alongside the newly arrived AIF, including the 2/14th. He again fought alongside the battalion at Gona. 'The battalion welcomed him as an old friend,' the 2/14th's unit history recorded. If young Len was looking for a role model, Honner was his man.

It was plain to all that the battalion was readying for a return to New Guinea. Len worried he would be left behind because, after suffering a slight injury in bayonet practice, he 'came up in big scaly sores all over'. He was packed off to see a skin specialist who told him he had psoriasis and was unfit for tropical service. 'I did not want to be accused of catching Gangplank Fever—a peculiar complaint which affects some soldiers when they find that an overseas trip is coming up. I asked him if he would park the papers somewhere until we had arrived in New Guinea so that I could at least get away and if the complaint got worse I could RTA (Return to Australia). He did better than that—he filed the report in the waste-paper bin.'

When the troopship *Duntroon* sailed out of Townsville on 31 July 1943, Len was on it. After an uneventful voyage, the 2/14th went into camp near Port Moresby and readied for the looming battle, wherever it would be.

CHAPTER 2

UP THE RAMU

'Nobody ever knows until the first shot's fired whether
they're going to be any good or not.'
Len Opie

At last Len was in a war zone. Proof was all around. The twin fuselages of a wrecked Lockheed P-38 Lightning sat under palm trees decapitated by its scything wings. Apparently the pilot walked away. Flying Fortresses and Liberators droned overhead each morning on their way to bomb Lae, Salamaua and Rabaul. One afternoon a stricken Fortress crashed into the sea. 'The next day we walked over to the wreckage,' Len wrote. 'We learned later that the only casualty was the tail gunner who was apparently trapped in the turret and drowned although the water was only knee deep when we were there at the same time 24 hours later.' Len's reaction to the poor Yank's demise was typical: he volunteered to go on a bombing mission as a replacement gunner. In what seems a highly irregular example of inter-service and international cooperation, the Americans occasionally allowed Australian soldiers to man .50 calibre machine guns in the bombers' bellies to spell the overworked US crews. Deploying his significant powers of persuasion, Len had a spot in the plane all lined up but the request was denied, again, as the Australians were on standby for action. Transport planes were already being loaded with jeeps and guns for the looming battle far inland.

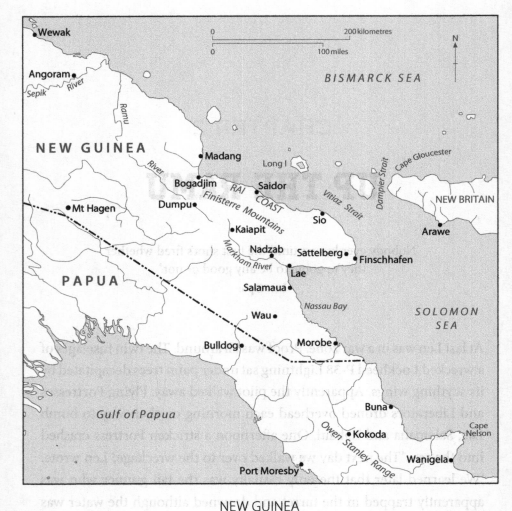

NEW GUINEA

The 2/14th was but a mere pawn in General Douglas MacArthur's stated aim of reclaiming eastern New Guinea by year's end. The plan was that the 9th Division—of Tobruk and El Alamein fame—would land on the Huon Peninsula and advance on the Japanese base at Lae, 30 kilometres to the west. Meanwhile the 7th Division would be airlifted to Nadzab in the Markham Valley, where it would attack Lae from the rear, and block any relief from enemy forces in the Madang area.

The bugle sounded reveille at 3.30 am on 7 September. Men of the 2/33rd Battalion filed into trucks and were driven to a marshalling area to await airlift from Durand's airstrip. At 4.20 am a Liberator took off from Jackson's strip and flew so low one Australian said he could have lit his fag from its flickering exhaust. 'Christ, it's going to hit us!' a digger yelled.

One wing clipped a tree and the plane crashed amid the 2/33rd's marshalling area, spewing more than 10,000 litres of blazing petrol over the Australians in their trucks. Three of the plane's four 500-pound bombs exploded. The infantrymen's grenades, mortar bombs and .303 rounds further fuelled the conflagration. 'The sounds of small arms, grenades and mortar bombs detonating and the stench of burning flesh will never be forgotten,' Lieutenant Colonel David MacDougal said 60 years later. Sixty-nine diggers—many who had survived the Kokoda campaign—were killed outright or died from their wounds over the ensuing days. Almost 100 were injured. A whole company wiped out. Photographs of the aftermath evoke a bushfire scene; tyreless rims supporting twisted metal, charred stumps and scorched earth; an Australian tragedy hundreds of kilometres from the front line.

Len escaped the inferno, as his tent was some distance from the strip. He blamed the disaster on African-American troops, who Len believed were angry at racism in the ranks and sabotaged the plane by putting sugar in its fuel tanks. He stated unequivocally in his diary and in an interview that 'Negroes' had been executed for the treacherous act. The source of his contentious charge is unknown, and probably never will be, for an inquest found nothing to support his assertion. 'The Court . . . is of the opinion that it will always remain a mystery. There is, however, evidence that it was unlikely to be the result of engine failure. The pilot had considerable experience and there is no evidence of any neglect on his part.'

Soon it was the 2/14th's turn to fly to the battle raging to the north. At 9.30 pm on 14 September the troops were rounded up, Len said, from assorted 'American picture shows, two-up schools and jungle juice depots' and shepherded to the airstrips where there was 'many a nervous look at the spot where the 2/33rd disaster had occurred'.

Presently they filed onto the transports—well drilled in this exercise after practising in imaginary planes scratched out in the dirt—and were flown to the battlefield.

'So that was the end of sleep,' Len said. 'For months.'

■　■　■

The storming of Nadzab was a grand display of US military might deep into the second year of its war. First, four dozen B-25 Mitchell medium bombers wheeled into the valley to disgorge 60 fragmentation bombs swinging from parachutes, before strafing anything that moved with the eight .50 calibre machine guns shoehorned into their noses. Then the A-20 Havocs zoomed in to lay smoke to cover the three battalions of US paratroops dropped from 96 Dakota transports. Twenty-eight heavy bombers pounded an enemy strongpoint between Nadzab and Lae, and the whole aerial armada of bombers and transports was shepherded by more than 100 Lightning, Thunderbolt and Airacobra fighters, prowling at three levels, the highest at 20,000 feet. More than 100 tonnes of bombs and nearly 50,000 machine-gun rounds saturated the area. And watching it all, in three circling Flying Fortresses, was General MacArthur and his staff. All that was missing was a band playing 'The Stars and Stripes Forever'.

It seemed over the top, and perhaps it was, for the landing was unopposed. The only casualties were two paratroopers killed after their chutes failed to open and one who died when he fell after he was snagged in a tree. Thirty-three men suffered minor injuries. Australian medics helped set the broken limbs while the engineers and pioneers readied the airstrip for transports bearing the 7th Division from Port Moresby.

Soon the Australians were leapfrogging the US paratroopers and surging down the Markham Valley to the Lae fortress, encountering stubborn Japanese resistance along the way. In one such fight, five soldiers of the 2/25th Battalion were killed by a well-concealed machine-gun nest. Acting alone and without orders, Private Richard Kelliher charged into the open and hurled two grenades into the post.

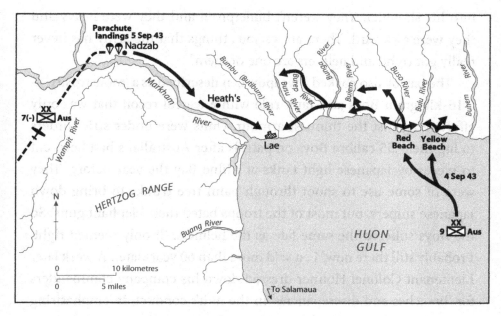

ATTACK AT NADZAB AND LAE

But some Japanese survived, so Kelliher returned to cover, grabbed a Bren gun, and attacked again. And again. On a fourth sortie he carried his section leader, Corporal William Richards, back to safety. Kelliher was subsequently awarded the Victoria Cross.

Len's 2/14th Battalion was one of the last of the division's units to arrive in the valley. When it touched down at Nadzab on 15 September 1943, the 7th and 9th Division pincer movement was squeezing the Japanese defenders at Lae. The heads were at a loss what to do with the 2/14th so decided to send Len and his mates on a glorified emu parade—a patrol in full equipment. The men had been ordered to wear their steel helmets at all times, 'so at the first stream we crossed we threw them all in', Len said. Designed in 1915 to protect its wearer from shrapnel, the standard issue steel helmet was fine on the Somme but was next to useless in the jungles of New Guinea, where artillery was an accessory rather than king of the battlefield. 'They were useless,' Len said. 'My platoon sergeant, he got two holes through his steel helmet into his shoulder. They weren't bulletproof and they were heavy and they were awkward. There are various things that the army has never really got right, and helmets are one of them.'

The patrol also packed a weapon Len described as a 'monstrosity'— a 16-kilogram Boys anti-tank rifle with a fearful recoil that was only effective against the thinnest armour. Units were under strict orders to lug their .55 calibre Boys on patrols after Australians had been cut to pieces by Japanese light tanks at Milne Bay the year before. They were of some use to shoot through palm tree trunks to bring down Japanese snipers, but most of the troops hated their 'elephant guns'. So the Boys suffered the same fate as the helmets. 'It only seemed right. Probably still there now,' Len said more than 60 years later. A week later Lieutenant Colonel Honner dressed down his company commanders for 'breaches and discrepancies' in the unit's conduct, in emphasising particularly 'the action of dumping gear'.

The vanguard of the 7th Division found Lae littered with dead enemy soldiers but otherwise deserted when it entered the shattered town on 15 September. However, it was far from safe. Soon the men were diving for cover from swooping US fighter-bombers. The soldiers frantically arranged anything white into an X—'forward friendly troops' and then a Y—'you are hitting our troops', to no avail. If that was not enough, shells, so-called friendly fire, started exploding, as no one had told the 9th Division artillery that the 7th Division had captured the objective. Finally the planes withdrew and the guns fell silent; at the end of it all Lae had been taken at a cost of 547 Australians killed and wounded. At least 1500 Japanese had been killed.

But what had happened to the rest? A captured document suggested the enemy had slipped through the gap between the Australian divisions and was making a dash for the north coast. The race was on to catch more than 10,000 Japanese soldiers before they could regroup. The fresh 2/14th was scrambled into the mountains to head them off—at last Len would see the action he had so craved since enlisting more than a year earlier.

Quickly the battalion filed into the jungle, each man carrying three days' rations, ammunition, a groundsheet, gas cape, mosquito net and personal gear—more than 30 kilograms all up. Thankfully the Boys rifle and helmets were no longer a problem. After being held up by innumerable creek crossings, they camped at the foot of a mountain range in jungle so thick not a chink of moonlight penetrated the canopy. Most of the men had never seen action, so it was a trigger-happy crew that settled down for the night. The unit diary recorded prosaically, 'Private Mohr of D Company was accidentally wounded during the night.' Apparently he had been answering a call of nature. 'It was black and you couldn't see in front of your hand,' Len said. 'He was wandering around so somebody just shot him. It was the first night, you know, just nerves.'

They climbed into the ranges the next day and spent a more comfortable night in kunai grass on the summit. In the morning they plunged into the Busip River valley and soon heard firing up ahead. D Company had been ambushed, and three men were down. The Australians took cover. One man grabbed his head. His mates thought he was done for, but the bullet had passed between his ear and his skull—leaving only a red scorch mark. Did he long for his helmet rusting back in the creek?

A Company readied for the gathering fight. In his haste, one soldier dropped his Owen submachine gun and it discharged, the bullet hitting company runner Frank Finnigan in the groin. While he was a rifleman, not a medic, part of Len's role was to carry medical supplies, including morphine. His mate Lou Francis also carried a pouch of medical gear, including the section's only syringe. Len and Lou rushed forward to administer first aid, arguing about who had the morphine needle. It mattered not, for the bullet had smashed into Finnigan's stomach. He was dead within minutes. Len went back for help and when he returned his comrade was lying beside the track, a handkerchief over his head, his grave already being dug. Len wrote that 'poor old Finney' was 'about 40', but the official record has him aged 29. Twenty-nine-year-olds seem about 40 when you are only nineteen. D Company's unseen fight up the track fizzled out. The battalion history recorded, 'Pte Frank Finnigan of A Company was killed during this engagement.' Again the official record did not tell the full story.

The 2/14th was fording the fast-flowing Bunzok River when orders arrived recalling it to the Nadzab area. The bulk of the enemy had escaped so the unit was needed for the advance up the Markham Valley. Speed was of the essence, with tragic results. Len wrote, 'In the rush, one of our section, George Hubner, fell off the bridge into the river and was swept away. "Cactus" Retallack, brother of our platoon sergeant, Joe, tried to run down the bank to save him but the undergrowth was too thick and the current too strong.' Hubner drowned.

Len's company was yet to see an enemy soldier but had already lost two men—one accidentally shot dead and one drowned—and another accidentally wounded. And all for nothing. The Japanese had slipped out of the trap.

As the unit regrouped at Camp Diddy, about 15 kilometres from Nadzab, the reason for its withdrawal became clear. The Japanese who had escaped Lae were joining a group that was advancing from Madang on the north coast. The Australians were being sent to meet them in the vicinity of Kaiapit, further up the Markham Valley. The 2/6th Independent Company—a commando unit—was dispatched to seize the village and its vital airstrip. The commandos had orders to move quickly. They fell upon the village in an old-fashioned charge against an entrenched enemy. After a sharp fight, the Japanese fled, leaving 30 dead. The commandos held off counterattacks before fixing bayonets to drive the enemy away. When the fight was over, more than 200 Japanese were dead. The Australians had lost fourteen men.

In the first six months of the Pacific War the Japanese had seemed invincible. As historian Peter Brune has written, the spell was broken at Milne Bay and on the Kokoda Track in the second half of 1942. Spells and curses are no match for well-trained and supplied Australian commandos. When a US general learned of the great victory at Kaiapit, he flew in a plane load of treats—soft drinks, sweets, cigarettes and books—for the exhausted commandos.

Len was in for a shock when the 2/14th landed at Kaiapit. 'We learned that our old foes Westendorf and Hallion had both been killed, the former on the 19th and Hallion the following day.' Westendorf was killed leading the initial charge. 'I have visions of him waving that great Mauser,' Len wrote. It appeared Len did not mourn his old instructors. Nevertheless, 'his men killed eleven Japanese where he fell', the official historian wrote of Westendorf, who, like Hallion, was clearly a courageous man in spite of any failings claimed by Len.

Japanese dead lay all around, and Len was appalled to see a comrade setting to work prising gold teeth out of the corpses. 'I am glad to say that the gold proved to be amalgam.'

The battalion spent three days improving the Kaiapit position and patrolling before joining the brigade's 'sprint to the west'. The Markham Valley was a broad and relatively flat expanse running north-west between the Finisterre and Bismarck ranges. It was covered in kunai grass with patches of trees along watercourses and palm clumps around villages. It was hot and humid but the going was much easier than the mountain fighting generally associated with the New Guinea campaigns. In the early days of the advance the brigade encountered only enemy-delaying actions while the Japanese bought time to prepare defences in the mountains. Len marvelled at the 'daily parade' of high-altitude Japanese bombers 'glittering silvery white in the sunlight' on their way to pound Nadzab.

The force of 3000 Australians streamed up the valley, outflanking enemy positions in the mountains as they went. The diggers moved swiftly. Curiously the battalion historian said the tail of the column moved twice as fast as the head, the result of a concertina effect. 'The difference is caused by obstacles. The time lost by each man must be made up by the rearmost troops.' Soon the brigade reached the Markham's headwaters, including the formidable Umi River, which was crossed in two-man rubber boats tied together in groups of ten. 'Confidence was not exactly boosted by the engineers telling us that they had only lost three boats the previous night,' Len wrote.

The 2/14th took the point position, and to speed its advance was supplied by 'biscuit-bombing' Dakotas dropping bully beef and biscuits. Often the drops left the bully tins mangled and reduced the biscuits to powder. Len had an idea. To relieve the monotony he put his hand to bully beef pie. 'I carefully ground up the biscuits and mixed them with water to make a crust, then laid that on top of the bully in the dixie, already mixing some water with the bully,' he wrote. 'I put it over the fire to cook. Ten minutes later, "Shorty" Gwyther, my eating companion, who had watched the preparations with growing exasperation, reached over to retrieve his dixie of water, so he said, and knocked the lot in the fire which went out. There ended what could have proved to be a gourmet meal and I never attempted it again.'

Relations between Len and some of his platoon mates remained tense. There is some evidence to suggest he was still being bullied. On one occasion the men were about to tuck into a rare issue of fresh meat when Len was sent on an errand. 'I got back about six o'clock at night and I said: "Where's my meat?" And they said: "Well, bad luck about that, we've eaten it." And they gave me a tin of bully and I was so mad I ate the whole tin. And that's unheard of [as] normally a meal is a third of a tin of bully and three biscuits, and I was so mad I ate the lot, but I had a bit of tomato sauce with it.'

On 30 September the battalion, at the head of the advance, sent patrols into the village of Marasawa. The enemy had fled, leaving the area in a filthy state. The village was torched to cleanse the mess. According to Len, Honner had issued a general order banning fires. 'One of our chaps started to boil up a brew on the embers of a still burning fire when the CO came along and blasted him for disobeying the order and told him to throw the water out. This was to have ironic consequences a day or so later.' Finding enough water for the 3000-man force soon became a problem. Now the troops were where

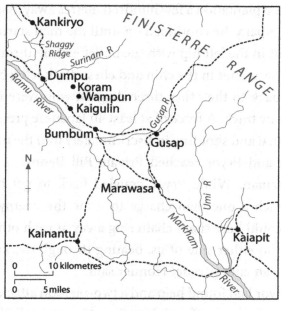

RAMU

the Markham Valley ended and the Ramu Valley began, although the change was imperceptible; the flat valley floor merely started draining to the north-west instead of the south-east. Len noted drolly the native name for the Ramu was 'Death Valley' because of the prevalence of malaria, dengue fever and scrub typhus.

Onward the columns marched, with the 2/16th on the left flank and the 2/14th on the right. On 4 October Honner sent A Company on a northern sweep to attack a village called Wampun, but it too was unoccupied. Mindful of recent defeats, the Japanese command was reluctant to be drawn into battle. 'There were a few shots fired but there was nobody to fire at,' Len said. When it was apparent there was no enemy to be found, Len and his comrades were instead ordered to head up the valley to look for water, as the supply situation was becoming desperate.

Meanwhile, Honner embarked on a water-hunting sortie with Sergeant Tom Pryor and three rankers. Heading into A Company's general area—so he thought—Honner saw men stripping leaves from trees in a banana plantation a few hundred metres away. Assuming they were his A Company, he continued on until the men started shooting. Honner was hit in the left hip with the bullet exiting through his right buttock. Pryor was shot in the chin and chest. Both left a blood trail as they crawled back to the other three diggers, who were further back along the narrow track. A force of at least 40 Japanese pressed forward, beating the kunai and shooting indiscriminately into the undergrowth. Soon Honner and Pryor reached Private Bill Bennet, a 28-year-old Townsville barman. While Pryor crawled back to get help, Bennet offered to launch a one-man charge to draw the enemy away from Honner. 'We could hear them chattering away at each other, and they marched past on either side of us, beating through the kunai grass—spread out like an emu parade,' Honner said.

By now, Pryor had found help and a two-platoon attack was quickly launched. The enemy suffered heavily—25 were killed—while the battalion lost five wounded, one of whom died the following day. Honner's unfortunate little sortie had inadvertently achieved what the entire brigade had not; it had drawn the enemy into the open. But Honner's war was over. He was one of the 2nd AIF's most vener-ated battalion commanders, but Len appeared unimpressed with his first CO. He was especially puzzled by how Honner had mistaken the Japanese cutting banana leaves for his own troops. 'Now A Company was a somewhat wayward child in the battalion, but why we should be doing that when we were patrolling is one of life's little mysteries. The official history states, "As they ignored his approach Honner assumed they were from McInnes's company." Well, of course they weren't.'

Len missed the firefight. When the first shots rang out he and his section-mates dumped their packs to run to the battle but they were too late. To add to the insult they were made to trudge back to get their packs. 'Our platoon commander had sent us out but he hadn't gone himself. And when we got back he and his little group had taken all their gear and moved forward about half a mile. And we said: "Where's our gear?" And he said: "It's back where you left it." So that's when we decided: "As far as we're concerned you can go; we don't want any more to do with you." We had to trek back another half mile to pick up all our gear and then go back again after dark, where his mob had already dug in for the night and got themselves a hot meal and everything. We were one hot and hungry section, having to eat a cold tea and dig in. So we decided we could do without him. No, we didn't find any water, either.'

As far as Len was concerned, the legendary leadership provided by the 2nd AIF's junior officers was a fallacy, a myth. Perhaps the section's open disobedience had something to do with the unnamed lieutenant's removal and replacement soon after Honner was evacuated wounded. Honner himself was replaced by a succession of temporary COs until original 2/14th officer and Syria and Kokoda veteran Phil Rhoden arrived back from a training unit to assume command.

The advance resumed the next day and after a hot and trying march the men were delighted to find the Surinam River running strongly. Their water woes were over. They bypassed the village of Koram, which was believed to be occupied by the enemy, and dug in north of Dumpu. Here they waited while the 9th Division seized Finschhafen on the north-east coast. Advancing behind its screen of fast-moving and hard-hitting commando squadrons, the 7th Division was ahead of schedule. It had covered 140 kilometres in eight days as the crow flies (although one digger pondered 'how far if the crow had military boots on?').

During the lull at Dumpu, one of the unit's chief scroungers, 'wily old bushman' Private Bill 'Yogi' Kerr, led two men into camp carrying what appeared to be a pig strung on a pole. Closer inspection revealed the 'pig' was a pair of trousers loaded with tropical fruit, and Kerr was the man who had supplied the trousers. 'To attempt any description of Yogi without pants, and with his thin legs bared to the mirthful gaze of his platoon, is too delicate a task for this history,' wrote the battalion's historian.

At Dumpu, four US scout and messenger dogs arrived to be trialled. They were adjudged to be 'highly trained' but 'did not stand up to fire' so apparently were dishonourably discharged. How dare the

dogs be scared of a bit of Japanese shooting! While the advance had
stopped for now, danger was all around. Lance Corporal Ian Langton
was killed in action on 6 October, and Private George Pottinger died
of the wounds he suffered during a sharp exchange of fire on a patrol
the next day.

Len gave an insight into the anatomy of an infantry patrol in an
interview with the Veterans' Affairs Department after the war. He
described in great detail how, in a company-strength patrol, the leading
platoon would deploy a forward scout followed by a second scout, then
the Bren gunners followed by the riflemen. A 'tail-end Charlie' brought
up the rear to guard against an attack from behind. The troops walked
at least five paces apart to limit casualties in an ambush. But not too far
apart. 'If you lose the fellow in front of you, you're in all sorts of trouble
because the next time you run into him you might think he's somebody
from the other side,' Len said.

Len was usually second scout and his principal role was to protect
the leading scout and to watch for his hand signals such as an inverted
thumb for 'enemy', and cupping a hand over an ear for 'stop and listen'.
A good scout had a keen sense of smell, too, as the Japanese smelled of
'unwashed bodies and sour rice'.

The men of the 2/14th were perpetually wet. Wet from the rain;
wet from fording the multitude of rivers and creeks; and wet from the
heat and humidity. Len found the army-issue groundsheet was next to
useless against the rain at night. Anti-gas capes, worn as ponchos, were
much more effective. 'The gas cape was impermeable,' he said. 'I've put
that on soaking wet at night and woken up bone dry in the morning.
On the other hand I've put it on dry and woken up soaking wet in the
morning, depending on the body heat, you see.'

At the end of a day's march the soldiers would dig rectangular
two-man weapon pits, which doubled as a bed. 'Some people didn't like
it because you were virtually digging a grave,' Len said. The Japanese dug
circular foxholes. On one patrol, A Company found one-man foxholes
abandoned so recently that almost every one had photos and personal

belongings spread on the parapet. 'They wanted some memories of home as they prepared to die,' Len said.

In the first week of October the Australian command decided it was time to leave the relative safety of the Ramu Valley and tackle the enemy in the Finisterre Range. The South Australians of the 2/27th climbed into the mountains to cut the Japanese line of communications to their outposts along the range. The 2/14th followed in support, with the bulk of the unit on flat ground at the foot of the range. A platoon commanded by Lieutenant Nolan Pallier scaled a hill that led to a razorback spur. Presently the enemy was seen on a hill at the top of the precipitous ridge, and Pallier's force was ordered to attack. Before they set off, the enemy position was shelled by 25-pounders, raked with Vickers machine-gun fire, and bombarded with mortars. Len described how a mortar bomb 'cooked off', that is, misfired. 'The charges must have been damp because the bomb came out of the barrel with a pallid "woomph" instead of a bang and rose about 30 feet in the air before falling back to the ground. Of course the act of exploding from the barrel is required to arm a mortar bomb, but now was not the time to query technicalities and the whole gang headed for a strategically located weapon pit. I wasn't the first in but I certainly wasn't the last because about a dozen others must have landed on top of me. The bomb plopped into the soft earth and just sat there.'

Oblivious to the pantomime in the mortar positions below, Pallier's platoon readied for the attack. They ate a hurried meal, checked their weapons and no doubt said their prayers. The attack would go in along the razorback—the heads had decided there was no other way, and Brigadier Ivan Dougherty was demanding immediate action because the 2/27th was hard-pressed and running low on ammunition. Pallier's plan was to climb as close to the enemy's foxholes as possible under cover of the barrage. With some understatement, the official history recorded that 'the situation confronting the attacking platoon . . . was not encouraging'. It had, in fact, all the makings of a suicide mission.

The platoon members certainly thought so. 'We realised that . . . there would be many of our cobbers left lying around before it was all over,' wrote Corporal John 'Bluey' Whitechurch, a veteran of Syria and the Owen Stanleys.

Out they went, clambering along either side of the narrow ridge while 25-pounder shells screamed over their heads to crash with unerring effect on the hill ahead. The machine guns and mortars added to the din. The Japanese did not dare pop their heads out of their foxholes into the storm of lead. To add still more firepower, Pallier left a small group to give covering fire from a small pimple halfway to the objective. The platoon crept forward, unmolested by the fire they knew would surely come.

The 25-pounders fell silent. The Vickers and mortars continued for a while before they too stopped just as the platoon neared the crest. Then a shot, and another. Soon it was a fusillade. The Japanese sent down a rain of grenades, but most rolled harmlessly down the hill, sometimes helped by a well-aimed boot. Only one man was wounded. The Aussies hurled their own grenades, then leapt at the enemy. 'One of our chaps gave a shrill, bloodcurdling yell that startled even us, and was partly responsible for some of the Japs running headlong down the hill in panic,' Whitechurch wrote. They tumbled over the sheer drop to their doom.

The fire was fiercest on the right flank. Sergeant Lindsay 'Teddy' Bear and Corporal Ted 'Hi-Ho' Silver, both veterans of Syria and heroes of Kokoda, confronted a foe emerging from a foxhole. All three fired simultaneously. All three missed. Bear, already wounded, lunged forward with his rifle and pitchforked the unfortunate enemy soldier over the cliff with his bayonet. He quickly bayoneted another. The hill was won.

Bear was wounded three times in the fight. He was awarded the Distinguished Conduct Medal to go with the Military Medal he'd won at Isurava the year before in an action in which he was also wounded three times. Silver and Whitechurch—another 2/14th original—received

Military Medals. Kingsbury was also from this section, whose eleven original members were awarded a VC, DCM and four MMs. The platoon lost three men killed in the attack and another five wounded, including Pallier. Two of the dead lay back on the pimple. It seemed the enemy was intent on silencing the covering fire when the attackers swarmed into their position.

Len was in a group of men sent up to carry down the dead. He came across a corpse all 'bluey grey' with a 'waxen sort of pallor'. Len could identify him only after checking his paybook. 'I'd had a disagreement with him a couple of days earlier,' Len said in an interview many years later. 'That's when I learned that I could put the hex on people because having hexed him he ended up dead this day, so that's one of those things.'

The interviewer was stunned. 'How can you put the hex on somebody?' he asked.

'If you don't like them you put the hex on them,' Len said. 'I found out it worked. It's happened a couple of times so perhaps I've got the ability, I don't know. It might be coincidence.'

After the Pallier's Hill attack Len's war took a turn for the worse. He was evacuated with malaria, one of scores of men from the battalion to succumb to illness. Back in Port Moresby his hospital bed was next to a scrub typhus ward. Each morning he counted the pairs of boots set outside—one per man who had died in the night. By the time he had recovered, the Ramu Valley was secure and the 2/14th was back in Port Moresby. Gary Cooper turned up to rally the troops. Len said it was 'not very successful as he didn't do anything but say "waal you guys" and eventually he was booed off the stage'.

The battalion was sent home for a break; Len spent some of his furlough in hospital recovering from his malaria. When his leave ended the army sent MPs to the Opie residence to arrest the deserter— who was actually on a troop train heading back to the war. Another army bungle. A rare written apology followed, and the black mark was struck from his record but more foul-ups were to come.

War, like babysitting, is sometimes described as utter boredom interspersed with occasional moments of terror. So it was for the next year as training resumed in Queensland. New Bakelite grenades issued to the troops were considered inferior to the trusted Mills bomb, until one disembowelled a soldier. During another exercise a man was given half a stick of gelignite to simulate an artillery explosion; it blew his hand clean off. Len was nearly blinded by an explosion in a booby-trap drill. These horrific incidents aside, camp life was dull. The most important decision among the ranks was whether to drain a 9, 18 or 27 gallon keg around the nightly campfire. Somehow Len managed to survive the grenades, gelignite and his boozing mates to receive the gold watch his parents sent up for his 21st birthday. It was promptly stolen by a comrade while Len was showering. 'That was the 2/14th Battalion,' Len said. 'That was my experience of my so-called mates about to risk their lives together.' Presumably another hex was cast.

Intensive training in amphibious landings was less dangerous than handling the latest grenades and gelignite, but was almost as unpleasant. When most of the platoon was throwing up in their landing craft, the poor wretches were chided by Len's old foe Hugh Dalby for fouling the boat. 'If you want to be sick, at least do it over the side!' Presently, Dalby was also doubled over on the deck. All the while two other diggers ate greasy bully beef with their fingers while teasing their miserable mates.

As they piled in and out of all different types of landing craft the men speculated as to their next destination. Malaya? Sumatra? The Philippines? The army had proved a disappointment for Len. He had barely seen an enemy soldier in New Guinea. As the stubborn Japanese were prised out of island after mountain bunker after coral atoll, Len was running out of time to prove his worth as a soldier. His chance came in the last seaborne invasion of the war, where the AIF unleashed all it had learned in five years of war into one last grand show.

CHAPTER 3

BALIKPAPAN

'A Company were the bad boys of the Battalion . . . 8 Platoon
were ditto in the Company.'
Len Opie

In mid-1945, a year after D-Day, Len set sail in the biggest Australian invasion force since Gallipoli. The entire 7th Division would storm the Borneo city of Balikpapan; more than 20,000 fighting troops plus another 10,000 in supporting arms, all beneath a mighty air force and carried to the beaches in an armada of 200 ships. It was the last major seaborne assault of the war and was launched even as the atomic bomb parts were being assembled for the US's coup de grâce in a few weeks.

But why invade Borneo, 4700 kilometres from Tokyo, when Japan was on its knees and was about to turn up its toes? The answer was politics. The Australian government rejected the entreaties of its generals to abandon the invasion, which clearly would do little to defeat an enemy whose cities were being burned to a cinder by US firebombers, and who had a new foe—Soviet Russia—to its north. If earlier landings at Tarakan and Brunei seemed a waste of 369 Australian lives—including arguably the greatest digger, Tom 'Diver' Derrick, killed at Tarakan—the Balikpapan operation seemed idiotic, given the objective was a 'ruined oil refinery and a virtually abandoned seaport'. At least one high-ranking officer feared a bloodbath of Gallipoli proportions.

Japan was done for but Australia bent to General MacArthur's will, which was to gain valuable practice in beach landings ahead of Operation Olympic—the invasion of Japan itself. MacArthur also wanted to use the idle AIF troops to restore the Netherlands East Indies government in the name of US prestige, freeing his GIs to find death and glory in the merciless drive to Japan itself.

The Australian generals' opposition to the invasion seemed to steel them to ensure as few of their men as possible were killed in the attack. The whole show was planned to the finest detail. As they steamed into battle, the troops were briefed thoroughly by officers waving batons over giant aerial photos and sand models of the beaches. Len liked nothing better than a good model, and he said the ones on his ship were 'beautifully constructed . . . the fog of war was finally lifting'. The preparation extended to a thorough softening up of the target; more than 5000 tonnes of bombs were dropped on Balikpapan ahead of the landing. When MacArthur saw the plan for the attack he reportedly ordered the bombardment be tripled. Three aircraft carriers were sent to support the invasion fleet that sailed from Morotai on 26 June. Len, on a Landing Craft Infantry (LCI), in typical fashion, talked his way into a job as an anti-aircraft gunner on the deck so he could escape the stifling heat below.

Len spoke for many when he recorded his dread about the attack. When the war in Europe ended, the UK government revealed that if the Germans had invaded Britain in 1940 they would have been met with blazing oil on the beaches. Balikpapan was an oil port. Desperate Japanese soldiers and lots of oil was a dreadful prospect. All ranks were allowed topside before Len's ship made its run to the beaches. This was no doubt a deliberate move by the brass to ease troubled minds, for there was no wall of burning oil, only palls of smoke billowing from a pulverised city and ruined refineries.

As the landing craft prepared to dash for the shore, rocket ships loosed off a deafening barrage and bombers zoomed in for one last low-level strike. It is a wonder there were any targets left given five cruisers and fourteen destroyers had been shelling the enemy non-stop for two hours. The first wave of troops clambered into their Landing Vehicle, Tracked (LVTs), a boat-meets-tank amalgam also known as an 'alligator', and dashed for shore under a deafening bombardment. Liberator bombers made one last run as the surviving Japanese gunners opened up with airburst, only to invariably be immediately silenced by the navy.

In another Gallipoli parallel, the Australians were landed in the wrong place ('as usual', Len said). Like Gallipoli, some claimed it was a deliberate late change of plan. Whatever the explanation, no one in the first wave was killed or wounded. As was their wont late in the war, the Japanese allowed the enemy to land unopposed before opening up from pillboxes and dugouts inland. A stiff fight was under way when Len landed 30 minutes after zero hour. His LCI, a small ship of 234 tonnes, steamed past destroyers blazing away with their 5-inch guns, the gunners kicking the smoking, ejected cases over the side. Len could not have been too perturbed; his vast collection of photographs includes shots he apparently took of the battle as his craft neared the shore. The ship dropped its ramps as soon as it touched sand. 'We were up to our chests in water, they didn't want to nudge in too hard in case they couldn't get off,' Len said. 'So they just eased up and we ended up soaking wet, and then we just flopped down on the beach waiting for orders to move up.'

They moved inland and soon MacArthur, Brigadier Dougherty and a 'retinue of perhaps 80 hangers on' arrived, whereupon a Japanese machine-gun crew sprayed the area with bullets. 'Even the Brigadier, no slouch himself under fire, ducked for cover, grabbing at the General to do likewise,' Len said. 'But MacArthur just brushed him aside and remained upright until he had seen what he wanted, then turned back. The remarkable thing was the number of his entourage who had suddenly discovered urgent business back on the beach so that when he arrived back, at least half of them must have been waiting for him.' MacArthur's many critics often labelled him 'Dugout Doug' for allegedly avoiding the heat of battle. So much for that, wrote Len.

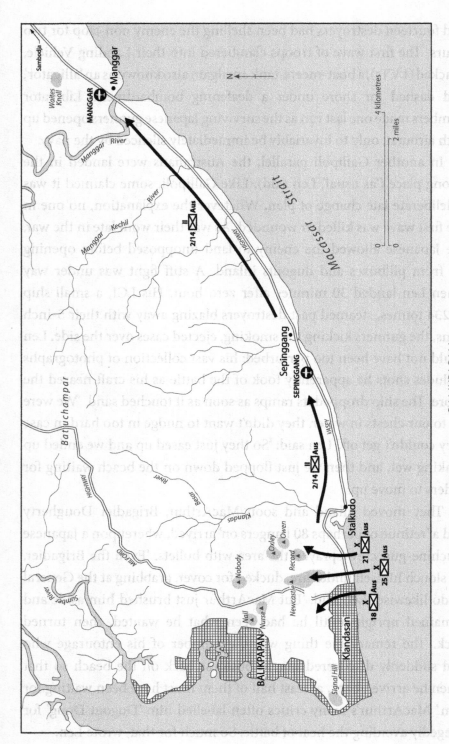

The landing had been a success. The division had met but was over-coming strong resistance on the left and in the centre of the expanding beach-head. The 21st Brigade's job was to secure the right flank then drive up the coast and seize two airfields. The 2/14th encountered only sporadic fire and fleeing enemy soldiers, but a commando unit sent to scout inland suffered heavy casualties in an ambush, fanning fears the enemy was keeping its powder dry. The battalion crossed a river then set up camp for the night. The burning refineries flickered and glowed in the distance and the men were troubled by no more than desul-tory fire after nightfall. That was no help to the unit's chiropodist and battalion original, Corporal Ken Clark, who was killed overnight. 'He was greatly respected, even by the roughest diamonds in the battalion for his deep spiritual faith and clean, Christian living and his death was a saddening shock to all,' the battalion historian wrote. But he gave no explanation for Clark's death and Len's diary contains only a prosaic mention of the incident. The 2/14th's unit diary is more revealing: 'Killed by fire from sentry post.' Friendly fire from a jumpy comrade by the sound of it. Usually Len would record such a misadventure. Perhaps Private Opie was especially sad and shocked by Corporal Clark's death, as he cried when shown a picture of Clark's grave decades later.

The battalion's B Company captured the first airstrip the following day against scant opposition. When would the enemy stand and fight? The men grew keener for action after they buried natives tortured and mutilated by the retreating Japanese. C Company leapfrogged to the head of the advance and pressed on to the larger strip, Manggar airfield, 10 kilometres along the coast. Covered by the guns of a US destroyer shadowing the advance, and with bombers and fighter-bombers a mere radio-call away, the battalion moved swiftly along the coast. The Japanese stopped momentarily at a small river but fled when Hugh Dalby's C Company showered them with mortar bombs and brought the navy's guns to bear. 'The Japs fired a few shots but did not wait for the bayonet,' the battalion historian reported. Snipers posted high in trees lining the main road were shown no mercy. One was brought

down by a rifleman at a range of 250 metres and another came down
'in pieces'—the mortar men knew their craft so well they could lob a
bomb onto a treetop. The advance resumed and presently the company
captured 'two fowls, two machine guns, a bicycle and a cow, but left
the cow'.

Soon it was the turn of Len's A Company to take point in the
advance along the coastal road, designated Vasey Highway in honour
of the division's beloved late general, who had died in a plane crash the
previous March. 'Highway was a courtesy title, because, although it was
bitumen, it was only one vehicle wide and completely potholed, but it
made for easy walking,' Len recorded. Potholed, and cratered too—a
C Company soldier had trodden on a landmine before A Company
took the lead. A river covered with a sheen of oil was forded and later
in the day the men were delighted when a partly demolished bridge
across a larger, crocodile-infested torrent was intact enough to allow
them to cross by foot. The men dispersed into an open formation and
advanced along the airstrip. They stopped at the end of the 1 kilometre
runway and awaited instructions—still there was no sign of the enemy.
Dougherty was with his forward troops and climbed the airstrip's
control tower to get the lie of the land. He was wearing his red brigadier's cap so if any enemy was around surely they would not neglect
so rich a prize. It was nearly noon and the troops decided it was time
for a brew-up in the open. The men had captured their objective in
just three-and-a-half days after advancing almost 15 kilometres along
the coast. 'There was a buoyant feeling of security,' the unit historian
recorded. 'The Japanese . . . had allowed the battalion to spread all over
the airfield without challenge. This was a good war.'

Len's section was nearing the end of the runway when all hell broke
loose. Heavy artillery, field guns, fast-firing cannon, large bore mortars,
machine guns—you name it, the Japanese on the high ground above the
Manggar airfield fired it that day in July 1945. The Japanese emerged
from deep, concrete-reinforced bunkers to plaster the enemy with
everything they had. An airburst cracked above Len and a comrade

fell, red hot shrapnel in his back. The forward troops scrambled into a revetment at the end of the field but Len was trapped in the open so had no option but to hit the deck. He was alone save for a panicky digger who started having visions of Japanese soldiers in their midst. There was nothing imaginary about the enemy soldiers seen scurrying to their guns at the end of the runway; they were quickly dispatched by the Australians sheltering in their ditch. Elsewhere the men of A Company found what cover they could in craters and drains. Seeing this, the Japanese gunners lifted their sights to the control tower.

There they wrought a terrible toll. Three artillery officers and a bombardier were killed or mortally wounded and several others wounded, including Major Gerry O'Day, commander of D Company. Despite the risk, Graham Thorp, a 25-year-old gunnery officer posted to coordinate the naval fire, climbed the control tower—a spindly structure that resembled the RKO Pictures motif, although the only flashing lights on this tower were Japanese airbursts—to direct counter-fire from the ships. The tower sustained two hits and one of its legs was shot away, but Thorp stayed at his post. Meanwhile, Sergeant Lindsay Ferguson, a 2/14th military policeman unimaginatively nick-named 'The Sheriff', broke cover to carry a wounded man across the bridge to safety. He was awarded the Military Medal, and Thorp the Military Cross.

Lieutenant Colonel Rhoden grappled with a thorny problem; how to silence the guns and dislodge a full battalion of the enemy on the high ground north of the strip. He decided to sit tight, pinpoint the positions, then bring to bear the massive ordnance at his disposal. He went about dealing with each gun in turn by concentrating his fire. The 2/14th unit diary called it 'weight of metal rather than weight of human lives to achieve an objective'. An artillery duel raged throughout the afternoon, with the 2/14th joining in with mortars and small-arms. 'The enemy had lost interest in A and B companies and concentrated his fire on the area of the tower and the bridge,' Len wrote. 'So we just sat and listened to the battle proceeding over our heads, unable to see anything except to our immediate front, and the day and the night passed that way.'

In the morning Rhoden unleashed his full firepower. The naval and land bombardment was supplemented with Liberator strikes. But the enemy's emplacements were reinforced with concrete and some guns were protected by steel shutters. A sole 6-pounder anti-tank piece was brought up and became perhaps the biggest sniper gun in history. It scored several hits from its hiding place near the river but failed to quell the fire. Three Australian-manned Matilda tanks were brought up on barges and landed behind the control tower. All three were immediately knocked out by one enemy gun. 'The Japs then began to mortar us and we could hear the rounds getting nearer to us,' Len said. 'Though fortunately almost one round in three was a dud and the others did no damage except to our nerves.'

A Company was withdrawn under the cover of darkness to positions near the bridge. Len and his mates slept beside water-filled foxholes vacated by D Company, which was sent forward to prepare for the inevitable attack.

On the night of the 5th, the 6-pounder was replaced with a 25-pounder field gun; its high explosive shells silenced two guns and wrecked some of the Japanese bunkers. In the morning the Japanese were introduced to a new and horrific weapon—napalm—that would become infamous in another jungle war twenty years later. Fourteen Lightnings smothered the hill with liquid fire and the Liberators came back for yet another turn. All up, 120 tonnes of bombs were unloaded on the enemy. When the infantry was at last called upon, on the afternoon of the 6th, Rhoden decided thirteen men were enough to take the main gun position. Thus warfare reverted to the time immemorial method of infantry seizing enemy ground. The men crept unseen to within 40 metres of the enemy. Lance Corporal Henry Waites shot a sentry and up the sodden slopes the men charged. A sapper carrying charges to blow up the enemy's emplacements was shot dead. Waites grabbed the explosives but he too was cut down. The diggers threw

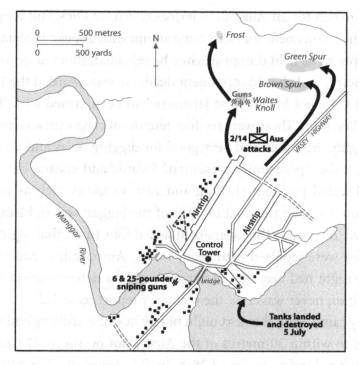

MANGGAR

their grenades, crested the hill then lobbed the dreaded phosphorous bombs into the enemy's dugouts. The feature was taken and about 50 surviving Japanese fled. It was christened Waites Knoll in honour of the brave lance corporal who died from his wounds. Two platoons were sent up to bolster the garrison. It was raining heavily as the men of the 2/14th braced for the inevitable counterattack.

It came soon after nightfall. Armed with petrol bombs, flame throwers, machine guns, small-arms, swords and spears, more than 100 Japanese fell on D Company in a banzai charge. Standing in trenches flooded to their chests, the men fired when they could; the rest of the time they were cleaning the mud that jammed their small-arms and heaving grenades into the darkness. They were alone; all communications with the rear had failed so for once there was no supporting fire. Shouting insults in English, some of the enemy made it into the trenches and hand-to-hand combat ensued. An officer wielding a sword was no match for an Australian bayonet. Private Dick Hill fought off two of the enemy before a third came at him with a spear. His magazine was empty so he held the spear while he reloaded, shouted 'get out you silly bastard', and shot his opponent dead. He was awarded the Distinguished Conduct Medal. 'The Japanese had been armed with "banzai sticks"', Len said. 'These were six-foot lengths of cane with an iron spear tip, roughly machined and very good for digging holes and no doubt, people, if the opportunity presented.' Swords and spears. For all the radio-directed pinpoint shelling and new weapons such as napalm, the infantry war in the final months of the biggest war in history had regressed 200 years. The Japanese attacked four times that night. Each time they were repulsed with heavy losses. 'Ammunition had run low and the night had been full of danger but their determination to hold the position never wavered,' the company report recorded.

They came again the next night but by now the artillery had ranged its guns to within 30 metres of the Australian positions. D Company fired from behind a curtain of 25-pounder explosions. More than 100 Japanese soldiers lay dead while the Australians lost five killed and five wounded. The Australian artillery was magnificent but an error by its or the battalion's officers left all but one of a twelve-man patrol killed or wounded by friendly fire.

Meanwhile Len was preparing to move. D Company needed a rest and it was A Company's turn in the firing line. The relief took place early on 8 July and after a quiet day Len and his mates were attacked by soldiers wielding shanghais. 'We were dug in for the night,' Len said. 'They'd come along, probably one, I don't know how many, but the ground was clay based and they'd just make little balls of clay and then flick them at you. They'd make enough noise that you'd hear something and wonder what it was and then after a while we realised that that's what they were doing. We had the choice of throwing a grenade at them which might or might not have killed them. In hindsight we should have done it but the other thing was of course it gave your position. When you throw the grenade, the spring striker lever springs up and it gives a twang anyway so it means they'd know where you are before you've even thrown the grenade. It gives your own position away so the easiest way is just to lie doggo, which we did and then of course they went away.'

By seizing and holding a toehold in the high ground, the Australians had silenced the knoll's two guns and bled away the enemy's strength by routing its counterattacks. But the Japanese held two spurs to the right and a small hill dead north of Waites Knoll. The next phase began with a relentless artillery barrage, more Liberator raids, napalm strikes and strafing. Six hundred shells rained down on the main feature, designated 'Frost'. Len's moment was drawing closer. At 12.30 on 9 July his platoon attacked Frost. It was unoccupied—all the Japanese were dead or had fled. Whether Len was disappointed or relieved to once again miss a fight is unknown as his diary entry is brief and matter-of-fact. 'And that was that, the battle for Manggar was over.'

Len might have been denied a fight but he was not going to miss out on the spoils. He set about carefully pouring the powder out of enemy shells and souveniring the base of a large casing for later use as an anvil. He helped himself to a briefcase containing a map and four Japanese flags. Thinking the map might be important, he asked Lou Francis to take the briefcase to the intelligence section, with strict instructions to return the flags to Len. 'I eventually received the empty briefcase and to the end of his life Lou claimed the flags as his,' Len said. 'In fact, 45 years later I heard that his widow had passed on the remaining flag to one of her daughters. I learned a valuable lesson there—the hard way!' No one was souveniring curious glass flasks that when smashed gave off a peculiar smell—many years later Len was told it was cyanide gas.

'The battle for Manggar airfield will go down in history as a magnificent feat of Australian arms,' wrote a sergeant who sent sanctioned despatches to the home press. The battalion diary said the unit's training had moulded 'an almost perfect fighting machine'. Both assessments are, of course, wrong. The battle, if it can be called a battle, was a great feat of US airborne firepower, although the Australian artillery played a key role. And while many skilful and brave individuals performed brilliantly, the 2/14th was some distance from being 'almost perfect'. Ken Clark would not have called it perfect. Nor would the men shelled by their own artillery. Despite its fine record and its glory in the Owen Stanleys, the 2/14th was regarded by some as the third-best battalion in the brigade. (As an aside, Len wrote that, 'A Company were the bad boys of the Battalion . . . 8 Platoon were ditto in the Company'.) Still, history is written by the winners.

After Manggar the battalion's war was a static affair with the occasional patrol. Even they were sometimes preceded by artillery bombardment. July slipped into August and the patrolling continued even as rumours of a new US super bomb started circulating. On one patrol 8 Platoon 'went off the map' and into a Japanese ambush. Bullets whizzed through the thick scrub and two went through Sergeant Sandy Perkins's steel helmet and into his shoulder. Len patched him up while the others returned fire. About twenty Japanese soldiers with two machine guns had the platoon well and truly pinned down. The scrub was too thick to throw smoke grenades to mark targets for the artillery so Lieutenant Norm Gugger simply pulled the pins and they withdrew under the cover of the smoke. They stopped on the beach, where it seemed like the whole battalion was swimming or playing volleyball.

Signs mounted that the end was near. The platoon was recalled from another patrol because the brass wanted to avoid unnecessary casualties. The clincher came when a crowd from battalion HQ came up to the forward positions and PA speakers playing 'Goodnight Irene' were hung in the trees. 'We thought, there's something funny going on,' Len said. 'And then we heard about this so-called big bomb, you know, that everybody was talking about.'

The war was over. The Japanese were rounded up and put in compounds where they bowed in the Emperor's general direction at the same time each day and waited to be rescued. Australian non-combatants appeared from rear areas to jeer the Japanese behind the wire. Len and his mates told them to cease and desist, forthwith.

Len's diary is silent about his reaction to the news of peace. He did once say his World War II experience was 'a waste of time'. He had barely fired a shot in anger or otherwise. 'I'd have done a lot more—I applied for the commandos and I didn't get them and I applied for the parachute battalion, which didn't go away anyway, so that was a good job. But with all the excitement that was going on in other places, it wasn't anywhere we were. I was in two campaigns, but apart from Manggar, which was a decent battle and lasted for three or four days . . . New Guinea was just a waste really.'

The fighting force was at the peak of its powers but had no one to fight. The men were in limbo; they lolled on the beach, nude until a nurses unit set up camp nearby, and fashioned sailing boats and surf-boards from the detritus of war—planes' belly fuel tanks made good canoes. All the while they scanned the horizon for the troopships that would take them home. 'One fellow in our platoon had found a huge pair of Japanese artillery binoculars and in between regaling us with tales of his girlfriend and threats as to what he was going to do if she hadn't remained faithful (not that [that] seemed to affect his activities as he had told us ever since Strathpine days), he rigged up a support and spent his time looking out to sea,' Len wrote. The battalion's louts took the interlude as an opportunity to get their own back on Sandy Perkins for breaking up a fight on the Tableland. Ignoring the fact their sergeant had been recently wounded, they threw him into a deep, water-filled anti-tank ditch. Once again Len was disgusted with his comrades' behaviour.

Twenty-one 2/14th men were killed at Balikpapan. About half had died accidentally or from friendly fire. Len told the sad story of Lieu-tenant Frank Doyle, who led the attack on Waites Knoll only to be killed when an Owen gun accidentally discharged on 22 July. He was about to be sent home under a scheme to repatriate men who had been in uniform five years with two years overseas service. Ken Clark would have also been eligible. After being buried where he fell, Clark was moved twice to make way for a road before his comrades buried him on the beach in a formal service. He was then moved to a temporary war cemetery, then a permanent war cemetery. 'He had more moves than the Regimental Aid Post,' Len wrote.

Balikpapan had been regained at a cost of 229 Australians killed and 634 wounded. More than 2000 Japanese soldiers died. Asked many years later about the campaign's worth, Len said it was easy to be wise after the event, given the Manggar strip would have been a key air base had the war continued. 'Now, if they hadn't have dropped the A bomb we would have had to go into Singapore so it wouldn't have been a side show,' he said. 'If we'd had to go into Singapore it was a different story, so it's alright people saying that it was a side show and we shouldn't have gone into Labuan and Balikpapan, but that's in hindsight and you don't know.'

His thirst for adventure yet to be sated, Len acted in a typically unorthodox fashion. Hearing Dougherty was about to leave for Macassar in the Celebes to administer occupation duties, Len saw an opportunity. Between the New Guinea and Balikpapan scraps he had learned some rudimentary Malay after picking up the book *Malay Made Easy* in his Port Moresby hospital bed. He lay in wait outside the brigadier's tent and 'button-holed' him. 'He was always very approachable and when I said: "You are going to Macassar and will need an interpreter and I'm it." He replied: "Well, I hadn't really thought about it, but I suppose I will and I will make arrangements and see you over there." Whereupon we went our separate ways. A couple of days later I was called up before the company commander and was greeted with: "Opie! You bastard!" "Who, Sir? Me, Sir?" "Yes, you! You know the chain of command and how to go about making a request! I've just been chewed out by the CO over you! Pack your gear and report to Brigade Headquarters!" "Who, Sir? Me, Sir? Yessir!" Half an hour later I was on a truck on the way to Balikpapan.' He sailed the next day. The job included interpreting conversations with Japanese prisoners. 'How Len organised that posting is a bit of a mystery,' Brigadier Laurie Lewis said. 'I, for one, never heard Len speak Japanese.'

What followed was five months as a virtual freelancer interpreting in war crimes investigations and for Australian diggers charged with various misdemeanours. He was unimpressed with the 'lazy' Dutch, whose empire was about to succumb to Indonesian nationalism, but seemed to thrive in his surroundings. Dougherty and his Macassar Force won praise for its firm but sensitive handling of disarming and repatriating the Japanese while not intervening in the looming revolution.

Len disembarked in late February and when he was discharged in August 1946 he had been paid about £660. He resumed his happy life as a mild-mannered and nondescript clerk during the day and a model-railway enthusiast on weekends. But Len had a taste for war. Something told him that a volatile post-war world would soon give him another chance to fight.

CHAPTER 4

KOREA

'I decided to make the Army work for me when I went
to Korea.'
Len Opie

The early Cold War's simmering tensions boiled over on 25 June 1950, when seven divisions of the Korean People's Army (KPA) flooded over the border to punch through the Army of the Republic of Korea's (ROK) paper-thin defences. With the republic riven, and the US indolent, Kim Il-sung saw his opportunity and struck with all his might. Whether the invasion was sanctioned by the Soviets and Chinese remains a moot point, but it appears the North Korean leader was confident of the communist superpowers coming to his aid if he ran into trouble. After ignoring North Korea's obvious belligerence before the invasion, the US sought and received the UN's approval to respond and had troops on the ground within a week of the attack. Australia decided to send its sole infantry battalion, then on occupation duties in Japan, into the fray, and called for volunteers to fill its depleted ranks.

World War II veteran Ben O'Dowd called it the last call of the bugle. When the bugle sounded in 1914 it was heard by the men who formed the 1st AIF. When France fell in 1940 almost 60,000 Australians joined up in two months. When the clarion call rang out again Len Opie, now 26, immediately decided to enlist. He was motivated as much by the

pervading fear of communist expansion, the yellow peril of the propa-
gandists, as by his thirst for adventure. 'I may as well go and meet them
up there as wait for them to come here,' he told his parents. He didn't
like bullies. Hated injustice. Abhorred tyranny. And he had no time for
communists.

Len walked into his boss's Adelaide Steamship office and dropped a
note on his desk. 'I hereby apply for three years leave of absence starting
today.' He then walked out and headed straight to Keswick barracks. The
service numbers for this new army started at 400,000 and Len received
400,006. He was the fifth South Australian to enlist; the first man was
designated 400,001 instead of 400,000. Len was offended by the minute
error. 'This is typical of the army, you know, they can't ever get things
right,' Len said. Allan Bennett was given number 400,017 and well
remembers his first encounter with Len, who said, 'What happened
to you? Did you stop for breakfast?' Once again Len's chest was
deemed too shallow for an infantry man but the examining doctor was
an old St Peter's boy so let the tape slip a little. 'I was off the leash
with no more worries in the civilian world! Because of all the time
I'd wasted in World War II, I thought this time I'm going to make the
army work for me instead of me working for the army.'

Len was given a 1916 rifle by a recruiting officer of a similar
vintage, Major Frank Allchin, who was in the first wave at Gallipoli
and a Rat of Tobruk in the last war. Within a week the recruits were on
the overnight train to Melbourne en route for the Puckapunyal camp
near Seymour in central Victoria. After the first day's training the men
quickly headed for the bar and Bennett was as thirsty as any of them:
'We'd been out in the paddock all day and he was sitting there on his
bed. "Are you coming up to the canteen, Len?" He said: "I've never
drunk, smoked or swore in my life and I'm not going to start now." I
thought God Almighty, what sort of bloke have we got here? I went up
to the canteen and I said, "I don't know what to make of him." Well it
didn't take long to work out what sort of bloke he was in Korea. It didn't
take long to prove what he was worth.'

Most of the men were, like Len, World War II veterans who wanted another crack at fighting. As such, 'K Force' wore a motley assortment of medals and colours. Len noted one in particular who had no right to wear a medal awarded to those who had defended Australia in the early days of the war. Another who bore a DCM said he had no need to wear the others. He was told to put it away, as was another who wore a German Iron Cross, captured presumably. 'One well-known character described himself variously as an ex-RAF Wing Commander or Group Captain with DSO [Distinguished Service Order] and DFC with service on the North West Frontier of India,' Len said. '[He] was shot down when he insisted on pronouncing Peshawah as PESH-A-WAH, but he still carried the act on, fooling even the commanding officer, even after the Korean War.' Jack Gallaway was an instructor sergeant who recalled K Force as being as diverse as its medals. 'Some told lies about their experience in the infantry,' Gallaway said. 'They were no infanteers, some of them. I got a bit sick of them so I took them for a gallop out past the rifle range and back again. Opie was the only bloke who didn't whinge about it. He was quite cheerful about the whole thing. He thought they probably deserved it.'

Yes, discipline was an issue but most of the men knew the pointy end of a .303 or had fired a Bren in the last war. So the training was essentially a refresher course with lots of route marches to toughen up civilian bodies. On one march a truck skimmed dangerously close to the column, prompting 'Tiger' Wilson, an ex-fireman who, Len said, was well known to the police in Adelaide, to throw his bayonet at the truck driver, who rolled up his sleeves, shaping for a fight. The platoon commander, Lieutenant Peter Johnston, turned a blind eye while the pair disappeared into the scrub. 'In about five minutes the driver reappeared, blood pouring from his nose and looking very much the worst [sic] for wear, and got into his vehicle and drove off,' Len said. 'A few minutes later, "Tiger" came out of the scrub, coughing and retching. As he had obviously had the better of the deal, we asked him what was up? "I put my false teeth in my pocket to punch him up and when I put them back in my mouth there were some strands of tobacco sticking to them and I've swallowed them." We marched back to camp and nothing more was heard of the incident.'

The brass, including the Chief of the General Staff, Lieutenant General Sydney Rowell, visited the troops to see how the recruits were getting on. Len's section was disassembling a Bren when the dignitaries strolled up. The trouble was, all of Lieutenant Johnston's men couldn't put the Bren back together again, much to the embarrassment of the company commander, battalion commander and brigadier. 'Well, a general can only spend so much time wasting it, so with a sad shake of his head and a muttered comment he passed on,' Len wrote. 'These were the people that were going to save Australia from the Red Menace. I might mention that by the time the platoon commander had finished with us, we knew how to strip and assemble the weapon.'

Cake and scones with strawberry jam were laid on for the next VIP to visit, the army minister. Nothing was left to chance this time. No more Bren jigsaw puzzles. The officers carefully choreographed a mock attack using Bren Carriers supported by mortar fire. When the attack force went in, the mortar team fired into a tree directly above them, wounding two, and the Bren carriers and their crews became stuck in barbed wire, the crews gingerly extricating themselves. 'So the whole exercise was called off,' Len said. Welcome to Australian soldiering, *Dad's Army* style.

'Ready or not,' Len wrote, when after a few weeks at Puckapunyal K Force went to Sydney to fly to Japan. The need was urgent as the North Koreans had swept all before them. Supported by 150 tanks, mostly Soviet T-34s, the invaders had swarmed over the 38th Parallel into the heart of the south. Seoul fell in four days and much of the ROK army was cut off when a key bridge on the Han River was blown up in a panic, killing 500 South Koreans in the process. The US ground troops thrust into the fray were abysmally trained and unfit, Australian officers in Japan reported. Outnumbered, outgunned and routinely outflanked—the GIs preferred to drive to battle in jeeps, leaving the hills for the enemy—the Americans were pushed into a pocket at the

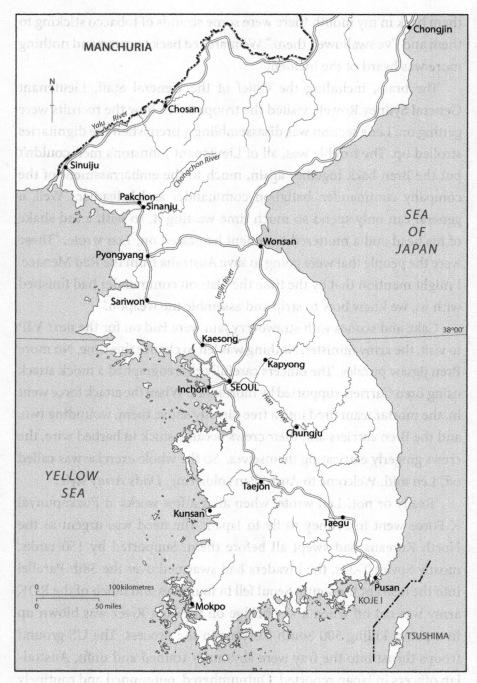

MANCHURIA

Yalu River

Chongjin

Chosan

Sinuiju

Chongchon River

Pakchon
Sinanju

Wonsan

SEA
OF
JAPAN

Pyongyang

Imjin River

Sariwon

38°00'

Kaesong

Kapyong

Inchon

SEOUL

Han River

Chungju

YELLOW
SEA

Taejon

Kunsan

Taegu

0   100 kilometres

0   50 miles

Pusan

KOJE I

Mokpo

TSUSHIMA

KOREA

foot of the Korean peninsula. There they held firm on a 230-kilometre front, the Pusan Perimeter or Pusan Pocket, and brought their superior air power to bear.

In the meantime Britain had sent two infantry battalions from Hong Kong; the Australian battalion in Japan—brought to strength by Len and his fellow recruits—would join them to make a British Commonwealth brigade. MacArthur was supreme commander of the UN force.

When they arrived in Sydney Len and his comrades were warned that anyone who spoke to the public would not be getting on the plane. 'We were rushed aboard Super Constellation VH-EAD *Sir Charles Kingsford Smith*,' Len wrote. 'There were lots of reporters there, but the need for such secrecy escaped us. It was almost as if we were mercenaries going off to fight some unlawful war. The Korean War certainly did have its detractors later on, but why the veil of secrecy so early was somewhat of a mystery.' No bully beef for them; they were 'treated to a sumptuous steak dinner' as soon as they were in the air. After staging at Darwin and Luzon, where they had a drink with GIs who asked them what language they spoke in Australia, they flew over the still-ruined Hiroshima and arrived in Iwakuni on 12 September. They were billeted in the Transit Hotel before being sent by train to the 3rd Battalion, Royal Australian Regiment (3RAR) barracks in Hiro. Len's draft of 40 men brought the battalion to its full strength of 960 troops. The arrivals' first contact with their new battalion was a VD lecture— stay away from 'Big Tits Betty' they were warned—and a brief welcome from the adjutant. They barely had time to settle in before being sent on night manoeuvres in a typhoon. The complaints about watered-down stew were unfair on the 'babblers' (the cooks), Len wrote, so heavy was the rain. They settled into a training regime as hard as anything Len had encountered in the last war.

Immediately there was tension within the battalion. While K Force comprised World War II veterans, the Australians of the British Commonwealth Occupation Force (BCOF) troops were mostly men who had been too young to fight in the last war. 'BCOF's main object in life of course was to show the flag and impress the natives with the accent on ceremonial,' Len wrote. The BCOF men resented the newcomers' often coarse ways and sometimes superior airs, while Len and his mates thought the BCOF men were better on a parade ground than a battlefield. 'We were immediately struck by the immaculate appearance of the troops; knife edge creases in starched uniforms, blancoed webbing and trousers bloused over gaiters with lead weights,' Len wrote. 'These were circlets of cloth-covered lead which weighed the bottoms of trousers neatly. They quickly became a bone of contention as in a brawl they could be used as weapons, wrapped around the fist and, as of course we in K Force did not have them, the comment became current that one could tell BCOF because "they wear lead weights and sleep with their mates" . . . . that was the cause of many fights.'

Still, the men needed to get over themselves and quickly. They would soon depend upon one another for their survival. The battalion commander, Lieutenant Colonel Charlie Green, a highly decorated and respected World War II veteran, had a problem: how to blend the K Force and BCOF men into a cohesive, harmonious unit.

He decided A and D companies would be almost entirely K Force, C was mostly BCOF, leaving only B as a mixture of the two. Green had commanded a battalion in New Guinea aged 25, and in just two weeks managed to fashion 3RAR into something resembling a front-line fighting unit, despite the inner rivalries. Green drummed out two company commanders he deemed not up to the task, and another officer was 'demoted on the spot' for 'leaving the troops without food'.

Len must have impressed someone because he was made a section commander in 11 Platoon of D Company. Tiger Wilson, the man who had brawled with the truck driver at Puckapunyal, had until then been the self-appointed leader of Len's little group, so was somewhat put out about being overlooked. 'He hid his disappointment, apparently deciding that he would be the power behind the throne or whatever,' Len wrote. The section was complemented by Bill Nimmo, Paddy

Trump, Scotty Gordon, Leslie 'Ossie' Osborn, Francis Cullen, Harry Munt and Keith 'Mo' Gwyther (a cousin of Shorty Gwyther of the bully beef pie episode in New Guinea). Osborn had been captured in Crete but escaped and fought alongside the Russians. Wilson was appointed Len's second-in-command and proclaimed the section would henceforth be called 'The Warriors'. It was a rough and ready group that Gwyther said 'had a lust for killing'.

It fell to Len to allocate which two would take the Bren gun. The medium machine gun was a section's most important weapon; it was crucial for close quarters support in attack or defence. Gordon and Gwyther were mates, so Len offered them the job. They refused, saying they wanted to be up with the other troops, not stuck in the rear covering their mates. 'For Pete's sake!' Len said. 'When we go into action the Bren gives supporting fire, and the distance from front to back of the section is probably 20 yards,' Len said. 'Where did you think you'd be—back in B Echelon?' (B Echelon is a supply area, usually well back from the front line.) Gwyther became the gunner and Gordon his number two. Len typically carried an Owen submachine gun, a weapon familiar to him from his time in New Guinea and Borneo.

The 24th US Division had fought a delaying action that had bought MacArthur time to pour troops into the Pusan Pocket. The defenders were now supported by 500 tanks and most of the North's planes had been systematically destroyed by the superior UN air forces, including the RAAF's 77 Squadron. The UN ruled the waves, too. All was in place for the crowning moment of MacArthur's career—a flanking manoeuvre that changed the war. With the enemy fully committed to smash the pocket, MacArthur landed a strong force at Inchon, the port of Seoul. Reeling from this grievous wound, and weakened by three months' continuous fighting, the enemy could not contain the inevitable offensive in the South when it came in late September. By the time 3RAR was piling aboard its troopship in Japan, the Inchon and Pusan forces had linked at Osan, south of Seoul. It seemed Len was about to miss yet another fight. Gwyther summed up the men's mood.

'So there we were, a whole mob of battle-hungry guys swearing and cursing because the Inchon landing had just happened, and we reckon the war's just about over. Blokes are betting fivers and tenners that we won't fire a shot.'

Still, Lieutenant General Horace 'Red Robbie' Robertson delivered a stirring speech as the rain pelted down on the ranks assembled on the wharf. The battalion band played and the men sang along, albeit with non-army-issue lyrics. 'We're a pack of bastards,' they sang, as one of the bastards, immune to the pomp or perhaps because of it, climbed a dockside crane and refused to come down. The *Aiken Victory* sailed at 7.45 pm on 27 September and Len and 'The Warriors' celebrated the occasion by devouring a bucket of strawberry ice-cream stolen from the galley. When they arrived at Pusan the following afternoon they were greeted by two army bands, Korean women in traditional dress, and children bearing flowers. The battalion boarded a train and disembarked at Taegu, 170 kilometres up the peninsula. Wrecked US tanks lay all around.

Len and his section were directed to an apple orchard, where every inch of ground was used by the economical locals—the Aussies dug in among rows of lettuces, radishes and onions. The fighting might have ebbed to the north but two divisions of cut-off enemy troops were said to be in the area. The battalion was now part of the 27th Commonwealth Brigade (the composition or fate of the previous 26 are unknown), comprising the 1st Battalion of the Argyll and Sutherland Highlanders and the 1st Battalion of the Middlesex Regiment. The two British battalions had performed brilliantly in the Pusan Pocket and the diggers were glad to be in the same brigade. After an uneventful few days when they were shunted from hill to hill on dusty roads, Len was called to platoon headquarters, where he was ordered to dig in by a road. When he returned the section was gone.

Fed up with the lack of action, the men had hitched a ride to the front. Len said Wilson was the 'self-appointed leader of the push'. Effectively he and the others had deserted. They figured the war would soon be over so they might as well take their chances with the consequences. Len was a section commander without a section. He returned to the HQ to tell Lieutenant Peter Johnston that the digging would take quite some time as he had to dig six foxholes in addition to his own.

'Why?' Johnston said.

'Well, the others have all gone,' Len said.

'What do you mean, your section has gone?' Johnston said.

'They've gone and I'm going to look for them!'

Johnston gave Len until nightfall.

The section leader sans a section hitched a ride with a Middlesex battalion truck heading north. After a while he hopped off to intervene in an 'interrogation' of two Korean peasants by two men armed with fixed bayonets. Len's code of honour meant he often found himself at war with his own side when soldiers threatened to mistreat prisoners or civilians. Len was ticking off the would-be war criminals when the Middlesex CO arrived on the scene. 'What! You've lost what?' exclaimed Lieutenant Colonel Andrew Man, a career soldier who was something of a martinet. 'My battalion has been in Korea four weeks and I have not lost one man and you've been here one week and you've lost—how many did you say?'

Len was getting nowhere so headed back to base where he found four of the absconders—Gwyther, Nimmo, Trump and Gordon—back where they belonged. But there was no sign of the others, including Wilson. Len paid the price—he was stripped of his section leadership. His command dwindled to the two Bren gunners and a rifleman. The bitter blow was given its proper perspective that day when Captain Ken Hummerston and Private Ken Sketchley were killed when their Bren carrier ran over a mine. They were the battalion's first casualties. Sketchley was only twenty.

Meanwhile, the deserters were front-page news back in Australia. Wilson had blabbed to a war correspondent, whose dispatch found its way into the Melbourne *Age*. 'We joined up to fight, but when we arrived we found our unit too far away from the front line, so we just took off and headed for the noise of the firing.' Wilson must have had good ears, as the firing was some 100 kilometres away at the time. Presently he and Private Ernest Stone were the last remaining free-lancers as Munt and Cullen had headed back to base. '[Munt] had been a jockey and I don't know how he had ever been accepted for K Force,' Len said. '[Cullen] carried what appeared to be a portable altar with a picture of the Virgin Mary in his pack. This must have helped give him absolution because he was the greatest gambler in the platoon with the foulest mouth.'

Presently the new section commander arrived, a 'big boof-headed character' packing a Tommy Gun. This ex-military policeman was allegedly a former professional wrestler who had arrived to 'straighten the section out'. Len was unimpressed. Others shared his opinion. One usually temperate sergeant told Len years later that the man was 'a big loud-mouthed false alarm'.

With the KPA in full retreat, the war was shifting ever northwards. To catch up with the fighting, the 27th Brigade was airlifted to Kimpo, Seoul's airport. As well as the Dakotas so familiar to the World War II veterans, C119 transports were lined up on the runway awaiting their human cargo. Anyone familiar with the 1960s TV show *Thunderbirds* would note how these massive beasts with their twin fuselages closely resembled Thunderbird 2. Even the good fliers among 3RAR were discomfited by seeing a C119 lose both its fuselages upon landing, by US pilots so young they resembled Boy Scouts, and being handed parachutes and given hasty instructions about how to use them. 'We weren't too impressed when we each received a parachute—not all the same type, either—and with the help of the crew strapped ourselves into them,' Len said. 'We boarded the aircraft and were rigged to a static line which meant, as was explained, that all we would have to do was jump if necessary, no fooling around with ripcords. That's all?'

The battalion remained at Kimpo for three days to allow its trucks and jeeps to catch up. Len's section was put on water-truck duty but found a brewery, pulled the plug on the water, filled the tank with beer and 'peddled it to anyone who would pay for it'. On 9 October a long convoy clattered out of Kimpo, crossed the Han River via a pontoon bridge and rolled past the wrecked Soviet T-34 tanks lining the route through Seoul. Without the luxury of US transport, columns of ROK troops flanked both sides of the road, filing past ranks of KPA prisoners heading in the other direction.

The Australians arrived at the border between North and South Korea—the 38th Parallel—in a cloud of dust at dusk. There they found the 1st US Cavalry Division and its two Australian recruits, Wilson and Stone.

Accounts differ slightly as to how Lieutenant Colonel Green dealt with the absconders. But most describe an incident that seemed to influence Green's decision. Three immaculately turned-out MPs arrived at Battalion HQ just as Green was shaving before a jeep's mirror. The MPs, in white puggarees and webbing, had arrived from Kure to take the deserters back to Japan for court martial. 'MPs are unloved under any circumstances, but in this situation, their spick-and-span appearance was particularly offensive to the eye of an infantry man,' Jack Gallaway wrote. Green was the definitive infantry man. 'Who the hell are these men?' he barked through his shaving foam. It was a rhetorical question. 'Send them back to where they came from.' The next day Wilson and the others were heavily fined—one account said five pounds, Len thought it was three—and sent back to the ranks. Len's section was back but the Tommy-Gun-toting former MP remained in charge.

Having pushed the KPA back to the 38th Parallel, where it had all started back in June, MacArthur and his masters at the UN had a choice: be content with a decisive victory and a return to the status quo, or launch its own all-out invasion. The North's army was humbled but not beaten, and MacArthur had permission from his UN masters to cross the border and systematically roll it up. When President Harry Truman asked his general about the chance of China coming to North Korea's aid, MacArthur replied, 'Very little.' If it did it would be soundly defeated, MacArthur said. ROK troops crossed the border and were soon followed by the GIs and then the Commonwealth Brigade. Len made a note of when he entered North Korea—5.22 pm on 12 October. They drove past a sign that read, 'You are now crossing the 38th Parallel courtesy of the First Cavalry Division.' They soon came across a truck with four US corpses in the back. Len was more concerned about the meagre rations—the sporadic issue of bully and tins of fruit—until 14 October when the section breakfasted on Rice Bubbles, prunes, pineapple, ham, eggs and bacon, scones and cake. 'Perhaps we were being fattened for the kill,' he said.

The early days of the great push were something of a disappointment to Len and his section. D Company went on a series of patrols that branched off from the main thrust. Once they came across a smouldering village, deserted save for an old woman wandering with a grenade in her hand. They prepared to ambush whatever was causing a cloud of dust in the distance, to be told by the source of the dust—Yanks in jeeps—that they must have been the northernmost UN troops in Korea. When they finally joined the axis of the advance, their days were spent bumping along rutted, potholed and—after heavy rain on the night of 15 and 16 October—muddy roads, in trucks chasing an enemy that was in full retreat. The town of Kumchon was taken with little opposition and the brigade pushed on to Sariwon on the road to the northern capital of Pyongyang. 'The method of advance was that each battalion in the brigade would take its turn on the point for however long it took to reach a major bound,' Len wrote. 'Within the battalion, each company would take its turn in front and in the company, the point platoon would ride on tanks, sometimes the whole company, while the companies coming behind would be mounted on TCVs [troop carrying vehicles]. If we struck opposition, everyone deployed, then climbed back on whatever mode of transport we were using.' The GIs only left the road to prise the North Korean Army (NKA) out of the hills when there was no alternative. The Australian infantry was happy to fan into the hills, often with little or no air or artillery support. 'Boy, you guys sure know what you are doing,' an incredulous American said as the diggers dismounted to deal with an ambush. 'The American mode of advance was to race along the road until they took fire or even if they saw a house ahead or to a flank, when they would pour a welter of artillery, mortar or automatic weapon fire into it,' Len said. The Americans called this method 'reconnaissance by fire'.

Sitting astride the main road north and at the top of a peninsula all but cut off by the UN advance, Sariwon was a magnet for both the advancing and retreating forces. North Koreans continued to stream into the town after it was captured by the Argylls on 17 October. In the dark the exhausted NKA troops mistook the white-faced soldiers in their midst for Russians who had come to their aid. 'Russkis, Russkis!' they cried with delight before the 'Russkis' opened fire. About 200 North Koreans perished under roadside banners of Stalin, Mao Tse-tung and Kim Il-sung. 3RAR was sent to block an escape road. The 2IC, Major Bruce Ferguson, was waiting to meet a supply detail in an apple orchard when he heard hundreds of marching feet coming his way. 'Russki?' asked one of the marchers, to be answered with a burst of machine-gun fire. Both sides went to ground with the stalemate only broken when Ferguson told them they were surrounded—they most certainly were not—and nearly 2000 emerged from cover with their hands up.

With Sariwon secure the race was on to get to Pyongyang. The Australians hoped to be the first into the North Korean capital, but the 7th Cavalry—of Custer's Last Stand infamy—led the way, shooting first and asking questions later. The US soldiers' disregard for civilians was fomenting in Len a distrust of his allies. 'The Americans seemed to take a delight in the destruction of the Korean houses, even to throwing rocks through windows if their vehicles stopped in close proximity to a dwelling,' Len said. 'To them, all Koreans were "gooks" rather than human beings. [This was] despite the flood of refugees in the South and the fact that as we went north, crowds lined the roads, cheering and waving flags, sometimes ROK, often Nationalist Chinese and even UN, and we were being treated as liberators rather than conquerors.'

Neither GI nor digger did anything about a grievously wounded KPA soldier when D Company set off with the 7th Cavalry on 18 October. '[He] had been partly run over by a tank but was still alive, although nobody seemed inclined to finish him off and he was alive as we moved off,' Len said. The diggers' hopes of at least joining the 7th Cavalry in being the first into Pyongyang were dashed when 3RAR was diverted to the coast, ostensibly to protect that flank, but in the Australians' eyes to allow the Americans the glory of seizing the capital alone. Len and his section cursed their rotten luck over their lunch of a square of jam tart each.

After a sharp fight, A Company cleared a village, which was 'practically destroyed in the process' by US tanks. Amid the din of strafing attacks on enemy positions and desultory fire from infantry and tanks, the section ate their dinner of diced carrots and peas and dug in for a cold night. Len had been in Korea barely three weeks but he was quickly learning how to keep dry and warm. After digging his foxhole each night he would line it with rice straw if any was available, and would snuggle into his cocoon with his boots still on. The temperature can drop to zero in North Korea in October and the Australians were yet to receive their winter gear. Until then they had to make do with only denim pants and tunics. He needed a good sleep this night as the section would take point in the morning.

After being roused at 4 am, D Company climbed aboard Sherman tanks and they clattered forward in the rain. They dismounted at a village and 11 Platoon was ordered to attack. Len's section was on the left and he came across a bunker behind a house. His Owen gun jammed so he lobbed a grenade through the door. The fight was soon won but Len was livid when he learned one of the men had bayoneted an old woman. The culprit kept his own counsel. The section leader and Wilson went back to direct the supply trucks to their position and the platoon pressed on without them. Len was to soon learn the section leader, who had been sent to straighten the section out, had a habit of disappearing when a fight was brewing. Movement was seen to the north-east. 'Go over and have a look at that haystack over there, take your section and do a patrol,' Johnston said to Len. They set out towards a haystack standing among spindly trees at the far end of a 250-metre-long paddy field. Len arranged the ten men in extended file, with Gwyther's Bren team in the centre and two of Len's chief antagonists, Stone and Cullen, on the respective flanks. Out they sloshed into the paddy field.

When they had closed to within 60 metres they saw four enemy troops moving towards the haystack and another two setting up a mortar. Len's men had crept forward so stealthily the enemy had no idea they were about to be attacked. But then Private James 'Curly' Neville mounted a paddy bund and yelled 'come here' in Japanese and another word that meant 'very much the reverse', Len said. Unsurprisingly, the enemy was unconvinced. They opened fire with two machine guns, forcing the section to splash down behind the bund and reply with all they had. By the sounds of Gwyther's account of the action, Len's fire was the most accurate. 'You can hear the bullets go zing, zing, zing as he rakes the corn stack,' Gwyther said. 'There we are up in the heart of Korea, pumping lead into we don't know what. Maybe it's as well we didn't.' By some miracle no Australian was hit. A tremendous boom solved the mystery of the haystack: it was a T-34, a 'tank in sheep's clothing', as Gwyther described it. The force of its 85 millimetre gun firing at the Shermans in the rear sent hay flying and Australian pulses racing. 'There we were looking almost right down the barrel of a gun that looked as big as a sewerage pipe,' Gwyther said. The tank's machine gun added to the heavy fire directed at the Australians, while others of the tank crew blazed away with submachine guns from hatches. Len kept his cool. He sent Neville and Cullen off on a flanking manoeuvre to the right while the rest of the section gave covering fire. The Shermans opened up and quickly scored a direct hit, disabling the tank. Cullen leapt onto its hull, banged on the turret hatch, and promptly shot the commander. The other four members of the tank crew were taken prisoner and sent to the rear.

With the fight won, the section went back to the main group where Len had to deal with more trouble. The prisoners had been stripped and tied to a jeep bonnet. 'Who did that?' Len said. 'I did,' a digger replied, adding that they were only 'gooks'. 'They're not gooks, they're enemy and they're captured and give them their clothes back. You weren't even on the exercise anyway.' The prisoners, now clothed, were interrogated and revealed they had been ordered to remain behind with the tank, which had a flat battery and no petrol, to delay the enemy. The action was seen by a host of officers and war correspondents but Len was surly about no one bothering to thank him, and no reports of the fight made the Australian papers. 'This episode was dealt with rather tersely in the Official History: "D Company and several US tanks fought another small action against some North Korean tanks", which I suppose really indicates that if you want to get in the history books you should introduce yourself to the author. They put us on trucks and shot us up north again. So we'd been up since four o'clock, we never got a word of thanks for taking this tank and capturing the crew, we swanned around up in the trucks for about two hours and got back about one o'clock. We didn't have any breakfast, we didn't have any lunch and we didn't get a word of thanks. That's gratitude for you.'

Notwithstanding the lack of recognition, and despite the run-ins with Cullen and the digger, Len had passed his first leadership test. He had excelled under fire by directing a textbook section attack on a powerful foe. Gwyther was certainly impressed, writing in his account of the action, 'If we'd had a battalion full of men like him we'd have shifted a stack of commies.'

With Pyongyang safely in US hands, 3RAR returned to the main advance. Once again the American predilection for self-promotion was evident. As they drove through the capital they passed under banners reading: 'You are now entering Pyongyang courtesy of 1 Cav Div.' The Australians were playing catch-up again, as the fighting had moved well to the north. MacArthur had committed his previously unused paratroops to battle, landing them behind enemy lines in a bid to trap the fleeing enemy. As he had done all those years ago at Nadzab, MacArthur watched proceedings—this time with selected war correspondents—from his personal plane. The operation did not go as smoothly as at Nadzab; soon the paratroops were in trouble and called for urgent help. The 27th Brigade quickly swung into action. All three battalions would press forward to relieve the beleaguered Americans. Advancing along the main northern road flanked with apple orchards on the right and paddy fields on the left, Green was told there would be no air or artillery support because the Americans were too close. 'All the fighting had to be done with infantry weapons and nothing else—the Bren gun, the rifle, the bayonet and the grenade,' 27th Brigade CO Basil Coad said. 'This was down the Australians' street.'

Indeed it was. C Company dismounted from their tanks and charged straight up the hill at the North Koreans. The Battle of the Apple Orchard had begun. Some of the North Koreans replied with bursts from their submachine guns—Soviet burp guns—but most fled before the bayonet. As they broke cover they were slaughtered by the Australians and fire from the supporting tanks. 'The enemy were equipped with high-powered automatic weapons but we outshot them and had ammunition to spare when the battle was done,' 3RAR's Sergeant Jack Harris said. Bleary-eyed enemy soldiers exhausted from the fight with the Americans emerged from culverts lining the main road, only to be quickly shot down. 'He raised his head very slowly,' Harris wrote of a soldier who peered over a paddy field bund, 'like some fabled genie or sprite to take a look and I took him with a quick shot through the skull . . . the head did not flinch or move and just as slowly as he had raised his cranium to look, so he now lowered it, dead to the world.' Harris described it as a 'brutish affair'. While hulking diggers carried dishevelled civilian children to safety, a US Sherman tank commander yelled at Harris to haul a wounded horse off the road. Harris looked into the stricken horse's 'huge brown eyes', pleading for it to budge. When it did not, the tank commander ran it over. He was fortunate Len was fully involved elsewhere on the battlefield.

Green's HQ group pressed up hard behind C Company and soon found itself under attack. The veteran of North Africa, Greece and New Guinea calmly issued orders and manoeuvred his battalion even as the enemy was shot down all around him. 'The CO had organised his own little battle,' Len said. Green and his staff were relieved by D Company and Len's section was sent into the fight soon afterwards. Here came something with a historical precedent in the Australian Army—ratting. When the World War I diggers stormed the French village of Pozières in 1916, they 'ratted' the Germans out of the ruined town's cellars. 'Several people were gathered around a hole in the ground,' Len said. 'The next moment a shot rang out [and] an American driver jumped back with a bullet wound in his chin. Out of the hole—which turned out to be a bunker—leapt a North Korean, who was promptly shot by the driver's mate. Somebody tossed a grenade in and a minute or so later three of them shot out and fled down the hill away from the road and through the orchard to the cries of "there they go" and bursts of fire. During the morning a total of 22 little men in baggy winter clothes popped out of that bunker. At one stage, coming back to it after replenishing my ammunition, I noticed what looked like a corpse lying just outside the bunker, except that I did not remember it being there five minutes before, so I fired a couple of exploratory rounds and noticed a slight twitch. When I fired a burst, he arched backwards like a scorpion, almost touching his head with his heels.'

Trapped between the Australians and Americans, the North Koreans tried to break out through the flanks. Eleven Platoon was sent north to try to make contact with the Americans but was soon fully occupied with the enemy's attempts to break out of the pocket. They were cut down by Australian rifles and American tank fire. Another D Company platoon took to the rice paddies to flush out hiding KPA soldiers. The Englishman, Coad, thought it was a jolly good show, preferring to compare it to an English hunt rather than plain old ratting. 'I saw a marvellous sight,' he said. 'An Australian platoon lined up in a paddy field and walked through it as though they were driving snipe. The soldiers, when they saw a pile of straw, kicked it and out would bolt a North Korean. Up with a rifle, down with a North Korean, and the Australians thoroughly enjoyed it! They did that the whole day, and they really were absolutely in their element!' Len was certainly in his element. Korea was his best war, and this was the best day so far of his best war. 'The apples were big, red, crunchy and delicious. We filled our pockets and then our shirts . . . eating with time off for firing at the North Koreans. Our platoon tally for the day was 46.' The battalion had suffered only seven wounded— including one accidentally shot by a comrade—while killing 180 and taking 250 prisoners. Among the enemy corpses was a colonel in a strange uniform studded with red stars. Was he Chinese? The men of D Company were too busy enjoying the spoils of victory. 'To round off the day', Len said, 'we captured the North Korean paymaster with a truckload of bank notes.'

The Middlesex men took the lead while the battalion was afforded a brief rest. Soon the Australians were on the move again and entered the town of Sinanju after lunch on 23 October. They were welcomed as liberators by the locals, who showered them with apples that were gratefully received by a force that had outstripped its supply lines. The rations were supplemented by similarly unorthodox means, Len reported. 'We were sent out on patrol to the west and came upon a local who confronted us with a double barrelled shotgun when we approached his home. When we managed to convince him that we were not unfriendly, he let us in and we found that his wife was about to give birth. He spoke a little English and it transpired that he was a schoolteacher, so we moved on as he seemed to have [the] matter in hand with some help from the local ladies. He also gave us some eggs.'

After being delayed by the enemy's demolition of three bridges across the broad and fast-flowing Chongchon River, the advance resumed on the 25th with 3RAR in the vanguard. They pressed forward to the twin objectives of the villages of Kujin and Pakchon, 3 kilometres further to the north. The main road crossed another large river, the Taeryong, and again they found that the North Korean engineers had blown the 300-metre-long bridge, although this time enough of the structure remained for infantry to cross. Green sent a patrol across and immediately 50 of the enemy emerged from the bushes, hands raised. But as they approached the Australians, North Koreans deeper in the bush opened fire on foe and former friend alike. The shooting was inaccurate but the patrol commander, Lieutenant Alby Morrison, decided to withdraw across the bridge, taking ten of the surviving prisoners back for interrogation. It was late afternoon and the US tank commander and a US signals NCO attached to the Australians advised Green to delay any attack until dawn. Green told them he was attacking immediately. After a strafing run from F-80 Shooting Star jet fighters (aptly named as they were outclassed by enemy fighters as soon as they entered the war) and an artillery and mortar bombardment, A and B companies clambered up roughly fashioned ladders onto the bridge proper and picked their way across beneath a bright moon.

Meanwhile, Green sent D Company north to seize Pakchon and, hopefully, to find another river crossing. Once again the locals lined the streets and cheered. Others appeared to be forming up for a welcoming parade. 'We screeched to a halt and moved back to find that it was indeed a parade—a company parade of 87 North Korean soldiers preparing to move out, presumably to attack us,' Len wrote. 'They were equipped with rifles, SMGs [submachine guns], pistols and plenty of ammunition, but offered no resistance as we disarmed them and collected their gear.' The Australians explored the town before the bulk of the company, escorting 225 prisoners, returned to the battalion just in time to see A and B companies start out across the Broken Bridge.

Australian war correspondent Harry Gordon clambered up the jerry-built ladder and onto the bridge with the first wave. He recorded the chatter that helped ease their nerves as mortar-bomb spouts rose from the dark river below. They spoke of T-bone steaks, the uncomfortable newly issued long johns—it was bitingly cold—and one said,

'Cassidy rides tonight.' Another replaced Gordon's peaked cap—the kind worn by officers—with a slouch hat. The soldier was worried about 'drawing the crabs', that is, Gordon being picked off by a sniper who mistook him for an officer. When they reached the other side they fixed bayonets and charged the scrubby hills. Most of the enemy had fled, leaving men wounded in the early bombardments lying in the scrub with grenades—'living booby traps', Gordon called them. They were mostly dispatched before they could do any damage. Presently the diggers caught up with the main enemy force. 'Suddenly it was awfully noisy and confused, with the Australians firing at every moving silhouette and burp-gun flash ahead of them,' Gordon wrote. 'Sometimes there were quiet patches, then heavy bursts of rifle and machine-gun fire from the enemy. Throughout there was mortar fire, sporadic and mostly ineffective.'

The two companies dug in the best they could in the frozen ground and readied for the counterattack, which came about 10 pm. The North Koreans brought heavy machine-gun and rifle fire to bear on the Australians; the battalion suffered its first battle deaths, including Sergeant Donald McDonald, who bled to death after a bullet smashed through his groin. When his mates told him they could not find the severed artery to stop the bleeding, McDonald said, 'Oh, fuck it! Give us a smoke will you?' The cigarette smouldered in the dead man's lips.

The diggers held firm, although Green felt the situation was serious enough to warrant him sending another platoon across the bridge to help. About 4 am they heard the sound that most terrifies the infantryman—tanks. The men were on their own until the US engineers built a river crossing for their own tanks. 'Well, we've taken on tanks before without support,' one soldier reportedly said in a feeble but well-intentioned attempt to soothe their troubled minds. 'Remember Len Opie?' Len's section-versus-tank win the week before laid the ground for this first mention of his larger-than-life reputation.

One man said a T-34 lumbering towards the Australians was 'as big as a block of flats'. Another thought they better resembled the 'taxation

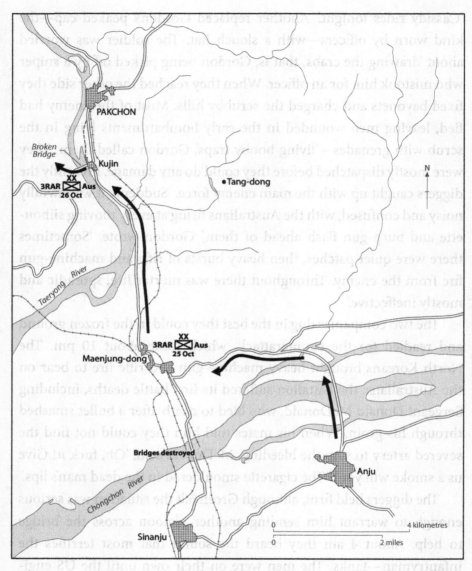

BATTLE OF PAKCHON

building'. The 3.5 inch Super Bazookas provided by the Americans were useless as their working parts were clogged with packing grease. So the Australians did as their comrades had done nine years earlier at a place called Tobruk; they lay doggo in the dark so as to deny the tanks targets. They saved their bullets for the enemy infantry advancing on foot or in jeeps—and one incongruously riding a BMW motorbike. The Shooting Stars reappeared with the rising sun and the enemy wisely turned tail.

Len was with his platoon in the battalion reserve on the other side of the river. 'It was a cold miserable night with a black frost, probably one of the coldest we had experienced, with the wind blowing down from Manchuria, a full moon, planes, artillery and small-arms fire and about 30 to 40 mortar bombs landed around us without exploding.' Other sources said they were shells, not bombs, but all agreed it was fortunate they were duds. At sunrise the section marched upstream to the ford built overnight by US engineers, who lifted their bulldozer blades when the enemy snipers opened up. The men made the crossing aboard tanks and started up the hill on the other side.

'Halfway up we shook out into formation and 6 Section was allocated the lead,' Len wrote. 'We received a couple of our own artillery rounds from the rear which had not cleared the crest facing us. Somebody called out: "Don't worry—they're ours!" Someone else said: "Who cares WHOSE they are, they're still landing among US" . . . the shooting stopped . . . over the hill we went. Unfortunately Charlie, who had stopped laughing long enough to aim at us with a machine gun, let fly as we crested the rise and with one burst hit five of 6 Section. Cullen was worst with wounds in back, chest and arm, Keith Gwyther, shoulder, Trump, both ankles, Nick Downing, chest, and Ossie Osborn, back and paralysed right arm.' By some miracle no one was killed but the broken and bloodied men lying all around were too much for even Len's excellent first-aid skills. While the rest of the platoon leapfrogged the stricken section to attack and silence the machine gun, Len jabbed each of the wounded with the syrettes of morphine he always had tucked under his slouch hat band (some of his fellow diggers thought the warrior had his own personal supply of detonators). 'He'd pop a bullet out of a fella in a flash,' 3RAR digger Reg Bandy said. When one of the men winced at the needle's jab, Len said, 'You're lucky to be getting it; it isn't easy to come by, so stop complaining!'

Len's diary account of the action in which he had narrowly escaped being killed or maimed is typically without embellishment. He records who was hit, then documents his disdain for the wounded man complaining about the needle. Gwyther was more florid in a newspaper article published more than three years later.

There were lots of things whizzing past me, so I angled down a bit into the low cover—small oak and young pine growth. I saw the gook getting down the slope only about 70 yards away. I brought the Bren up, gave him a burst, and down he went. Coming back down into the cover I felt a hearty slap on my right shoulder. The slap spun me around. I could see another gook crouched down in the short cover only six yards away. His burp gun must have been very greasy, because it was smoking heavily. All this happened in a flash. Twenty-eight rounds into him. I yelled to Paddy Trump . . . to keep right with me. Then I yelled to 'Ossie' Osborn, an experienced Bren gunner, to work his way down and get my Bren. We could not afford to have a Bren out of action. I struggled with my gun trying to hold it up. Paddy came across to hand me a magazine and that same gook with the burp shot him in the feet. The five shots that hit him in the feet did not even spread—that's how close it was. Paddy drew up his retractable landing gear in a hurry. 'Whoops', he said. I heard a noise behind me. Looking back quickly over my shoulder I saw Ossie coming. Then I saw the bullet go into Ossie's shoulder. 'I've got it', he said. By this time I had whacked the new mag on my Bren. I could only lift the front part of the gun; but I squeezed the trigger and gave that gook the whole 28 rounds. I poured every round into that heap of smoke from the greasy burp there in the low cover. There was a grunt and a groan and no more fire from there.

Len probably read Gwyther's account. He probably would not have been impressed.

The rest of the company came up and eventually occupied high ground on the battalion's right flank. Len's platoon commander, Lieutenant Johnston, asked him where the section leader had been during the action. 'I told him that I hadn't noticed and he said "a lot of people have said the same thing".' The wounded were evacuated and what was left of the section dug in close to platoon HQ because it was no longer in any condition to fight, at least until it was replenished with replacements. There was no more fighting to be done, for the moment in any case, as the bridgehead was secure, but eight diggers lay dead and 22 had been wounded. 'The dead were lined up alongside the road, with their heavy hob-nailed boots sticking out from under their ground-sheet coverings,' Jack Harris wrote. The North Koreans had lost 100 killed and 50 captured. Green was justifiably proud of his battalion, saying to his staff, 'After that they can send them by divisions. This battalion will hold them.'

The Middlesex battalion leapfrogged to the lead as the Brigade struck out for the Manchurian border, now just 100 kilometres away. The UN's dominance of the skies made life hard—and frequently short—for the North Korean tank crews. Len and his mates marched past a dozen wrecked tanks and two self-propelled guns on 27 October. 'The North Koreans with their armour were in the habit of harbouring in groves of trees which was all very well for concealment and defence, the only trouble was that the tank tracks leading in were clearly visible from the air and the job of the striking aircraft was made easier by the fact that the limits of the target were clearly delineated,' Len wrote. 'It was rather like an ostrich sticking its head in the sand.'

The enemy decided to make a stand at a mountain pass on the road to the next main town, Chongju. About a battalion, supported by tanks, was dug in on the pine-clad slopes either side of the cutting. Green called in repeated rocket, napalm and strafing strikes from the Shooting Stars and P-51 Mustangs, and brought down a bombardment from his supporting tanks. Green ordered a frontal attack—'up the guts'—and this time Len's D Company would take the lead. 'While we were waiting for the airstrike to finish we were regaled with reports of the number of enemy tanks—which ranged from 14 to 20 to 30—which did nothing to raise morale,' Len said.

Four Shermans clattered off followed by another four with the advancing company. Twelve Platoon was on the left, Len's 11 Platoon was in the centre, and 10 Platoon was sent on a flanking sweep to the right. The US airmen had claimed to have knocked out many of the enemy's tanks, but the advance started taking heavy fire, and a tank took a shell through its turret. Soon 12 Platoon was pinned down in the paddy fields and was taking casualties. Men were falling alongside Len, too. Amid the shelling and the shooting and the smoke he took note of another comrade's failings. 'As with so many of our actions there seemed to be someone who wanted to take charge and organise things: This time it was one Buster Morris, an ex-RAAF type who jumped on the tank supporting us and tried presumably to direct its fire towards 12 Platoon. Whatever it was, he got himself wounded in the back and head for his trouble.'

Meanwhile, 10 Platoon had fought its way onto the heights from where it quickly brought down enfilading fire on the enemy positions in front of the other two platoons. Len's 11 Platoon crested the ridges and in turn brought down covering fire to help their mates below on the paddy field but not before Sergeant Fred Bendell was dead and two others seriously wounded. Denis O'Brien's head wound was so bad the platoon medic reportedly said he had 'more brains in his hat than his head'. The medic bandaged him up as best he could. Alex Croll was probably going to O'Brien's aid when he too suffered a severe head wound. The decorated ex-RAAF air gunner was hit in the same place as he was struck by anti-aircraft fire over Germany. The wounds rendered him mute and he was paralysed on his right side but he led a long life and became an award-winning potter.

Soon the whole company was on the high ground, which was the signal for A Company to attack on the right flank. It seized its objective—and it did so without tank support, as the American company commander refused to fight. A Company CO Captain Bill Chitts told the recalcitrant tank man to 'get the fornicating things out of the fornicating road and he'd do it himself, which he promptly did'. Without tank support the diggers were forced to use the aforementioned bazookas, now free of their packing grease. The Australians brewed up three T-34s. The diggers had earlier been issued with British-made PIAT—projector, infantry, anti-tank—guns, but they were almost universally derided by the men. According to Jack Gallaway the PIAT kicked like a mule. 'It could only be fired successfully by A Grade front row forwards in robust health and with nerves of steel. Best effective range? Approximately 10 feet.'

Over in the D Company sector Len's section rallied to help their mates in 4 Section. 'They had Ray Blythe, Joe Longmore and Bill Rose killed in action and Buster Morris, Tom Bush and Lofty Richards wounded, while Jack Stafford was hit in the arm but only slightly wounded,' Len wrote. Stafford ignored his wound to silence an enemy post with his Bren, before setting a T-34 ablaze by shooting up a reserve petrol tank strapped to its hull. The Americans awarded Stafford their Silver Star. His mates had something more practical in mind—they gave Stafford their combined rum ration. It would have been welcome in the sub-zero night. Len chalked up another Australian win over the formidable Russian tanks. 'We were the only section to get two tanks.'

The Australians were expecting a counterattack but their losses meant they were thinly stretched to meet it. A band of signallers from battalion headquarters had been cobbled together to reinforce the depleted 6 Section. Despite this, Len's foxhole was flanked by large gaps in the line on either side. The shells shrieked in soon after 7 pm and the line was being peppered with mortar bombs and raked with machine-gun bullets. Bugles sounded in the murk below and then came the chorus of 'Banzai'—according to Len the NKA had the same battle cry as the Japanese. A tank spouted red tracers at the Australians from 30 metres. 'I saw two figures running towards my pit,' Len said. 'I fired a burst and dropped them but the larger of the two, whom I nicknamed Horace, continued to moan and carry on, ending up with his feet practically on the edge of my pit, so I fired another burst, changed magazines and eventually put almost a magazine into him. It took about 30 bullets from an Owen gun to stop him. He was still kicking and screaming even then.' Horace was not what you would call a stereotypical small and slight Asian. Len said he was six feet, five inches (196 cm).

The surging wave of North Koreans attacked across the company's front. The defenders waited until they were within metres before firing. Those not cut down swept over the foxholes only to be shot in their backs. The survivors encountered a battalion headquarters bristling with machine guns manned by men who knew how to use them. The North Koreans withdrew, to once again be shot to pieces as they ran back through the line of foxholes on the ridge. It was slaughter. An attack in the A Company sector was also routed. More than 150 corpses lay around the Australian positions, and in some cases *in* the Australian positions. 'Horace's companion in the attack was still moaning and crawling about so Reg [Bandy] obligingly put a bullet in him,' Len said. 'A little later, Sergeant Buck Buchanan, [the] 11 Platoon Sergeant, came along with a can of hot coffee from goodness knows where, but very welcome. He first offered some to Horace till I pointed out that (a) he was North Korean and (b) he was dead.'

Jack Gallaway's recollection of the incident differs slightly from Len's. As the signals platoon sergeant, Gallaway led the party that reinforced Len's section that night. 'I took a section of riflemen up to reinforce Buck Buchanan's platoon,' Gallaway said. 'I took a bucket of very sweet tea up to where Buck was because they copped most of it. They were very much at the heart of the attack. They lost a few wounded but they held onto it. Anyway, after dark I snuck up there. A bloke, who I discovered afterwards was Len Opie, had another bloke in the bunker with him and I said "does your mate want a cup of tea?" "Oh," he said, "he's not thirsty." I didn't know him from a bar of soap at that stage of the game. He was a very, very calm character. To me he was so cool.' Coffee or tea, Buchanan or Gallaway, the nub of the story is the same. The Opie legend was up and running.

That Len cut off the fingers—or in some versions, the ears—of his foes to keep as trophies is also part of Opie folklore. Len seems to have thought it had its genesis in Korea. After the Chongju battle Len was asked to produce the pliers that everyone knew he always carried. 'One of our killed in action, Bill Rose from 12 Platoon, was wearing a ring and the authorities decided that it would be nice to send it home to his widow. The problem was that, with rigor mortis, the ring wouldn't come off so the Opie services were called for. I had a file, but I pointed out that a ring in two or three pieces would be slight consolation to a grieving widow and as my pliers were side-cutting the solution was obvious. And so rose the legend of the severed finger.'

In the morning the men left their foxholes to stretch their legs. A young civilian was detained after he was found wandering around the trenches. 'Somebody thought of the bright idea of hanging him, but nobody had any rope and there was no likely trees in the area so I suppose he was handed over to the MPs because he disappeared,' Len said. Len combed the ground for epaulettes discarded by enemy troops trying to escape capture. He also souvenired the pipe of Horace's companion killed on the edge of Len's foxhole. He noted that the 'assault pioneers blew up Stafford's tank for the second time'. One of Len's section handed him a North Korean grenade. When Len asked where he found it, the digger replied, 'Oh it was in the bottom of your pit: I thought it must have fallen in.' Len realised just what had happened. 'It fell in alright—after Horace heaved it at me, but in the excitement of the moment he had forgotten to pull the pin.'

The battalion had lost nine dead and 30 wounded on the heights above Chongju. On the road below, bumper-to-bumper tanks, jeeps and trucks carrying the Argylls streamed by, the way now made clear by the Australians. The Americans would take the lead for the triumphant final advance to the Yalu River on the Manchurian border. The Australians moved up to a reserve position and dug in for the night. The nights were now extremely cold and the men welcomed an issue of US winter kit and Len was especially grateful for a balaclava from his mother that arrived with the mail that very evening. 'There was a rumour that 27 Brigade will be Divisional reserve and we are unlikely to see further action,' Len wrote. All through the lines that night the men reflected on a job well done and dreamt of soon being back in Japan. Or Australia.

Charlie Green was proud of his men. The battalion had done all that was asked of it, and more. 'Well, we've made it, Arch!' Green said to C Company CO Arch Denness. Green attended to his duties before retiring to his tent pitched on the side of a gentle hill. At 6.10 pm five shells landed just over the ridge. The sixth cleared the crest and exploded in a tree. There were dozens of men in the area and Green—asleep in his tent—was the only one seriously hit. A chunk of shrapnel sliced into his stomach. He was rushed to a US field hospital and while he was stretchered in, said faintly, 'I could use another blanket.' The born soldier fought hard for 24 hours. First Cavalry Division CO Major General Hobart Gay said, 'Colonel Green was the finest battalion commander I ever saw.' Brigadier Coad kept a photo of Green on his desk until his dying day. Dead at 30, Green was one of Australia's greatest soldiers. He deserves to be better remembered.

Len recorded only the basic details of Green's death. If he was affected he did not show it. He was more concerned with matters closer to home, such as the section leader exercising his vanishing powers to their full extent by being transferred to a rear unit. 'Which left me back as section leader of 6 Section,' Len wrote.

On the morning of 1 November Len was grumpy; he missed an anticipated church parade because he was sent on a patrol with no clear orders, no map and no radio. 'Why me?' he wrote. 'I was not at all happy, especially as once we moved away from the unit we could hear the sound of hymns being sung in the distance. It would all have sounded rather beautiful were I not in such a stinking mood.' His patrol headed further into the fog when a shot rang out. 'I saw an old man lying by the track. He was so badly wounded that I finished him off then went back to the section to find the culprit.' Len's diary records the shooter's name. 'He claimed the old boy was [from the] North Korean People's Army [and] had been running to avoid us,' Len wrote. 'I suggested he go over to have a look as the victim must [have] been close to 70, but it was too late by then.' Len was doing a lot of killing all of a sudden.

Upon his return to the lines Len was called before the company CO, Major Wally Brown, who told him to report to 12 Platoon as a section leader. 'Why me?' Len asked for the second time that day. He then crossed the boundary into insubordination. 'You sacked me three weeks ago because of what happened and I'm no better now. Why has this happened?'

'Oh, just try it for a fortnight,' Brown said.

Len soon learned the reasons for his transfer. Twelve Platoon had a leadership vacuum. The rankers had refused to acknowledge their section leader, much as Len and his mates had treated their boss. Their platoon sergeant had been hit in the recent fighting. Their platoon commander was a Duntroon graduate who had been blamed by the men for their heavy casualties when they were pinned down in the paddy field below Chongju heights. 'Well, I'm the new section leader,' Len told his new comrades, who were mostly veterans of World War II and wore ribbons from the Middle East campaigns—meaning they had seen a lot more fighting than their section leader. 'They were a grizzled bunch,' Len wrote. 'They took one look at me and said: "You'll do!" And that was that! Eight Section of 12 Platoon went on to become the best section in the battalion.'

Which was just as well for Len because the Chinese had swept across the border and the Americans were in full retreat.

CHAPTER 5

THE THIRD WORLD WAR HAS STARTED!

'He was the outstanding Australian soldier from the Korean conflict.'
Brigadier Laurie Lewis

The South Korean generals boasted they would wash their swords in the Yalu, the river that formed the North Korean–Manchurian border. Whether they did is not recorded, but apparently some GIs pissed in the river. A ROK unit had time to fill a bottle with Yalu water to be sent back to President Syngman Rhee before the South Korean soldiers were overrun by one of several Chinese armies that attacked the North.

MacArthur had been warned. He had dismissed the repeated noises out of Peking that China would act if the UN armies threatened the Manchurian border. The Chinese were already piqued by US support for Nationalist leader Chiang Kai-shek; MacArthur's hubris in invading the North was the last straw. American imperialism must be checked, the Chinese propaganda trumpeted to a nation weary of the long war with Japan immediately followed by civil war. But the years of conflict had shaped a class of hardened veterans who knew little other than soldiering. It was the Chinese generals' turn to show some swagger. The Americans can bomb us all they like but they will never defeat us, they said. Atom bombs? Bring them on, we are an agrarian economy—will they nuke the whole of China? Sure, a few million might die, but we are a nation of many millions, they said. Five million of those many millions were in uniform, and of those 130,000 to 300,000—estimates vary—swarmed across the Yalu in October and November 1950.

Somehow, this immense force surprised the Americans. Throughout history bold armies have exploited enemy complacency over the impenetrability of geographical features. In 1759 the British seized Quebec after crossing a river at night then scaling weakly held precipitous slopes. The Gallipoli August offensive gained the heights—albeit briefly—after the Anzacs and British negotiated the treacherous ravines north of Anzac Cove. In 1940 Hitler conquered France after attacking through the thinly defended Ardennes forests. So it was in Korea. The Chinese armies padded into the mountains that ran down the country's spine. The ranges separated the main axes of the UN advance, and were not defended in any strength. Travelling light, with each soldier carrying a week's rations, and always at night, they did not throw up tell-tale dust clouds or leave vast dumps of materials in their wake. They set forest fires to further shroud their columns. Teeming hordes, billowing smoke, scorched earth—Armageddon had arrived.

US and South Korean units broke and ran in the face of the overwhelming odds. The Chinese attacked swiftly before the Allies could bring to bear their air power, artillery and armour. It all seemed so primitive—bugles, bells, drums, flutes and whistles heralded their charges—but there is nothing so effective as surprise. Accounts of the battles tell of how the Chinese appeared out of nowhere and vanished just as swiftly. Whole US battalions ceased to exist as effective fighting units in the face of the relentless onslaught. 'The Third World War has started!' a US general exclaimed to Brigadier Coad.

When word of Chinese intervention filtered through to the men of 3RAR, one theorist contemplated lining up all the Communists in front of the battalion's Vickers guns. No matter how long the guns fired there was no way of wiping out the enemy, he reasoned. 'If we're not careful, we'll run out of bullets before they run out of Chinamen.'

The US columns continued to stream past the Australians, only now they were going the other way. 'Everyone was going south as fast as they could,' Len wrote. Including the Australians, who were ordered to surrender their hard-won ground and take up a blocking position north-west of Pakchon. The Chinese advance through the central mountains threatened to outflank and cut off all the UN troops north and north-west of Sunanju, where the Korean peninsula is at its narrowest. The 27th Brigade had led for much of the advance; now it was the rearguard. Before long 3RAR was defending the extreme left flank of the entire UN army.

Meanwhile, Lieutenant General Horace 'Red Robbie' Robertson, grappled with finding a replacement for Green. Major Ferguson, the battalion second-in-command, seemed the logical choice, but Robertson instead appointed Lieutenant Colonel Stan Walsh, an officer with limited experience of battle command. He had joined the battalion by the time it had arrived back at the Broken Bridge, which had been captured by the Australians less than a fortnight before. The situation was confused. Coad, expecting attacks from the west and north, positioned his forces in those directions, leaving a long north–south ridge to the east—his rear—unoccupied. The Chinese attacked through this yawning gap on 4 and 5 November, with Coad rushing the Argylls into the breach. Down the road US gunners were firing over open sights at the teeming Chinese infantry. Len likened it to circling a wagon train, John Wayne style. Coad ordered 3RAR to take the dominant heights to the east. As their kin from 77 Squadron in Mustang fighters zoomed in to strafe the hills, the men of A and B companies fixed bayonets, formed a line and charged the ridge. 'It was an all-Australian day,' Ferguson said. 'The boost to morale was amazing when we recognised the planes of 77 Squadron overhead. The squadron's support was the closest I have ever seen and we passed our congratulations to the pilots over our contact wireless.' The diggers suffered heavy casualties, but took

Len and his sister, Molly, were loyal siblings despite their differences. 'She was an extrovert. He was an introvert,' Molly's daughter Lee said.

A pipe? Len never smoked and was teetotal his whole life.

Len (right) was a 'rather earnest scout', a schoolmate recalled. As a soldier he was an expert scout.

Len in his cadet uniform. He applied for Duntroon but was rejected. If he was disappointed at the time he soon got over it.

On 10 May 1940, Germany invaded the Low Countries. Cadet Len Opie was being drilled in firing a rifle grenade in Adelaide's Victoria Park that same day.

Len (second in line) sets off for one of his wars. Undated and unlabelled, this classic image of diggers setting forth was probably taken soon after he joined up in World War II.

Up the Ramu and across the Uria. Len (second in line) and his comrades chased the Japanese up the Markham and Ramu valleys, crossing small rivers such as the Uria, before pursuing their quarry into the Finisterre Range. (AWM 060243)

The landing at Balikpapan. This picture is from Len's personal collection so was very likely taken by him, giving us a fascinating soldier's eye view of the attack.

A captured Japanese war artist in Macassar must have seen something in young Len. He painted this portrait after Japan's surrender.

Opie and his new comrades file through the Keswick barracks clothing store after signing up for Korea. Clothing—specifically the lack of warm clothing—was foremost in their minds during their time at the front.

Len's 11 Platoon section had a 'lust for killing', Mo Gwyther said. Here 'the Warriors', as Tiger Wilson called them, are on their final manoeuvres in Japan before heading for the Korean front.

Christmas Day, Korea, 1950. Len (back, right, in slouch hat) is about the only digger without a long neck, but he is sporting a very impressive moustache. His comrades were posing for the camera—the beer was frozen, although it made for very palatable ice blocks.

Len takes communion in Korea. While not a deeply religious man, his diary often refers to his disappointment at missing a church parade.

Korea was short of a lot of things, but not mountains. Here men of 3RAR keep watch on Hill 614 after it was taken in February 1951 by Len's section. (AWM HOBJ2080)

'His effort cleared the way for the advance of the whole brigade.' Brigadier Ian Campbell pins Len's Distinguished Conduct Medal on a chest that was at first deemed too shallow for fighting. (AWM 148150)

By the mid-1950s Len's chest was starting to fill out with campaign ribbons to go with his Distinguished Conduct Medal.

Len was afraid of heights—or at least he claimed to be—but spent hundreds of hours in the air in Vietnam. Here he has just landed at Tam Ky after a recce about a month into his first tour.

The scribble on the back of this September 1966 photo reads: 'Just back from Recce (in disguise).' Len's companion, a US captain (left), is dressed in a more conventional fashion.

Winning the hearts and minds: Len with his Revolutionary Development team leaders in Tam Ky, 1966.

the hill. A, B and Len's D Company dug in on the high ground while the rest of the Brigade withdrew down the road, which was defended by C Company and battalion headquarters. The enemy came for them after dark.

The bugles and whistles sounded as the artillery and mortars opened up at about 8 pm. The diggers' foxholes were raked with small-arms fire while heavy machine guns targeted the rear positions astride the road, which were also pounded with mortar bombs that set a farmhouse on the lower slopes ablaze. Poor Walsh, with his limited battle experience, was overcome in the confusion of combat, and ordered a general withdrawal. 'We climbed out of our pits and moved about 100 yards, which put us in silhouette from the burning building where an old peasant woman was running around screaming and carrying on,' Len said. 'We halted for some ten minutes then were ordered back to our original position, where we went with a minimum of delay and settled in again somewhat short of the crest.' An enemy soldier, probably thinking the Australians had gone, wandered up and, in Len's words, 'Toddy Pemberton dropped him . . . but he was still moaning, so after warning our people that I was going out, I moved forward and finished him off'. Len does not say how he dispatched the soldier.

Walsh's panicked decision-making had put the battalion in great jeopardy. The men were relatively safe as long as they remained dug in on the ridge, but faced a rout if the enemy charged while they were pulling out. Walsh contravened exactly what Len's cadet instructor had counselled against all those years ago: 'At all costs avoid a running fight!' This is exactly what happened in A Company's sector. A platoon commander was counting his men as they filed past him in the dark and realised there was something wrong when the number reached 45 and counting. He did not have that many men—Chinese troops were in the Australian lines and hand-to-hand fighting broke out in the dark. When the whole of A Company assembled the next day, 60 men answered the roll call; it had entered the battle with 110. D Company suffered few casualties as its CO, after pulling back a short distance as described by Len, thought better of it and decided to ignore Walsh's order. 'They chopped A Company to bits and they did the same thing to us but we managed to get back into our holes for the night,' Len said. Approaching dawn, as the fighting petered out, the last post rang out across the battlefield. The bugler's identity remains a mystery.

Twelve Australians were killed in the action, and 64 wounded. The enemy's dead were estimated at 200. Jack Gallaway claimed it was the first time the UN had beaten the Chinese in a head-to-head fight.

As was his wont, after the action Len surveyed the battlefield. 'One of the first things I did was to check my little friend from the previous night,' he wrote. 'I found he was a North Korean and that he had a body band rather like the Japanese belt of a thousand stitches, except that he had some coins tied into his belt. These I shared with Toddy as the kill was half his anyway.' Later the men were detailed to bury the dead. Len lost an argument with an adjacent section leader about who would bury one particular corpse. 'When I searched it, I found three fountain pens including a Parker plus some banknotes, which I happily showed my counterpart,' Len wrote. 'However, when I came to bury our friend I had some difficulty. The usual procedure is to dig a hole alongside a body and roll it in, breaking protruding arms if necessary with an entrenching tool, as it has always been my experience that rigor mortis, once having set in, does not go away, although it could be because of the freezing conditions. Whatever, this particular chap had been napalmed and when I took his arm to roll him into the hole, it came away in my hands.'

Another soldier tripped a hand grenade when he moved a booby-trapped enemy corpse. The digger was unwounded but covered in blood and gore. 'It was said he did not share a weapon pit for a week afterwards,' Len wrote. 'Some of our chaps had investigated the ruins of the burning house and found a pig snuffling around the ruins. With the expectation of pork on the menu they stalked it, but when they caught up with it, it was busily engaged in rooting about in a corpse, so it was left to its own devices.'

Walsh was sacked the next day, to be replaced by Ferguson. Len said there were several accounts of what happened. 'The official version is that Brigadier Coad drove up to Battalion HQ, took one look at Walsh, sacked him on the spot and ordered him to drive southwards in his jeep. Another is that Walsh spotted Fergie and said: "Well, what's the form?" To which Fergie replied: "I'm in and you're out! That's the form!" ' The third version is scandalous. Len said the officers—he used the term 'mafia'—mutinied. They held a council of war and delegated one of their number to ride a pushbike to brigade headquarters to tell Coad they would not fight with Walsh. Many years later Gallaway asked Walsh for his version of events. Walsh said Coad recalled him to brigade headquarters, where he was summarily dismissed. 'I went forward again and found to my surprise and anger that Bruce [Ferguson] had already been informed, which, of course, was a completely unethical manner of dealing with the situation.'

The reorganisation extended beyond the battalion commander. Len received a new platoon sergeant, Peter Smeaton, who was 'a very pucka type with a toothbrush moustache and a pistol which he kept in an oiled rag and was continually cleaning'. Len liked the look of the Luger and 'kept him and it in mind should he stop the odd bullet'. Twelve Platoon also had a new commander, Lieutenant Jackie Ward, who Len said was 'a little ex-jockey who had won an MC with New Guinea troops in 1945' and a good officer. 'His main claim to fame was that, whenever he sat around a fire, the smoke would gravitate to him, it never failed—he was like a magnet.'

The Chinese offensive stopped as quickly as it started. Some speculated the initial thrust was merely to test the UN's strength, or that the Chinese were marshalling for a greater push, or even that its troops—many of whom had been quickly moved from southern China—were being re-equipped with winter uniforms. Whatever the reason, the Australians were unmolested while they replenished their ranks with reinforcements from Japan, including drafts of more World War II veterans. 'When we came to put a section together the problem became who to make section leader,' Ben O'Dowd reported. 'Not because we lacked talent, but because we probably had an ex-sergeant major and a few ex-platoon sergeants as well.'

Lieutenant Reg Saunders, a World War II veteran and the first Aboriginal man commissioned in the Australian army, was among the new arrivals. Saunders had been great mates with Tom 'Diver' Derrick. It is said Saunders sensed his mate's death in Tarakan when he was thousands of kilometres away in New Guinea. The enemy's withdrawal meant any action was restricted to patrol fights, which was right up Saunders' alley. He was a sterling soldier who had a habit of delivering wry, self-deprecatory or bitter one-liners about his Aboriginality. Later in the war when a fellow officer surveyed barren country from a high hill and ventured it was 'no country for a white man', Saunders replied, 'No country for a blackfella either.'

Reg Anock was in a batch of reinforcements posted to Saunders' A Company platoon. 'I remember one occasion we were ready to go into the attack and a bullet landed at his feet and he said "look at me, I'm a white man"', Anock said. Saunders was a wag all right. When he once posed for a photo with an African-American GI, Saunders quipped, 'Fancy getting a photo taken with a black bastard like you.' He used to say the Chinese were afraid of blackfellas. It was not mutual. 'He wasn't frightened of anything,' Reg Bandy said.

When they were not on patrol the men were assailed by the cold. At night the temperature plummeted to as low as minus 15 degrees Celsius. Every soldier was issued with mittens with the trigger finger cut out for ease of firing. However, in the cold, bare skin stuck to metal as if it was coated with superglue. To further exacerbate the problem, the mittens were unsuitable for effective firing. There are stories of Bren gunners who fired a whole magazine to warm their hands. The frozen ground made for hard digging and rice straw to line foxholes was at a premium. 'Cold!' Len scrawled in his diary. 'Christ it was cold!' Len was seldom so florid. 'Once your feet got frozen they stayed frozen, and the same with your fingers. You didn't feel the cold like you feel the cold here, you just felt numb and coped with it.' Warm clothing—especially US 'pile' jackets—was highly sought after as the men put on layer after layer to try to keep warm.

Still there was no sign of any enemy formations of any consequence, and on 11 November, Remembrance Day, the brigade advanced slowly and cautiously north of Pakchon. It was a period of relative inactivity—occasional desultory shelling, rounding up surrendering North Koreans—and the ever-present cold was fertile ground for idle chat. 'There was another rumour—this time that General MacArthur had threatened to A-bomb the power plants on the Yalu if the Chinese did not withdraw,' Len said. 'In their turn the Chinese have denied knowledge that their troops are in Korea [replying] "possibly only some volunteers".' Another story doing the rounds was that a South Korean officer had been taken by a Siberian tiger in the night.

By now the men were regularly receiving issues of the popular US C-ration packs, which contained tinned meat and fruit, biscuits, coffee, sugar, salt, pepper, chocolate, cigarettes and toiletries. Len's comrades checked his pack for tinned apricots, as every time he ate them they went into action the next day. But the ration packs were often inedible anyway as the tins froze and even after being heated over a fire a 'solid block of ice' remained in the middle. Len and his section mates took turns hauling a tin of strawberry jam halfway across Korea and back in the hope of coming across a loaf of bread. However, the Thanksgiving meal put on by the Americans made 23 November a day to remember. Gigantic turkeys with cranberry sauce, shrimp cocktails, hard-boiled eggs, crabmeat, hot vegetables, plum puddings, fruit cocktails and mince pies—Gallaway said all that was missing was ice-cream, and it was too cold for that anyway. MacArthur declared they would be home by Christmas—doesn't every general in every war? He was preparing an offensive he believed would drive the Chinese out of Korea and end the war.

The Chinese allowed the UN armies to advance for barely a day before hitting them hard. Three ROK divisions collapsed immediately.

They swept past US units while GIs were curled up in their sleeping bags. Many of those not caught in their tents broke and ran. The 27th Brigade was in reserve around Pakchon when Len heard firing in the direction of the Argylls. The Scotsmen were 'horsing around', he guessed. The next morning Len was woken by Lieutenant Ward telling him to rouse the rest of the men, and quickly. 'What, did the Argylls play up last night with all that firing?' Len asked. 'No,' said Ward. 'The Chinese have broken through the line at Kunu-ri and we have to go there to help the Turks.'

The Turkish brigade had only recently arrived in Korea and was in reserve when it came under attack at Kunu-ri, at the apex of the line on the UN's left flank. This was the key point, a salient on a main transport route, which had to be held to avoid a rout. The diggers were issued with ammunition, packed up quickly, then boarded their trucks. On the way they passed a US convoy loaded with assault boats—presumably for the drive across the Yalu—going the other way, then truckloads of Australians. 'Where the hell are you going?' one of Len's mob shouted. The reinforcements yelled back that they were on their way to join 3RAR. 'Well, you'd better bloody turn around because you're going the wrong way!' a soldier yelled back. 'What an initiation to the country [that would be], to be captured before you even joined your unit!' Len said. 'Anyway, the drivers smartly screeched to a halt, turned around and trailed after us.'

They arrived at Kunu-ri, debussed in the mist, embraced the Turks and posed for photos with the foes of their fathers. The Turks marched off in the direction of the firing and the Aussies dug in. Campfires were prohibited lest they betrayed the soldiers' positions, but D Company HQ apparently ignored the order and accidentally burnt down their tent. Gunfire during the night had diggers grabbing their rifles, but it was only the HQ's ammunition going off in the fire. Len woke to news the position had been outflanked and a general retreat ordered. There were only enough trucks for two companies. B and D companies drew the short straws and so set off on the 30-kilometre march to Chasan, where the brigade would stand and fight. Photos of the columns show diggers with slouch hats squeezed on top of thick bala-clavas and wearing mittens the size of oven gloves. 'The yellow dust, despite the freezing weather, kept blowing in our faces,' Len said. 'All along the line of march there were fires, not that they did us much good. Our fingers began to thaw out . . . at the other end, our feet, which after 30 minutes of marching started to perspire and warm up . . . froze again so that when we started marching they took another half hour to warm up again. We passed a US artillery battery firing in all four directions, including the way we were going. This did nothing for morale!' The companies marched behind their own piper, lent by the Argylls to raise the men's spirits. The pipes had the opposite effect on Ben O'Dowd, who bore an Irishman's grudge against an old 'heathen' enemy.

The brigade's orderly and disciplined withdrawal was in stark contrast with the US 'bug-out', as the retreat became known. The Amer-icans were in disarray, and little wonder given the weight of men that fell upon them when the Chinese attacked. With the enemy swarming all around, the 2nd US Infantry Division followed the Australians, Scots and English down the road to Chasan. It came to a fork in the road; should they take the road to the west or follow the Australians down a shorter route through a deep mountain pass? This was fraught as the Chinese were streaming along the heights. They chose the pass, but it was too late. As they often did in attack, the Americans tried to bash their way through using weight of metal. Most of the metal was left to rust after being hit with a hail of bullets and mortar bombs from the heights. The Middlesex battalion attacked from the bottom end of the pass but was repelled, with heavy losses. Few of the Americans made it through; the rest took to the hills. Three thousand GIs were killed or captured. The day after the battle Len's section marched past some of the very few tanks that made it through the pass—they looked like they had been hosed down with blood. Meanwhile, the Turks chose the westerly route and made it to the safety of the UN lines unmolested.

As the big 'bug-out' gathered pace, Brigadier Coad visited Corps headquarters. In the battle room a large perspex map showed the Chinese formations swarming south. In the mountainous centre an enemy formation was labelled '2 MILLION?' Little wonder the UN was in a panic. All its planes, ships and tanks were proving no match for Chinese armed with little more than burp guns and mortars. MacArthur's great offensive became a rout, and the general's orders to pull back to the 38th Parallel were redundant because that was exactly what his armies were doing anyway. The Australians paused briefly to make a stand at a river crossing before having to withdraw when their flanks were exposed by retreating units. They saw more of Pyongyang this time around—from the other direction. 'The most depressing sights were when we went back through Pyongyang and saw the huge dumps of rations and supplies on fire,' Len said. 'Endless streams of refugees loaded down with all their possessions trudged along the sides of the road.'

All the while Len's standing grew. The men looked up to him, even though they no doubt feared him as well. When Len told a newly arrived recruit to watch over a would-be deserter, the greenhorn brandished an entrenching tool over his comrade's head for an entire night.

Now he was in command, Ferguson made a point of pressing some flesh. On 6 December, the retreat paused long enough for this to happen. 'He finally appeared and inspected us,' Len said, 'asking such questions as: "When did you wash last? How many Chinese have you killed with your weapon?" He looked rather disparagingly at my footwear: "And what are those?" "American paratroop boots, sir." "And what is the particular virtue of them?" "None that I know, just that I burned a hole in one of my [boots] and these were the only ones I could find. Anyway they are better for walking, sir."' Ferguson raised an eyebrow and continued on his rounds. At last a loaf of bread magically appeared and Len sent for the man whose turn it was to carry the precious jam. He had eaten it. Oh dear. Len drew a breath. 'Henceforth, so long as you are in 8 Section, which I trust won't be for long, as I would advise you to

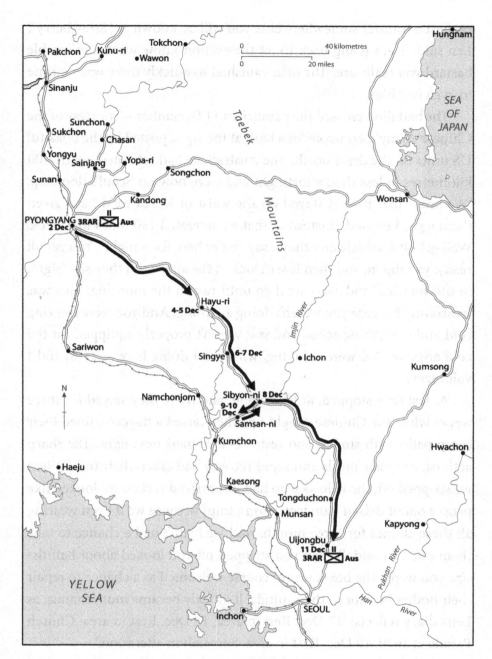

THE BUG OUT

request a transfer somewhere else, you will be known as "Strawberry",
Len said. 'I am going back to let the section know what a miserable
bastard you really are.' The man vanished so quickly there was no time
to even hex him.

The battalion crossed the parallel on 11 December—'courtesy of the
Chinese Army' Len wrote, in a barb at the signs posted by the boastful
US units on the drive north. The Australians had retreated nearly 400
kilometres in less than a fortnight and were now on Seoul's doorstep.
'We knew that if we'd stayed on the waist of Korea we'd have given
them a go,' Len said. 'Instead of that we retreated 190 miles in a week.
We'd get off a vehicle and they'd say "we're here for a night". You get all
ready, you dig in, and then five o'clock in the afternoon they say "right,
in the vehicles" and away we'd go until two in the morning. This was
frustrating because you weren't doing anything. And you were freezing
cold and everything ached and you weren't properly equipped for the
cold anyway. You were thinking, what am I doing here . . . why did I
volunteer?'

At last they stopped, at Uijeongbu, and there they stayed for three
weeks while the Chinese caught up. They raised a flagpole, lined their
camp paths with stones, and rested before their next fight. The sharp
actions, irregular meals and rapid retreats had taken their toll. 'When
we stripped off, the fellows who had just arrived reckon we looked like
people out of Belsen [concentration camp] because we'd been wearing
all these clothes for three months and we hadn't had a chance to take
them off,' Len said. 'When you stripped off you looked about half the
size you were.' The break was of course welcomed as a chance to repair
their bodies but not so their minds. It quickly became monotonous, as
Len's diary reflects: '17 Dec. Rest in area. 18 Dec. Rest in area. Church
Parade at 1630. 19 Dec. Rest in area. Snowfall in afternoon.'

The brigade's service had been noted at the highest levels. The
South Korean government decided to award it a presidential citation,
to be presented by 8th Army commander General Walton Walker. The
ceremony was arranged for 23 December, at brigade headquarters. But

Walker was killed when a ROK truck swung onto the wrong side of the road and collided with his jeep. Lieutenant General Matthew Ridgway, a veteran of the airborne attack at Normandy, assumed command in Walker's place. With a hand grenade pinned to one lapel and a first-aid kit to the other, Ridgway was imbued with fighting spirit. He immediately asked MacArthur if the supreme commander had any objection to him counterattacking the Chinese. MacArthur said the 8th Army was his, and he may do as he pleased. Ridgway rallied his demoralised army ahead of his planned offensive. He ordered the GIs to get off the roads and start fighting in the hills. Overwhelming firepower was all well and good except when you were outflanked and overlooked by the enemy. 'He was a breath of fresh air, a showman, what the army desperately needed,' a US infantry colonel said of Ridgway.

The Christmas of 1950 was one of great largesse for diggers who had grown used to going without. The US cooks laid on turkey with all the trimmings, and fruit cake, and there was beer—albeit frozen beer—so the men sucked on giant ice blocks of Fosters, Asahi and Kirin. The *Adelaide News* ran a rather incongruous front-page photo of the teetotal Corporal Len Opie—complete with thick moustache—tucking into his Christmas lunch while pretending to drink from a longneck of beer. That week the men were laid low by the cold; often they sought the refuge of their sleeping bags in the afternoons. A liberal issue of rum and whisky shared by the Argylls warmed many on New Year's Eve. Not Len, of course. He showed his disdain for drinking and drinkers in a 3 January diary entry: 'In the adjoining section were two characters who had managed to get some of the local Tiger Brand whisky during the day and had finished off a bottle between them. Now they were suffering. Every half hour or so the occupant of the sleeping bag would climb out and proceed to heave his insides out while the other climbed in and tried to warm up.'

Meanwhile the Chinese had beaten Ridgway to the punch. A fresh offensive was heralded by the usual trickle then stream of refugees surging south, followed by 'the familiar sight of ROK soldiers moving at a solid jog trot toward the south', Gallaway said. The brigade was sent north to act as a shield for the retreat, and had some hairy times while again fulfilling its task to the letter, with minimal casualties, before pulling back to Seoul, which was readying for evacuation. After yet another rearguard action, with D Company in the front line, the battalion withdrew across the Han River and took its place in 'Line D', more than 150 kilometres to the south. This is where Ridgway would stand and fight. As his UN armies dug in, MacArthur was making preparations to evacuate Korea.

Battle casualties, illness and transfers had reduced Len's section to five men, but he revelled in leading his little band on regular patrols to stay in contact with the next unit in the thinly held line, an ROK outfit stationed some 2 kilometres away. Len enjoyed the exercise and it helped keep the men warm in the blizzards that swept down from the north. The campaign histories are filled with tall tales such as warm water poured from a jug freezing before it hit the ground, but yes, it was cold. Len took to wearing long johns, service trousers and windproof pants all at once. Some men kept little braziers burning all night in their foxholes. Others kept a 44-gallon drum fire going 24 hours a day despite the paucity of firewood. As usual, some of Len's men bucked the system. 'I found out that some of my fellows were sleeping in Korean huts which were centrally heated,' he said. 'They have a fire underneath, they're raised about two feet off the ground and beautifully warm, but they didn't bother to tell me that they were doing it.' Every now and then a bundle of good cheer arrived from home. 'A parcel today from the Barossa fruit growers which will come in very handy,' Len recorded on 10 January.

About this time the Australian government declared an amnesty for all the diggers who had joined up to escape their alimony and maintenance responsibilities. 'Anyone was permitted to come clean and make allotments or otherwise straighten out their affairs,' Len wrote. 'Twelve Platoon had seven in this category.'

Len thrived as section leader. He had even been promoted to temporary corporal. But he also had frequent run-ins with his comrades, and was plainly horrified by some of their behaviour. He described how one of the earlier deserters absconded again. 'A great pity he wasn't shot when he first went as, like Strawberry, his only use was as a number on picket.'

One bleak night, during a thick snowstorm, Len asked another soldier to keep his head above the parapet so Len had a reference point when he returned from checking on the other troops. His companion instead withdrew deep into his trench, leaving a lost Len to spend a night in no man's land furiously exercising to avoid freezing. When Len made it back in the morning he angrily confronted his comrade, who shot back: 'You know, if you were in trouble, I don't think I'd help you!' Len replied: 'Like you didn't last night! The difference between us is that if you were in trouble I would have to help you because that is part of my job, so perhaps you had better move elsewhere!' The man duly transferred to another platoon. He took a Len hex with him.

The battalion's new medical officer, Captain Don Beard, joined 3RAR about this time. 'Due to the fact that he had little medication for the treatment of frostbite, his usual recommendation was to rub Barbasol shaving cream on the affected parts, so he earned the title "Barbasol Beard", Len wrote. Beard said Barbasol was useless for its intended purpose 'but it had some lanolin in it so it was my special treatment for frostbite'.

Beard and Len became good friends, which was unusual for a captain and corporal, a temporary corporal at that. 'I got reports about this Opie and he certainly was a great soldier,' Beard said. 'He was always smart—well, as smart as you can be in the snow. More so than most of the other soldiers. And he was tireless. He worked very hard. A great leader of men. Critical of people who did the wrong thing but very ready to support them if they needed support. He knew that if we were going to win this war we'd have to do it properly and well. Soldiers told me that he was a stickler for keeping personal weapons clean. And he was insistent on shaving every day.'

The day Beard arrived the battalion was engaged in a close action. It didn't help that Beard had a hangover from a farewell party in Japan.

'I was tired and I have to admit that I was not a little frightened about all this.' He asked a US orderly for directions to 3RAR's lines. 'We didn't know there were any Australians in Korea,' was the reply. When he finally found Ferguson the CO said, 'It's good to see you. We've got casualties who need looking after.' Beard was directed to the medical section in a 'ditch in the paddy field'. When he arrived at his post he had a moment of clarity. 'All fear vanished because I realised I was in a battalion and everyone was concerned about each other and everyone looked after each other—and you had Australians all around you. And that was a good feeling.' Apparently the alimony dodgers, malingerers and malcontents had fashioned something resembling esprit de corps.

Also newly arrived was a regiment of NZ artillery. However it was a less than auspicious entrance—the gunners dropped ranging shells in the heart of D Company's lines. No one was hit and the Kiwis 'did get better', Len said. Otherwise it was a relatively quiet and safe time. Some men were afforded leave in Japan and the rest had to be content with B-grade movies for entertainment. Len judged *The Glass Menagerie*, a 1950 adaptation of the Tennessee Williams play, as 'probably the worst film I can remember', although Kirk Douglas and Jane Wyman could hardly be called B-grade actors.

The men of 3RAR shivered in their foxholes, patrolled no man's land, and spoiled for a fight. The Chinese thrust had again petered out. The enemy was tired. The Chinese were not immune to the cold and as they thrust further south, they had to contend with the problem encountered by attacking armies over the centuries—stretched supply lines. And they were subjected to daily strafing and bombardment from long-range artillery. Ridgway marshalled his counter-thrust—in fact a series of operations—Wolfhound, Thunderbolt, Roundup and Killer. The latter was aptly named. It was in this fight that a killer from South Australia achieved his crowning battlefield glory.

CHAPTER 6

HILLS ARE FOR HEROES

'There's a VC if I've ever seen one.'
Captain Reg Saunders

Ridgway drew on the wisdom of generals past to describe his army's new method—methodical, plodding, advances en masse with no gaps in the line, along the high ground as well as the roads, all supported by creeping barrages and air strikes. The plan was to take and hold ground in steps, while killing as many of the enemy as possible. 'Crumbling', he called it. The same word was used by Montgomery in Egypt, and the tactics were similar to those applied by Monash in the last year of World War I. It was in stark contrast to the US practice of the early months of Korea, of sticking to the roads and surrendering the heights to the enemy. As in battles of the ages, the high ground was the key to victory. Heights such as Chunuk Bair at Gallipoli, the shallow Pozières ridge, or even molehills such as Trig 29, taken and held by the magnificent South and West Australians of the 2/48th Battalion at the height of Alamein.

Heights such as Hill 614: after a mostly uneventful start to their part in the Operation Killer advance north of the Han River, the Commonwealth troops suddenly found the way blocked by this precipitous peak. It towered over a pass to the next valley so had to be taken. 'This

2000 foot hill dominated the surrounding countryside in tortuous and rugged terrain where the snow still lay thick in sheltered hollows and the razorbacked ridges were slippery with rain,' wrote Norman Bartlett in *With the Australians in Korea*. Hill 523, a step in the climb to the 614 summit, was found to be unoccupied when 3RAR's B Company scaled it on 23 February. Late in the afternoon Ferguson sent a platoon along the razorback saddle leading up to 614, but heavy fire from the peak repelled the Australians, who withdrew with one man wounded. The peak was shelled overnight by the New Zealand 25-pounders and hit hard by US heavy mortars ahead of a planned morning attack.

Six Platoon of B Company headed up the narrow ridge the next morning, but just as the Australians neared the final approach they came under heavy mortar and machine-gun fire, and withdrew after losing one dead and six wounded. It appeared the summit was strongly held by a well-dug-in enemy. The approach was so narrow, with steep drops on either side, there was no opportunity for flanking manoeuvres. The bastion was holding up the whole brigade—now more than 3000-men strong after the arrival of a battalion of the Princess Patricia's Canadian Light Infantry. Ferguson and Coad called in air and artillery strikes and sent out probing patrols on 25 and 26 February. One party made it to within 20 metres of the crest before it too was repelled, with one dead and two wounded. 'One of the wounded rolled down off the hill wrapped in an orange air recognition panel, rather a spectacular sight,' Len said. 'By now each attack on the hill was attracting a large audience, including war correspondents.' The peak was bristling with machine-gun nests—two US planes were brought down by .50 calibre fire while strafing the enemy. Meanwhile, the battalion's crack sniper, Ian 'Robbie' Robertson, performed his deadly work. Robbie found a spot in the open—never behind a tree or rock, too obvious a target, he said—and set about reducing 614's garrison. 'He spent hours alone on the hillside, methodically picking off his marks, one by one,' Andrew Rule wrote in a 2004 *Sydney Morning Herald* profile of Robertson. 'He called it "switching them off".

As usual Len was not short of an opinion and freely offered it to his company commander, Captain Bill Keys, who, as Sir William Keys, was later a pillar of the RSL. 'I suggested to Captain Keys that we should try a night attack without preparation,' Len wrote. 'You'll get your turn,' Keys replied. Perhaps he knew that turn would come in the morning.

At 6.30 am Len was brewing cocoa against the cold; the winter was nearing an end but snowdrifts filled the sheltered hollows. 'Get your gear, Len, we're going on patrol,' Lieutenant Ward said, before Len could have even a sip. The platoon headed off and came upon Ferguson, the brigade major, Keys, and a large party of VIPs 'sitting as if to watch a demonstration—sitting like spectators at a game—which they were, except that we didn't know it at the time'. It quickly became apparent Len's section would lead the next attack on the hill. 'Captain Keys introduced us to the VIPs whereupon Fergie took over and said: "Now I want you to nudge along, but don't get into any trouble." By which time I realised that "getting into trouble" meant that we were next to have a go at 614.' Len laughed at his colonel before replying: 'Well, are we going to take the hill? You either want the hill or you don't.' Ferguson ignored the intemperate comment, but Keys was not impressed. Len couldn't care less.

Len's diary reveals nothing of his personal thoughts about the fearsome task. Eleven men had fallen in three attempts to take the peak. 'We weren't given any instructions at all except that there was a hill and we had to take it,' Len said. There was scant cover because the repeated air and artillery fire had stripped almost all vegetation from the battlefield. The attack would be made up a 'steep and narrow ridge line, over open ground for a distance of 200 yards'. So Len's thoughts are unknown as he led his small band up to crouch at the foot of the hill while it was bombed, shelled, mortared and raked with machine-gun fire. He crouched behind a rock the size of a kerosene tin as the US planes zoomed in to plaster the peak with napalm. It was a spectacular show for the war correspondents and men not involved in the attack, but the bombardment was mostly ineffectual as the Chinese simply withdrew deeper into their bunkers. Len waited for Ward's signal. This time the Australians would keep off the crest; instead they would climb across the grain on the south-eastern slope.

Go! The last shell shrieked over Len's head as he ran up the hill. 'There was arms and legs going all over the place,' recalled Private Allan Bennett, who, like much of the rest of the battalion, had a grandstand view of the battle. 'That was worth watching.' The battalion's Vickers guns blazed away at the summit while Len's section scrambled up as fast as they could. Despite the sharp climb and the need for speed, Len was weighed down with enough firepower to take on several Chinese armies. As well as his customary Owen gun, he had his ancient Keswick issue .303—number 16809—slung over his shoulder, and grenades. Bill Nimmo had taken the .303 when Len received an Owen upon his promotion to section leader. The Owen was good for close quarters fighting but the .303 had a greater range and packed more punch. As Len prepared for the fight, Bill handed it to him and said, 'You never know; you might get a long distance shot.'

'As I went across the grain of the hill I noticed a couple of heads peering at me from a weapon pit up the hill to my right, about 10 feet [away],' Len said. He hurled a grenade at the slope above the trench. 'It did the right thing and bounced into the pit just as it went off.' Immediately two men—one brandishing a Tommy gun—popped out of a foxhole 20 metres away. 'As I twisted to get out of the way of his fire, my foot caught in the fork of a small tree so that I fell pointing downhill with one leg in the air.'

Len's military career appeared about to end with him hanging upside down on a Korean hill. Despite his ungainly and precarious position, he started duelling with the Tommy gunner. 'I fired a burst and the chap disappeared, only to pop up again a few seconds later. This time I had a shot at him with the rifle and the same thing happened. By now I had freed my foot, so I estimated the time he would pop up again and fired at the parapet of his pit where he had disappeared.' Len shot the man between the eyes. 'I tossed another grenade in and continued on

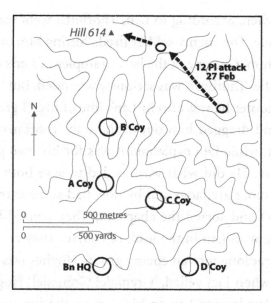

Hill 614 ▲

12 Pl attack
27 Feb

N

B Coy

A Coy

C Coy

0   500 metres
0   500 yards

Bn HQ   D Coy

HILL 614

my way.' But only after helping himself to the occupant's weapons. As well as the Tommy gun, the enemy soldier had somehow come upon a US Garand rifle and an M1 carbine. Len also grabbed some Chinese grenades, but left the Tommy gun behind. Presumably the Owen gun was also left, but not before Len pulled up a shutter door and 'filled the dugout up with a magazine'. At least seven Chinese lay dead.

The Chinese replied with their own grenades, rolling them down the hill. It reminded Private Osbourne 'Ossie' Hughes of another war. 'It was like fighting the Nips in the islands,' the ex-commando said. 'Everything started to happen at once. A chink threw three grenades and Len Opie threw one back to him. Then a Chinese appeared out of the ground behind me.' As the soldier took aim, Private Charlie Thorburn 'ran him through' with his bayonet.

'Charlie Thorburn was behind me and the next customer was in a one-man foxhole with the muzzle of his rifle sticking out,' Len said. He blazed away with the captured rifles and tossed Chinese grenades. 'As fast as his gun ran out of ammunition he picked up another weapon,' Hughes said. Hughes, Thorburn and Len were in the thick of three strongpoints when, according to Len, Thorburn went too close to the one-man foxhole. The enemy soldier fired, 'hitting him in the shoulder and dropping him'. Cue one of the best examples of Len's dispassionate coolness in battle. Thorburn was seriously wounded. But lying between Len and the shooter he was also in Len's line of fire. 'I grabbed him by his bad arm and dragged him out of the way.' Thorburn cried out in painful protest, while Len explained it was for his own good. He was not a cruel man. He did what was needed to save both their lives. 'I had called for more grenades and by now had some extras so I threw one into the pit and sorted the chap out.' They paused briefly before charging again, with Len in the lead, of course. They crested the peak and charged headlong into an enemy group. Hughes was blazing away with his Bren when Len yelled, 'Grenade! Grenade!' Hughes was flattened by the blast leaving Len on his own on the summit. It mattered not. The Chinese had fled. Hill 614 had fallen. And it had fallen not to a division, brigade, battalion, company or platoon, it had succumbed to a section—Len's section.

The rest of the platoon came up, followed by the whole of B Company. Robertson scaled the peak to check on the results of his sniper fire. He found 30 corpses in the area he had been targeting. One morning's work. 'And I'd been there all week. I got a feeling of horror. I never did the arithmetic. I still don't want to.' Many years after the war Robertson sent Len a photo of him cradling his sniper's rifle in his arms. It was accompanied by a short note that read, 'Enclosed is a recently surfaced photo of self and best friend in Korea.' No one knows how many men Robertson killed in Korea, not even the man himself. 'We weren't a lot of Hollywood macho idiots carving notches in our rifle butts,' Robertson explained. 'We were never body counters.'

Robertson wasn't patting himself on the back and neither was Len, who scouted to the left, off the crest, to deal with any enemy lying doggo in more foxholes. There were none, so he returned to the summit. There he stood face to face with a man who promptly had half his head blown away by a lucky long-range machine-gun burst. Len was unmoved. It was the man who had left Len for dead in no man's land the month before. The hex had another victim.

Thorburn, who was seriously wounded and unconscious, was taken to an aid station where he was put in a morgue tent with a dead man's tag on his toe. One shocked medic discovered he was very much alive.

Len suffered nothing more serious than grenade fragments in his hands. As usual, he searched for booty—pocketing the hex victim's .45 Colt pistol for a start—while the rest of the company swarmed onto the peak. Len wrote sneeringly about an officer who was 'determined to be in at the death'. Some of the company not involved in the battle were boasting of the conquest and posing for press photos. Hughes regaled a reporter with the story of the attack, describing Len as 'one out of the bag—they don't come any better'.

'There's a VC if I've ever seen one,' Reg Saunders reportedly said after watching Opie's attack from the Australian lines. Saunders knew something of such matters, being close mates with 'Diver' Derrick VC. 'Reg Saunders always claimed he should've had the VC,' Gallaway said. 'Lennie shot five blokes with five different rifles. Although Reg was inclined to gild the lily a little bit. But I knew enough about Opie to know that was true. Len Opie's aggressive attack and his skill at arms gave the lead to his comrades and caused the enemy holding the feature to flee.'

According to Reg Bandy, Coad, who was also watching, told Ferguson to immediately write a VC recommendation. 'He should have got a VC in my mind,' Bandy said. 'We'd been two days going to take the hill. He did it on his own.' Tom Muggleton said Len 'did a magnificent job because that hill was as bare as a road—no cover whatsoever'. Captain Colin Brown joined the battalion later in the war, but he wrote, 'Some who were in the battalion at that time told me it was a feat worthy of the Victoria Cross.' The Americans among the observing VIPs considered Len's feat worthy of the Congressional Medal of Honor, the US equivalent of the VC. 'If that man doesn't get a high medal we'll give him one of ours,' one said.

Len received a high medal, just not the highest. After several months of army muddling, he was awarded the Distinguished Conduct Medal (DCM), which is second only to the VC. The official citation reads in part, 'Corporal Opie unhesitatingly led his section in an attack on the three enemy strongpoints . . . seven enemy were killed by small-arms fire and grenades . . . by his unselfish devotion to duty, initiative and great courage, Corporal Opie made the capture of the position possible, thereby enabling the battalion, and subsequently the brigade, to continue the advance.' Gallaway said the DCM represented a 'conservative evaluation of the merit of the achievement—his effort cleared the way for the advance of the whole brigade'.

It is hard to think of anything like the act of bravery in Australia's fighting history. But he very likely was never recommended for the VC. An officer of the era said not many—if any—were in Korea. Why the officers up the chain of command did not write up a VC recommendation is a matter for pure speculation. Perhaps they were put off by quotas, perhaps they thought the deeds were inferior to those of World War II, or perhaps they were simply too busy fighting to do the paperwork.

Len's was the first DCM awarded to an Australian soldier in Korea. Only five were awarded in the three-year war. It changed his life. It brought him limited fame, though in no way fortune, and validated his worth as a soldier, if indeed it needed such endorsement. It probably emboldened him to challenge his superiors even more, as they would be loath to argue with a highly decorated war hero. Most of all it made Len feel like he belonged in the army, even though he was a volunteer and proud of it. When in uniform he always wore the infantry corps badge, rather than the regimental badge. This was his little joke. It was easy to assume he was a career soldier, but wearing the corps badge was his way of saying he was always a volunteer, and *never* regular army. 'He used to say "I never took the Queen's shilling"', Brigadier Laurie Lewis said.

Len also delighted in cocking a snook at martinets, parade ground soldiers and big-noters. He was no blower. In several hours of interviews with the Veterans' Affairs Department for an oral history project, he did not mention the Hill 614 action once. His 'stunt' set the Opie legend in stone. But, that afternoon in February 1951, he was grumpy about being sent to the rear soon after taking the hill. 'I never had a chance to check my results and even more annoying was the sight of B Company chaps having their photos taken, not for winning the hill but describing in living colour how they had nearly won it.'

Temporary Corporal Len Opie's only immediate reward for his heroism on Hill 614 was being allowed to sleep in until after eight the next day. That and being promoted to sergeant—temporary sergeant— and being sent back to 11 Platoon as its platoon sergeant. One of his first challenges was reining in a private of Irish stock who heard 'wee folk' in no man's land while on sentry duty. That was harmless enough except the private set about exorcising the spirits with grenades. 'The only remedy was to take all his grenades away,' Len said.

Len's stunt made headlines back home. *The Advertiser* reported on 2 March that 12 Platoon was the 'toast of the Commonwealth Brigade ... after scaling razor backed spurs' to seize Hill 614. 'Australian officers gave a lot of credit for the success to the leading section commander, Corporal Len Opie, of Medindie, SA, and his section privates, "Ossie" Hughes, of Victoria, and Charlie Thorburn. Opie with an Owen gun, Hughes with a Bren gun, and Thorburn with a rifle, charged among the Chinese weapon pits and dugouts. Opie seized a carbine and a rifle from two Chinese who tried to fight it out from their foxholes.' Details of his bravery were broadcast on the radio and reporters were dispatched to the Opie residence in Medindie. Mr Opie senior doesn't appear to have given them much, so the column inches were filled with minor detail such as how the hero went to Saints, served in the 7th Division in the last war, and was single. Still, the reporters apparently extracted a photo from the Opie family, so a smiling Len beamed out from the bottom of page one. The Melbourne *Argus* was more expansive, reporting that the 'tall, slim' corporal carried out a 'one-man attack on a razorback ridge' that had held up 'a whole brigade for a week'.

The array of weapons used by Len at 614 is at the heart of the Opie legend: his Owen, the borrowed .303, the US Garand rifle, Mills bombs, Chinese grenades and the M1 carbine, which became one of the most travelled and most interesting weapons in the history of the Australian army. After a long war with Customs—in which Len argued he wanted to use it as a 'sporting rifle'—the M1 carbine was returned to him after the war. He didn't fire it for another ten years, and then only when he loosed a few rounds into the sea off Yorke Peninsula for the sake of it. On Kapyong Day 1982, he donated it to the Woodside Barracks, where it was hung on a wall. Later it was mounted on polished wood and presented as an annual prize for 3RAR's best section. The Opie Trophy is awarded to this day and is regarded as a high honour by the winning section.

Hill 614 was in Allied hands, but Korea has no shortage of hills and the battalion was next ordered to take Hill 410. On 6 March, as dusk fell, Bill Keys gathered his D Company officers and NCOs and relayed Ferguson's orders while helping himself to Len's freshly brewed cocoa. A Company would attack at night and D Company would go in on a parallel spur before dawn. The men rose at 4 am. 'Our gear was frozen solid and took some folding up,' Len said. 'At 0500 we moved down the hill preparatory to the assault on Hill 410. It was all right until we were about 25 yards from the bottom where the slope suddenly became almost sheer and, after the first few had negotiated it, the snow became ice so that there was no way to climb down. Each person hung on to scrub and tree branches, then slid the rest of the way amidst a welter of gear. A line had been laid by one of the signallers and as I lost my footing, the line snagged my carbine magazine which came apart with the spring and bullets flying every which way. Once at the bottom we had the pleasure of watching the other victims and it was an entertaining half hour until we shook out, crossed the valley and commenced the ascent.' So began the 'Slippery Slide' battle, as the men of 3RAR were to call it.

A Company soon came under heavy mortar, machine-gun and rifle fire, and sustained heavy casualties. Company commander Ben

O'Dowd called for supporting US mortars to set about 'belting the enemy, accepting a few drop shorts in the process'. But with A Company pinned down, it fell to Len's company to take Hill 410. Eleven Platoon headed up the assault, with 12 Platoon on the left and 10 on the right. The company came under fire as it crossed the valley and soon the artillery ranger and his signaller were hit, effectively blinding the gunners supporting the attack. The consequences were disastrous. To gauge the range, the gunners fired a white phosphorous shell—which landed smack bang in 11 Platoon's ranks. 'The platoon commander, Lieutenant Battersby, caught some of the phosphorous and disappeared over the edge of the spur with burns,' Len wrote. 'I retrieved his walkie talkie and called up CHQ [company headquarters] advising what had happened and that I had taken over the platoon. Lieutenant Battersby took no further interest in the proceedings as he was busy picking bits of burning phosphorous out of himself with the help of the medic.' It got worse.

A shell screamed in and exploded with devastating effect in 10 Platoon. Three men were killed and another three wounded by the euphemistic 'friendly fire'—the gunners had misjudged the range. 'Bunny O'Neill, our instructor at Pucka, asked his companion for a light,' Len said. 'When he did not respond, Bunny nudged him, where-upon the chap rolled over with half his head missing.'

Most of the shells started to land further up the hill so the men pressed on after tending to their wounded. Len does not detail the ensuing fight but it is clear from other accounts that his 11 Platoon took the hill. 'After a brief sharp struggle, using grenades and small-arms, 11 Platoon overcame the demoralised enemy,' Keys recorded. Len strongly disagreed with Keys's claim that the wounded Battersby calmly 'rallied his forces', saying, rather, that his platoon commander arrived at the crest after the summit was won. But, as ever in Korea, victory did not guarantee safety. The 12 Platoon runner, Ian Hamilton, was shot dead by a sniper while they gathered their breath on the summit. Hamilton was one of twelve 3RAR men killed in the battle.

Thirty-seven were wounded. Battersby was evacuated, leaving Len in charge of the platoon. He and his men dug in as the snow fell.

Ridgway's offensive was going well. The Chinese had been driven back on a wide front and Seoul changed hands yet again on 14 March. Some prize, for the capital was a smoking cinder after nine months of war. MacArthur's career was in a similar state—he was sacked by President Truman after pre-empting his government's offer of a peace settlement with an entreaty of his own. Officially, his crime was insubordination, but really it was more about camels and straws. MacArthur was consumed by his own ego. He was replaced by Ridgway, whose Eighth Army was given to Normandy veteran General James Van Fleet. In any case, the Chinese refused to parley. The war would drag on. Such higher machinations were of no import to the men of 3RAR, whose sweat and sacrifice in the mountains had fed Ridgway's success. In late March, almost six months after setting foot in Korea, Temporary Sergeant Len Opie was sent to Japan for five days' rest and recreation. While his mates got drunk and caroused with geishas, he spent much of his time in hobby shops poring over model trains and planes. The hero of Hill 614 could not have been happier.

CHAPTER 7

KAPYONG

'My old man said to me that people said it was a little war.
A little war, when you lose 100 blokes overnight? You think
it's a little war when you lose 100 blokes killed and wounded?
It was murder.'
Allan Bennett, 3RAR

The 1951 Anzac Day preparations were in full swing. Trucks brimming with beer and fresh food cluttered up to the mess ahead of a gala barbecue. But first the Turkish brigade would join the Australians and New Zealanders for a grand parade in a traditional 'hollow square' formation—a ceremonial gesture to honour the dead after a battle. The hollow square represented a sanctuary for fallen comrades. The last time the Aussies and Kiwis were on the same battlefield on Anzac Day there had been no such formalities—they were busy being dive-bombed by Stukas as they fled Greece in 1941. Ten years later they would commemorate the solemn anniversary before hoeing into the grog and grub. The Turks' presence in the hills around a little village called Kapyong made the occasion all the more special. The three nations would compete in boxing and athletics, cheered on by comrades feasting on beer and barbecued meat.

As the day approached, diggers roamed the hills gathering the azaleas that had sprung out of the shrinking snowdrifts. As they fashioned wreaths for the Anzac Day service they thought of their fathers storming Anzac Cove and gave thanks for being with the Kiwi gunners and Turkish infantry. They were also grateful for the happy coincidence of being well behind the lines for Anzac Day. 'Life is really looking up,' Len wrote.

'We went down by this river . . . stripped off and swam and lay around in the sun, which was lovely as we'd only had one bath in four months,' Reg Bandy said. It was a time of plenty. The men had been joined by their own cooks for the first time since January. A press photographer asked Len to pose, mouth agape, with a huge turkey leg. It made a nice shot, but Len was grumpy again—he had to give the leg back after the photo was taken. The caption accompanying the photo in *The News* on 24 April was apt. 'Sergeant Len Opie, of Medindie, seems to be anticipating the flavour of the meat into which he is about to sink his teeth.' Indeed. He soon had greater cause to grumble. These salad days were rounded out by picture shows most nights. Len was settling down for a film when there was an almighty blast. A digger had flicked a match into a supposedly empty jerry can after lighting his cigarette. Bodies flew everywhere, mostly onto Len, who wore a boot in the face. 'In a very disgusted tone the projectionist announced, "That's it! You've stuffed up the projector and there won't be any film tonight!" So we wended our way back home. Nobody had been seriously hurt; my injuries were two bruised fingers which had been trodden on and a slight nose bleed, the result of the kick in the face.' Len was kept awake by the officers 'grogging on' but at least there would be another film the next night.

On the morning of 23 April, word filtered through that the Chinese had attacked the 6 ROK Division, which had taken the Commonwealth Brigade's place in the line. 'Panic ensued,' Len wrote, and the diggers were ordered to make ready for action. They moved out at 6 pm, past the stockpiles of food and beer ordered in for the Anzac Day party. 'We don't know whatever happened to that beer—we certainly didn't get it,' Doc Beard said later. The fog of war was especially thick that morning.

Ferguson was ordered to deploy his unit in a blocking position, but beyond that he was in the dark. He drew on an anecdote from the last war. 'I am reminded of a conversation I overheard between two Pitcairn Islanders of our company in the Owen Stanley Ranges,' he said. One, a private, was demanding the other, a lance corporal, fill him in on the military situation. The lance corporal replied, 'The trouble with you is that you think I know fuck nothing. In fact I know fuck all.' Ferguson felt the story worth repeating to Bob Breen when the historian asked him about the prelude to Kapyong.

The diggers were trucked 10 kilometres forward to dig in behind the ROKs. D Company scaled a long saddle to a peak designated Hill 504. There the men dug in, all except Len, who happened upon 'a large and very comfortable' foxhole from an earlier fight. A Company was further down the ridge, with C Company on a parallel slope directly to the rear, and B Company on a low feature on the other side of the north–south road. Most men expected the flap would blow over and they would be back in camp the next day. B Company's CO Darcy Laughlin, a 39er of the last war, was so sanguine he ordered his command tent be set up among the foxholes. 'Darcy Laughlin, who we called "The Master", he'd not only rigged a tent but was sitting back in an armchair having an evening aperitif, that's how casual they were,' Len said.

Whether Laughlin knew the battalion sat astride the traditional north–south invasion route is unknown. Since ancient times armies had stormed down the Kapyong Valley to seize Seoul. Now 3RAR—and the Princess Pats on distant heights to the west—were deployed as insurance in the unlikely event the large South Korean and UN force between them and the Chinese broke. The UN's recent bite and hold thrusts had put the Chinese on the back foot, so much so that few of the 3RAR rankers feared a counterattack of any substance. Unsurprisingly, Len was one of the few. The clues lay all around. On a visit to the battalion dentist he noticed two 17-pounders pointing up the main road. This, more than 20 kilometres from the front? 'I think I used to think more than other people,' he said. 'All of a sudden I got worried—they haven't got tanks so why is a 17-pounder pointing up north?' Another telltale sign was the smoke haze—the Chinese were torching the bush again. But most of the men sent up into the hills on the evening of 23 April thought they would be back in their camp the following day. As such they went forward with no extra rations or ammunition. Some made no more than token efforts at digging in. The ground was too rocky in any case, so some piled the rocks into sangars or rudimentary bulwarks instead.

There were not enough men to deploy a continuous defence. The Argylls were in Pusan awaiting a ship home, while the Middlesex regiment had been sent forward to protect the Kiwi gunners, who in turn were supporting the ROKs. So Ferguson deployed his companies as separate entities, their platoons sited to protect each other, rather than the other companies. They overlooked the confluence of the Kapyong River running from the north-west, and a smaller stream flowing from the north-east. The main road forded the river below their positions. Rising abruptly out of the paddy fields, the hills were covered with low scrub. Laughlin's B Company was in the most precarious spot, spread along a low ridge wedged between the river and the main road. D Company was on the highest ground, with 12 Platoon forward, Len's 11 Platoon in support, and 10 Platoon on the 504 summit. Two spurs— together shaped like a U—jutted out towards the valley. Twelve Platoon was on the right ridge, while the left led down to A Company's positions, some 400 metres down the hill. Len's 11 Platoon was near the base of the U. Len being Len, he was blueing with his new officer, Lieutenant Russell McWilliam, who had replaced the wounded Battersby. McWilliam, according to Len was forever moaning about the company commander, Norm Gravener, a hardened veteran who had enlisted in 1939. Len told McWilliam to put a sock in it, but if anything the officer's sniping increased. 'He and I didn't hit it off from the start,' Len said. 'His attitude was not conducive to good morale and I let him know.' Eleven Platoon's officer and platoon sergeant were on very bad terms as 3RAR hurtled towards its day of days.

The men of D Company scanned the valley from atop Hill 504. Presently a trickle of fleeing South Korean troops grew to a steady stream, then a flood. 'They were obviously panic-stricken and completely uncontrolled,' the 3RAR diarist noted. Then came the Kiwi trucks carrying not only the gunners but the Middlesex infantry. The line had broken and something nasty was coming down the road. Reg Saunders recognised a familiar sound—an army in retreat. 'I had heard it before, in Greece and in Crete and earlier in Korea. I must admit I felt a little dejected until I realised I was an Australian company commander and if my morale got low then I couldn't expect much from my troops.'

Next came the refugees, 'old men, women, children leading their animals and carrying their possessions on their heads,' Ben O'Dowd said. 'And this was bad news because we knew that in the dark, or semi-dark, the Chinese would mix in with the refugees and use them as a shield to get them onto our rear and cut us off.' Soon the road below the Australians was a mess of headlights, blaring horns and curses in several languages. As A Company's CO, O'Dowd faced a thorny problem: Chinese troops were indeed using the refugees as a human shield. Did O'Dowd dare fire? He asked Ferguson, who was directing the battalion from his HQ well down the valley, for, at the very least, permission to fire a burst or two over their heads. Ferguson refused, for fear of hitting the civilians, of course. Soon afterwards, Ferguson's batman brought his commander a mug of tea. 'He was drinking it when a bullet went through it,' Len said. Battalion headquarters was under attack—4 kilometres behind the so-called front line. The four rifle companies were cut off and the Battle of Kapyong had begun.

The first attacks fell on five US Sherman tanks posted up the valley from A and B companies. The Chinese were beaten off but quickly regrouped for another assault. For all their imposing might and power, tanks are vulnerable when deployed without infantry to stop the enemy getting too close. And these tanks—while notionally under Ferguson's command—were really acting as freelancers on the Kapyong battlefield. When he realised the tanks were in front of his company,

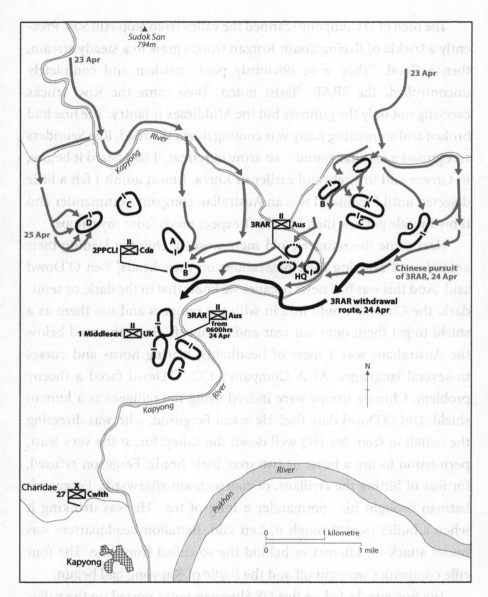

BATTLE OF KAPYONG

Laughlin sent a section forward to provide covering fire from a knoll. The diggers were too few and it was too dark to provide much help to the American tank men. Swinging open their hatches to better direct fire in the dark, four of the five tank commanders were hit, including the platoon commander, who was shot between the eyes. Soon the Chinese swarmed onto the hulls, searching for gaps in the armour. With turrets swinging wildly like frantic Daleks, the tanks' only defence was to hose each other down with their .50 and .30 calibre machine guns. 'As we had found often in the past, tanks do not like to be forward without an infantry screen,' Len said. 'The tanks withdrew with big Jim Young of B Company trying unsuccessfully to get them to stop. In the case of the particular tank commander with whom he was talking, the tank proceeded down the road followed by Chinamen who ran [past Young] as he hid in the ditch at the side of the road. After they had gone he made his way back to the company.' Young escaped and the tanks clattered back to battalion headquarters and beyond.

But there was no safe harbour to be found back at headquarters. The Chinese had flowed down the valley like water; the human stream lapping against the rifle companies, which were like boulders in a rising creek, before hurtling head-on into the signallers, engineers and military police that are part of any infantry battalion—but who rarely, if ever, are called upon to shoulder a rifle in anger. They were stiffened by fighting men from the Mortar, Anti-Tank, Machine Gun and Assault Pioneer platoons (although the latter two sub-units totalled fifteen men with four Brens—all the Vickers guns were forward with the rifle companies). As the routed South Koreans fled past in the dark, Anti-Tank Platoon Sergeant Fred From and his interpreter 'challenged every soldier who approached the perimeter—those who answered in Korean were invited to join the Australians, those who did not were shot'. Soon the Anti-Tank was a numerically very strong platoon indeed, although Len had a different take on how it press-ganged the South Koreans. 'They got a South Korean warrant officer. And every time a South Korean came by, he invited them to join the crowd. If they didn't want to be in it he whacked them over the head with a bit of four by two. They ended up with about 70 in the platoon and stayed there all night—didn't fire a shot. Apparently the Chinese were rushing past them.'

With its two 17-pounders and about 70 men, the Anti-Tank Platoon was bristling with firepower, but was too far from the heart of headquarters to bring its guns to bear on the hordes falling upon Ferguson. Outnumbered perhaps ten to one, the Australian cooks, drivers and dispatch riders circled the wagons and fumbled for their little-used small-arms in the dark. The official history said Ferguson and his men were in an 'extreme predicament'. It was uncannily similar to the behind-the-lines fight at Brigade Hill on the Kokoda Track nine years before, where Brigadier Arnold Potts and his staff fought a close-quarters battle with the Japanese. Potts and his men exacted a heavy toll before being forced back down the Track. This time the notion-ally non-combatant 3RAR men held the line, not that there was such a thing. And of course Potts had no tanks in the Owen Stanleys—the Shermans' machine guns mowed down the Chinese, and when the infantry started taking fire from the village astride the road, the tanks brought their main armament to bear. The result? No more village. Forty corpses were pulled from the rubble of one house.

Up on the ridges the rifle companies were hanging on, too. Each of the four companies had open flanks, meaning they were on their own. The men of B Company sent forward to cover the tanks must have felt very lonely indeed when a force of 30 Chinese charged at about midnight. Laughlin ordered them to withdraw, and somehow they scurried the 400 metres back to the company perimeter without losing one man. The enemy then worked over each platoon in turn, herald-ing each charge with bugle calls. B Company was surrounded and at one stage the Chinese penetrated as far as company headquarters, but a 6 Platoon counterattack turned the tide. When dawn broke Laughlin and his brave men were holding firm in their shallow gun-pits. By now the New Zealand gunners were back in business and their shells added to the carnage below B Company. Soon hundreds of dead and dying Chinese littered the Kapyong Valley.

From his headquarters in the scrub of the opposite slope, Ben O'Dowd pondered myriad problems. Ferguson was too far away—and too involved in his own fight—to exercise effective command, so O'Dowd, as senior company commander, took charge. Even if Ferguson had time to direct the battle, a critical breakdown of communications meant he had no means of doing so. 'The major cause of Fergie's confusion on the night . . . was a lack of communications,' Jack Gallaway confided to Len in a letter written long after the war. Gallaway, the signals platoon sergeant, was on leave during the battle, but investigated the matter thoroughly and told Len, '[I] was told then that this lack of communications was all the trouble but I found no one wanted to talk about the details.' O'Dowd was left to try to make sense of the chaos. It was clear the rifle companies were cut off. He knew his company held valuable ground, sitting astride Hill 504's lower slopes, between B and D companies. The first attacks came at about 10 pm, 'little probing movements', O'Dowd called them. 'Our soldiers shot them back into the dark and then the attack proper came in.'

O'Dowd's account of the attacks that night aptly illustrate the Chinese soldiers' tactics. First, whistles and bugles blared as the attacking force assembled. Then all fell quiet as they approached. The next noise was the 'rattle of metal striking stone', as Jack Gallaway described it. Grenades. The attack went in while the defenders were diving for cover from the grenade blasts. So the Australians had only a few seconds of firing before the Chinese were upon them. 'We were pouring rapid fire into them and cutting them down, wave after wave as they came down, until eventually the Chinese pulled back to re-organise and reinforce for another attack,' O'Dowd said.

The Chinese suffered heavily, but so did the Australians. During the lull, sergeants and corporals pulled the dead and wounded out of their gun-pits and ushered fresh men into their place. Then came the whistle and bugle calls, silence, a shower of grenades and another charge. Attacks fell on 1 Platoon, which was furthest down the hill, and company headquarters and 3 Platoon further up the slope.

At the epicentre of the fight was 1 Platoon. Wave upon wave of Chinese soldiers fell on the platoon's gun-pits. The defenders fired their

Brens, Owens and .303s as fast as they could into massed attacks. Soon the enemy was clambering over its own corpses to get at the Australians. 'It ended up in a lot of hand-to-hand fighting and they were generally only little fellas—so they lose,' Reg Bandy said. The diggers stood firm amid the searing splinters of metal and rock; held fast as the whistles and bugles sounded yet again; kept their nerve as the tracers flew and tumult mounted. Until it was too much even for them. Eventually Lieutenant Fred Gardner sent word to O'Dowd that his men were too few to stem another assault, so O'Dowd pulled what was left of the platoon up the hill to company headquarters lines. The Chinese piled into 1 Platoon's trenches.

O'Dowd was not overly concerned about losing the ground. He consolidated his headquarters, 3 Platoon and the remnants of 1 Platoon in a perimeter overlooking 1 Platoon's former position. As long as he held the heights he commanded the field. The attacks continued to fall on his perimeter and also against 2 Platoon further up the ridge, but by now the Chinese commanders—stung by their losses—preferred short, sharp rushes instead of the earlier rolling charges. The enemy fought smarter, too. Probing for weaknesses in the defenders' lines, it found the gap between O'Dowd's force and 2 Platoon further up the hill, and set up a machine gun in the breach. The gun poured fire down onto the Australians in the pre-dawn murk, and even when the sun rose, O'Dowd was unable to pinpoint the source of the fire. There was nothing for it—O'Dowd ordered 2 Platoon to charge. Down the diggers came, bayonets fixed, to wipe out the enemy machine-gun nest in a 'sharp, neat action' in which one Australian was killed. Perhaps emboldened by the success, O'Dowd then set 3 Platoon upon the enemy in 1 Platoon's old lines. 'They were greatly outnumbered but the Chinese didn't stop and fight, they took off for the road,' O'Dowd said.

In the words of the official historian, 'The enemy did not stay to give battle.' Sergeant George Harris described the turkey shoot that followed. 'We were just getting them in the back as they ran away . . . they were hiding in thickets or creek beds or down toward the river . . .

we were picking them up on the ground, picking them off everywhere. The Chinese were very stupid by staying there.'

A Company had held on, but at a great cost. Fifty men lay dead or wounded. O'Dowd was distressed by his men's suffering. With the company cut off, there was no way of evacuating his casualties. The men cared for their mates the best they could but it was a bitterly cold night. Medical supplies were scant and there were no doctors forward with the rifle companies. 'Certainly some who died would have survived had they been transported to proper medical care in reasonable time,' O'Dowd said. 'Some could have hung on had it been possible to keep them warm. This was an unhappy aspect of Kapyong.' It was barely better back at the regimental aid post, where Doc Beard and his orderlies treated the wounded while the battle raged around them. However, the Chinese respected the Red Cross insignia—the aid station was never directly attacked, even though stray bullets whizzed through the tent while Beard was 'putting dressings on, stopping bleeding and giving morphine and getting them out'. Beard had no time to be scared. 'People have said to me, "oh weren't you frightened?" And I'm not a brave man by any means, but somehow I wasn't frightened at all because I was too busy doing my own work. I didn't believe that any one of these bullets could hit me.'

The unit chaplains and a Salvation Army major gave invaluable assistance—the Salvo did sterling work as a stretcher bearer under fire. On one foray to the front he witnessed a bizarre exchange. A digger was taking pot shots at a distant enemy, who took off his shirt and waved it like a drill-range instructor to signal the marksman's misses, 'which highly amused the Australians and helped relieve the tension'. Sadly, according to Len, the enemy comedian was blown to bits by a US tank round. Later in the battle, Ferguson, Beard and the battalion intelligence officer, Alf Argent, went forward in Sherman tanks to assess the forward companies' plight and evacuate wounded, some of whom were strapped to the tanks' hulls. The Chinese fired on the tanks as they came up the valley, but did not when they started back with their wounded. Argent reportedly was so tired he fell asleep in the tank even as enemy bullets rattled into its armour. Len was incredulous. 'I defy anyone to fall asleep in the bottom of a tank!'

Up on the summit Len was also trying to sleep as the battle raged. D Company had been unmolested while the men of A and B companies and battalion headquarters had been fighting for their lives. So the company was put on a 50 per cent stand to—that is, one man on watch while another slept. Len turned in at about 9.30 pm while Paddy Trump scanned the murk for two hours before they would swap. 'I was not exactly in a deep sleep,' Len said. 'When eventually master Trump gave me a nudge, he said: "Well, it is two o'clock, so you can stay up for the rest of the night." My reply was: "I've got news for you, mister, the arrangement was two hours on and two hours off, so I'll be waking you at 4!" However, by 0400 the first probe came against 12 Platoon and that was the end of the snooze.'

Stiffened by a section of Vickers gunners and overlooking a steep slope, 12 Platoon was in a commanding position and drove off the initial attacks, each presaged by the usual bugle calls, whistles and grenades. But still the Chinese came and the defenders were heavily outnumbered. 'My old 8 Section under Corporal Bill Rowlinson took the brunt of the attack and soon had casualties,' Len said. 'Directly in front of the section was a drop away . . . a false crest which prevented a clear sight so that the Chinese were protected until they breasted the rise but it also meant that when they did they were fully exposed.' Australian losses mounted as the enemy mortars found their range. After half-a-dozen assaults seven Australians lay wounded but the slope below was littered with 30 dead Chinese. War correspondent Hal Richardson specialised in colourful reportage but his account of Kapyong was almost as pyrotechnic as the battle. 'Peering through narrowed eyes,' Richardson wrote, 'a group of Chinese, their weapons smoking, came over a ridge nearly on top of an Australian position. "Surrender," shouted the Chinese leader. "Surrender be damned," cried back an Australian, and the Chinese vanished over the hillside in a shower of crackling explosions as the Australians hurled grenades after them.'

Len's platoon was about 200 metres back up the ridge, but nowhere was safe—the Chinese were swarming all around. 'Every time we popped our head over to have a look at A Company there'd be a burst of machine-gun fire,' Len said. At about 5 am an infiltrator was shot even further back, at company headquarters. Another was captured by 10 Platoon close to the summit. Len was keen to get forward to help his old section but McWilliam stopped him, triggering another argument. Len skulked back to his hole 'for a doze . . . as we were not doing anything'. McWilliam grabbed a Bren and went down to 12 Platoon on his own, further enraging Len. 'He did not stay long and when he came back and found me resting he remarked that I didn't seem to be taking much interest in the proceedings.' Len replied, ' "Well, since you wouldn't let me help with the casualties and we are probably in for a long day and night I decided to have a sleep and I think it would be a good idea if you stopped fighting the company commander and concentrated on fighting the war." And that was about the last time I remember speaking to him.' Len made himself scarce by scampering up to company headquarters to check on the fighting there.

While Len and McWilliam conducted their own war the real one continued on 12 Platoon's front. The situation was becoming desperate. If the Chinese seized the heights, they could fall upon A Company and roll up the Australian line. 'If they could tackle that thing sitting on top and come down on top of us the rest would just fall like apples off the end of a branch,' O'Dowd said. The diggers were holding but not everyone was covering himself in glory. 'It was noticed that leaves and twigs were flying off branches directly over one of the pits,' Len said. 'One of the less aggressive members of 8 Section was lying in the bottom of his pit with his Owen pointing straight up and he was firing to keep from feeling lonely. I could never understand why he was trusted with an Owen submachine gun.'

Len's former comrades of 8 Section held the key to the battle for Hill 504. The full fury of the Chinese attacks fell upon their post, on the left flank of 12 Platoon's perimeter. Many of the wounded fought on before being evacuated to company headquarters. Rowlinson was wounded but refused to hand over command. 'He displayed outstanding leadership and bravery in holding the section together during the successive attacks,' the official historian reported. On the right of the line, Private Ron 'Tosh' Smith's pit 'bore the brunt of each enemy attack' but Smith stood firm in spite of a serious wound. Medic Ron 'Nugget' Dunque managed to get all six of the section's wounded out before his forehead was creased by grenade shrapnel. He continued treating the wounded, with little regard for his own injury. Lance Corporal Harry Richey was killed while, Len said, 'rushing around getting the wounded out of their pits'. He was shot while carrying a comrade in a fireman's lift. The casualties mounted. Private Noel 'Kid' Heathwood was seriously wounded. Len said he died of his wounds after being given the wrong blood at the Indian Field Ambulance attached to the brigade. The Australian War Memorial has a photo of Heathwood with his three sisters, Connie, Audrey and Daphne, on the day of his embarkation at South Brisbane Railway Station. The siblings' smiles are enough to break the hardest heart.

The Chinese regrouped before attacking again at 11.30 am. Wave after wave of Chinese soldiers fell on the hill for the next two hours. By now the New Zealand gunners were in position at the rear and they soon found the range. Kiwi observers and Captain Gravener himself brought down fire within 50 metres of the Australian foxholes. In the A Company lines a Kiwi artillery spotter decided to shoulder a musket. The artilleryman sniped at the enemy with great effect and refused to leave his post even after he was wounded. Diggers and Kiwis were commemorating Anzac Day a little early.

As with Gallipoli, Kapyong had its bungles. Gallipoli's follies are well known—landing on the wrong beach, underestimating the tangled terrain, the charge at The Nek . . . Less well known is the curious case of

B Company's withdrawal from its low ridge on the left flank at Kapyong. The fiasco is shrouded in mystery. Accounts differ as to the genesis of the stuff-up, but the bare facts are these: at about daybreak, someone ordered the company, which was holding firm in its trenches and had suffered a casualty, to yield its ground, cross the valley and enter the friendly fold on the opposite slopes. Laughlin's men scurried across the open ground, guns blazing at the Chinese all around, and made it safely to the other side—collecting 40 prisoners along the way. The last platoon was arriving when they were told to turn around and go back. The order had been reversed. They had to take positions voluntarily vacated minutes before; positions that were now brimming with Chinese troops. A section charged a knoll and was mown down almost to a man. Then a full platoon—with much of the rest of the company providing covering fire—stormed into the maelstrom and took the knoll at bayonet point. Inspired by their leader Lieutenant Len Montgomerie, who had served as a commando in World War II, the men of 4 Platoon slogged their way up the hill with bomb and bayonet. Many of the enemy fought to the death. When the Australians were ordered to stop at a second hillock, more than 80 Chinese lay dead. The Australians had lost three men killed and nine wounded. The Chinese, dead and living, could have the damned hill—the attack was called off. 'Those who saw Montgomerie's attack described it as one of the finest and most aggressive actions they had seen at a platoon level,' historian Bob Breen wrote. Montgomerie was awarded a Military Cross and Corporal Don Davie a Military Medal for showing 'complete disregard for his own safety'. When it was over, B Company crossed the valley for the third time that day, and disappeared into the sanctuary of the battalion perimeter.

Like a cat presenting a fresh pigeon to its owner, Laughlin showed off his cache of prisoners to O'Dowd, who, to Laughlin's disappointment, was unimpressed. 'The alternatives were to turn them loose, shoot them, or take them with us,' O'Dowd said later. 'They had been observing us all day and knew too much to turn them loose, and shooting them, apart from the humanitarian aspects, would not go over too well with the authorities. So I got back to Darcy and reminded him that he had captured them, so he could look after them. He crossed me off his Christmas card list with a "thanks a lot".

Up on the summit, the gallant but heavily depleted 12 Platoon was also pulled back to the relative safety of its sister platoons' lines above. It had taken a heavy beating, and Gravener did as O'Dowd had done with his own 1 Platoon the night before. This showed constancy in the Australian middle command that came from experience under fire and superb training. And Gravener, like O'Dowd, employed defence as a form of attack—and this is how he did it: first, the platoon, in broad daylight, snuck away so silently, so skilfully, that the move was undetected by the Chinese command. The enemy pounded the empty foxholes with mortar bombs, before about 30 soldiers charged the position. 'They launched a full scale attack against nothing,' Norman Bartlett wrote. Second, Gravener brought down all the firepower at his disposal—NZ artillery, company mortars, Vickers machine guns, and the Brens, Owens and .303s of Len's 11 Platoon. The Chinese paid a heavy price for the vacant territory. There was a rider, however—the surrendered ground was ideal for forming up to attack 11 Platoon, and Len and his mates hunkered down ahead of the attack they knew would soon come.

By now Ferguson had managed to extricate his hard-pressed battalion headquarters and attached sub-units down the road to relative safety, allowing him to concentrate on directing his forward companies. This was when he went forward with Beard, in a tank, to assess the situation. He asked O'Dowd if he could hold for another night. O'Dowd was sceptical. He was running short of ammunition and B Company's withdrawal had opened a yawning gap on the left flank. Then there was the problem of the wounded, who were suffering terribly.

Meanwhile Brigadier Brian Burke, who had assumed command after Coad was promoted to major general and given his own division, decided to pull the battalion out. The brigadier reasoned the Australians could not hope to survive another night out on their own. Because the Chinese held the main road through the valley, Ferguson ordered O'Dowd to pull the battalion out through D Company's position, thence down a long ridge in a sweeping movement to avoid the main enemy force. Hill 504 was the key to the battle and now it was the pivot for the retreat. And the whole withdrawal would be covered by Len's 11 Platoon, which was handed the poisoned chalice of being the battalion rearguard. News the battalion would pull out reached Len about 4 pm. 'We thought, why, we're holding all right?' he said. 'We might as well stay.' The Chinese realised what was afoot when they saw the lower companies heading up the hill. The full might of their effort fell upon D Company. 'Don Company got it all day,' O'Dowd recalled. An enemy soldier poured fire on Len's platoon from the shelter of two rocks that formed a perfect V to rest his machine gun. When the battle was over the Australians found a huge pile of spent cartridges behind the rocks.

To ease the pressure on his company and keep Chinese heads down while the other companies filed through his lines, Gravener called in an air strike. A spotter plane was scrambled to sweep the area and pinpoint the Chinese positions. Two US Corsairs circled like water bombers contemplating which part of a bushfire to strike, except in this case the bombers were not putting a fire out—they were starting one. The single prop fighter-bombers carried a payload of napalm. The Australians on Hill 504 watched as the planes cruised overhead. 'We were all just standing around as the aircraft came over,' Len said. The Yank pilots were cutting it fine, many thought, as the planes flew directly towards the summit—then released their canisters.

The friendly fire started a very unfriendly one. Ammunition exploded and weapons were cooked in the blaze that raged on the summit. The company's radio operator Private John 'Sandy' Winson dashed into the flames to save his set, which was the only link with O'Dowd down the hill. He was mentioned in despatches for his bravery. The company second-in-command, Captain Michael Ryan, ran into the open—under fire—frantically waving an aircraft identification panel to head off another strike. Down the hill, B Company's radio operator Kevin Hatfield watched in horror. 'I immediately called control and told them that the planes were going to bomb the hill,' Hatfield said. 'By the time I had looked again one of the planes had dropped napalm. Control must have got on to them because they broke away and wiggled their wings.'

Up the hill, 10 Platoon scattered in a mad panic. One digger broke an ankle jumping over a small cliff. Others stood their ground and tried to shoot the canisters down, as if they were at a clay pigeon range. Len said one mortar man ambitiously loosed off a few bombs into the sky. Of course it was to no avail, the napalm cloud of billowing orange flame engulfed 10 Platoon. Australians burned to death. 'Give the bastards the heat treatment,' Edward 'Harold' Giddens used to say when the enemy was hit with napalm. He was badly burned that day on Hill 504. According to Len, when he was stretchered away, Giddens said, 'The bastards gave *me* the heat treatment!' George Harris said Giddens showed a lot of guts that terrible day by urging the medics to see to the others first. 'Some of those burnt by the napalm were like roasted meat,' Harris said. 'Their faces and hands had been barbecued. Giddens was particularly bad. His hands had been reduced to stumps and he had some shocking facial scars.'

Two diggers were incinerated. 'Nugget' Dunque went to work again among the wounded, but was wounded a second time, by a grenade that detonated in the inferno. He was sitting stunned and sorry for himself when an 'apparition' emerged from the smoke, the 'sticks and stones' penetrating his translucent feet as he walked. 'His fingers were all burnt off, his feet were burnt off,' Dunque said. 'The flesh was hanging off his face. He was something to see. And I was sitting on the company head-quarters, sitting down, and this apparition came and sat next to me. And I didn't know what to say or anything because I couldn't recognise him. You couldn't . . . the flesh was hanging off his arms. And I turned to speak to him, and he said, "Jesus Christ, Nugget, you're having a rough day." I recognised him by his voice then. But anyway, he lived.'

Not all the casualties were as serious. 'Norm Gravener had half his moustache singed away,' Len said.

Len watched the conflagration on the slopes above him. His 11 Platoon was in quite a spot. Above him, hell. Below, lurking Chinese keen to make the most of their good fortune. 'The Chinese came leaping over the ridge,' Len said. The rest of the company started pulling out as Len and his men settled over their gunsights. 'The Chinese launched their heaviest attack of the day,' Len wrote in his diary, without elaborating on the action. Jack Gallaway said the Chinese 'ran into a hornet's nest . . . the diggers repulsed all attacks and inflicted heavy casualties upon the enemy'. First, the Chinese charged straight up the hill. When that was repulsed with heavy losses they came at the diggers from the vacant right flank. McWilliam and Len swung their force to meet the new threat and the Chinese were again sent packing. Gravener said the action was 'the most determined we had experienced . . . the enemy fairly ran headlong into our forward lines and, on the right, had gained the cover of a spur but could not breach our position'. Small groups of Chinese crept up from the right all afternoon but Len and his men held firm, allowing the battalion to steal away up and over the hill.

B Company led the way, followed by A and C. O'Dowd called a barrage, including smoke shells, on to B Company's old positions to mask the Australians' withdrawal. The companies leapfrogged one another on their way down the escape route, covering each other as they went. It was a perfectly executed withdrawal under fire, anything but the 'running fight' Len's drill sergeant had cautioned against all those years ago. At about 4 pm the word came for Len's platoon to pull out. Six Section gave covering fire as the rest of the platoon thinned out and scampered up the hill. 'We eventually cleared the feature as the Chinese came over the crest at the far end, to be met by shells from the New Zealanders,' Len said. This was thanks to Private Winson and his rescued radio set. Bill Nimmo and Dunque were two of the last out, the former helping the wounded latter, who described their escape as a 'three-legged race' with the enemy in hot pursuit. 'We saw these characters all up on our hill and we thought that we're going to cop it now. And I said to Bill "come on let's move then". Just as they were streaming down the hill the New Zealand artillery got the lot of them. Bang, bang, bang. I saw the whole front row of these people disappear. Scores of them, just disappear.'

Gravener was full of praise for his rearguard. 'The last platoon out, of course, was 11 Platoon,' he said. 'The thinning out of 11 Platoon got us that final clearance . . . gave us the break we needed. It was possible to bring the guns down the ridgeline. Drop 50, go on, drop 50, go on—that's the order we were giving.' As they pulled out, Len was keen to ensure they had their aircraft identification panel in case they were attacked again by their own planes. 'I was alongside Teddy Hearn and as we were moving back with some speed, the air panel in his haversack fell out and unrolled on the ground. We were both trying to pick it up while at the same time treading on it.' Slapstick under fire.

Next came an incident that grew into one of Len's greatest grudges. As 6 Section filed past, Len asked about his old comrade Mo Gwyther. He was told Gwyther had made his way out with the stretcher parties bearing the napalm victims. He had not. According to Len, Gwyther had been told by a mate to sit tight while he investigated what was going on. The man never returned, so Gwyther did not receive the word to pull out. The first shell of the Kiwi covering barrage knocked Gwyther out. When he came to at about 8 pm, the platoon was long gone. What came next defies explanation. He reached into his haversack, pulled out a bottle of beer, and opened it. The Chinese, who were all over the hill, heard the noise and captured him.

Dunque's story differed from Len's. 'One of the blokes from 11 Platoon . . . he was taken prisoner. Anyway, I saw him about ten years later. In Melbourne. I said: "Listen, where were you? I was the last man off that position, and I never saw you around there." And he said: "No, but I saw you. I saw you and Nimmo, getting along." And I said: "Why didn't you call out?" He said: "Because I noticed you started in a half run. I saw you do this and I looked over there and there was millions of these buggers. I thought Jesus, if I call out to him, he'll only come over and get me and then we'll all be done. She'll all get done." So when he looked over and he saw me, and he saw these thousands of Chinese, I can remember at the time, I said to Bill: "For Christ's sake, look at that." And there they were, lining up the top of the hills. Ten deep.'

Gwyther underwent all manner of privations—in between escaping and being twice recaptured—until his release two years later. He was mentioned in despatches for his 'outstanding conduct while in captivity'. Len was livid about the loss of his mate. Perhaps another hex was cast. 'Despite the fact that people claimed to have seen him with the stretcher parties on the way down the hill, the only person who knew the truth wasn't saying anything,' Len said. 'Forty years later [Gwyther's trench-mate] committed suicide and I like to think that his conscience finally caught up with him.' This was no one-off vent. Len said in a later interview, 'I'm glad to say that that fellow committed suicide within the last two or three years and I like to think his conscience—if he ever had one—finally caught up with him.'

Len said the Chinese did not pursue the Australians further down the hill, but O'Dowd disagreed. 'The Chinese followed immediately, of course, but they ran into Charlie Company,' he said. The companies continued to leapfrog each other—one taking a blocking position while the others withdrew. Much of the gear was carried by Chinese prisoners pressed into service as porters. 'I was moving back and forth in the column in the dark . . . and at one stage I found myself in the middle of a bunch of Chinese carrying weapons,' O'Dowd said. 'The hair stood up on the back of my neck until I realised that they were our Chinese, some Chinese we had captured earlier, and they were being used as stretcher bearers. So I stopped the first escort and took him apart because these Chinese, some of the Chinese, were carrying weapons and his comment was rather dry: "Well, you don't expect the bloody wounded to carry them do you?" He disappeared into the dark.'

The Chinese prisoners had surrendered in droves during B Company's back-and-forth forays in the valley that morning. 'For some reason or other a whole bunch of them flooded up to [CSM] Blue Bradley for protection, he was like a mother hen,' Len said. 'They adopted him. When it came to taking out the casualties, A Company had had about 50 per cent of one platoon, we haven't got enough people for carrying the weapons and the equipment so we gave it to the Chinese. Well the Chinese are good unionists you see . . . once you've got a Chinaman, he doesn't try to escape. He's fought his fight. He'll do whatever you'll tell him to do. So they trailed along with old Blue Bradley, completely outfitted with Australian equipment, and weapons. When they got down to the bottom of the hill around midnight, there's Young from B Company waiting, and all of a sudden he sees almost a platoon of people fully armed . . . fortunately he twigged that they weren't enemy.' Well, they were, just not a hostile enemy.

Len's platoon was one of the last to cross the river to safety, at about 11 pm, and passed through the Middlesex lines on the far bank under the eye of Ferguson, before bedding down at 1.30 am—on Anzac Day. Saunders might have been a veteran of Greece and Crete but said 'at last' he 'felt like an Anzac and I imagine there were 600 others like me'. Not so, for one tearful young Bren gunner told Saunders, 'I feel bloody awful, skipper. It's Anzac Day tomorrow and we're running away from the bastards.'

Notwithstanding its heroics on the heights, the withdrawal was perhaps 3RAR's most successful action of the whole battle. Gwyther was the only casualty in a manoeuvre expertly planned and directed by O'Dowd and flawlessly executed by the troops. O'Dowd was justly proud of his men—they had stopped the Chinese thrust on Seoul. 'They had, without artillery support, without wire or mines, they'd taken on wave after wave of Chinese, in the dark at very close quarters and beaten them,' O'Dowd said, before singling Len's company out for special praise. 'They had withstood attacks all day long using artillery and their own weapons and they'd also had a napalm attack go in on them, but they still held firm. The Australian soldier proved that he was well worth the title of digger.'

The Chinese next attacked on the left flank, where they were also blocked by the Canadians. Its momentum slowed and the Chinese offensive petered out. 'At the centre of the UN front, the line stabilised, and held,' war historian Max Hastings wrote of 27 Brigade's stand at Kapyong. 'The surviving attackers withdrew. One arm of the Chinese offensive was shattered.'

Ferguson was awarded a Distinguished Service Order just a week after the battle. The official historian rained lavish praise on the CO for being a 'battalion commander in the finest traditions' of the AIF. The same writer also wrote that Ferguson was a 'good performer at concert parties'. Some of the diggers—including Len—felt 'Fergie' erred in setting his headquarters so far back. But Gallaway defended the CO in a letter to Len after the war. 'The critical judgement which enabled 3RAR to win at Kapyong was the one made when the CO selected the ground on which to fight—and this decision was Fergie's and his alone.'

The battalion's valour also earned it a high honour—a US Presidential Citation, which some have compared to a unit Victoria Cross. It entitled each member of the battalion to wear strips of blue silk on both sleeves of their uniform. Strangely, and unfairly, the award did not extend to the 32 men killed in the battle. Another 59 were wounded, and two others joined Gwyther in captivity. Kapyong veterans interviewed for this book struggled to talk about the battle. Allan Bennett called a halt to his interview when asked about Kapyong. 'I just get the shakes sometimes,' he said.

A month after the battle there was a call for volunteers to return to Hill 504 to bury the dead. The man who left Gwyther behind stepped forward, but Len was having none of that so took his place in the burial party. 'The padre climbed Hill 504 with us and we found the bodies of [Jack] McBride and Harry [Henry] Richey, both with their boots removed,' Len said. 'I was rather surprised that the padre merely tossed a handful of earth on each and said a prayer. I went along the top of the feature to where Mo Gwyther's pit was. It was empty with no sign of a body. His web belt [was] cut in half at the back together with the sheath of his "Samurai" knife lying alongside the weapon pit. It was obvious that he had been taken prisoner.'

Len came upon a fire-blackened rifle with fixed bayonet resting against the parapet of a trench. He bent down, picked up a discarded Bren barrel from the dirt and walked back down the hill.

CHAPTER 8

KILL OR BE KILLED

'Len Opie was a cold-eyed killer.'
Jack Morrison DCM

Stung by their heavy losses, the Chinese generals regrouped for another offensive. A hard lesson was learned at Kapyong—next time they would leave the Australians alone. Reg Bandy said a captured Chinese officer had revealed under interrogation that, 'We look up a map and look where the British and Australians are and we go somewhere else.' The UN used the lull to straighten its line by advancing where it had been forced back and ceding some ground where it had repelled the enemy attacks. Realising that total victory was now out of the question, a political solution was sought by both sides and eventually, after much squabbling about the ground rules for parleying, formal peace talks started. But there was no truce. The combatants felt the more ground they held, the more bargaining power they had. Conversely, too much aggression might threaten the peace talks, so Ridgway reined in his strategy to conduct only limited offensives.

It might have been mostly quiet on the Korean front, but as ever with Len, there was plenty of action off the battlefield. Deciding he could no longer serve under McWilliam, Len quit his post. 'I finally have had enough of Mr McWilliam and his continual bitching about the OC behind his back to the troops and handed my resignation in, requesting reversion to the ranks and transfer back to 12 Platoon. Captain Gravener called me in and we had a discussion lasting one-and-a-half hours during which he advised me to hang fire, stating that the problem would sort itself out shortly.'

It did, in two ways. First, Len was appointed to command 10 Platoon, whose lieutenant had been transferred to Japan. Len would be in charge until a replacement officer arrived. Clearly he was being noticed in high places. Len's rank at the time was unclear; a diary entry about this time records he was still 'private temporary sergeant'. Second, the McWilliam matter was settled later in a rather old-fashioned way—Gravener thumped him. 'One day the OC, having had all he could stand, took McWilliam around to [have] a set to,' Len said. 'McWilliam rather fancied himself but he didn't know that Norm Gravener had been a fighter in his younger days. The result was that McWilliam had his lights punched out and shortly thereafter was transferred to C Company.' Platoon sergeants 'resigning' at the battlefront and company commanders flattening lieutenants—welcome to dispute resolution Australian army style, circa 1951.

Another kind of fight was also missing from the handbooks. The Australians and Kiwis had discovered that the stalks left in the ground after the rice harvest were 'ready made missiles', Len said. 'This practice had started at the end of winter, as soon as the thaw commenced. The rice straw could be pulled out of the ground with large lumps of mud sticking to the roots and whenever we or the Kiwis were static and the others—or Americans—drove past, we pelted the vehicles and occupants. The Americans never understood or appreciated the custom, but the Kiwis and Australians never failed to have fun.' One day, in an attempt to stop a mud fight, Ferguson and the New Zealand gunners' CO drove into the middle of an all-out cross-Tasman war, only for their jeep driver to beat a hasty retreat when both sides pelted their commanders. 'The VIPs departed at speed,' Len said. 'Eventually the inevitable happened—somebody had an eye damaged by a piece of rock in one clod of mud—and word came down that the practice was to stop.'

The real war dragged on. The opposing generals might have called a halt to major offensives, but there were still skirmishes along the line, patrolling and limited advances. In May, Len was in charge of a section sent forward to occupy a rocky outcrop. On the way there they encountered a small force of Americans sent to attack a hill about 400 metres further forward. The Aussies scaled their peak and watched the GIs start to cross the valley ahead. Trouble lay on the other side. 'From our vantage point we could see Chinese preparing to receive the Americans so we fired our Bren guns over the Americans in the general direction of the Chinese, to warn the friendlies rather than with the expectation of doing any injury to the Chinese.' The Yanks were either blind, deaf, stupid or crazy brave, for they continued to amble forward in single file until the Chinese dropped three of them. The rest quickly turned tail, leaving the three wounded men in no man's land. When the Americans asked if they could camp with the Australians for the night, a livid Gravener refused outright and immediately sent a patrol to bring in the three wounded men. 'The patrol finally collected the wounded and brought them back, returning by 0200 with some very unhappy Americans, having been literally left for dead by their own people,' Len said.

It fell to the Australians to seize the hill. Len's platoon climbed down and started across the valley. 'Just short of the feature there was a hold-up and I went forward to see what was the matter,' Len said. 'It turned out to be an argument between the two leading section commanders as to who should lead the assault. Having sorted the problem out, we went forward again, to find that the Chinese had evacuated the feature during the night, leaving one dead.' One of Len's men poured the dead man's sack of millet over the corpse's face, saying 'bloody gook' as he did so. Len railed against such disrespect for the dead. 'I made him clean it off the Chinaman's face. I informed him that, as he hadn't killed the Chinaman, the body did not belong to him and he was entitled to a proper burial—which I made him carry out.'

Having left the Australians to capture the hill, the Americans showed their gratitude by lining them up in a tank's sights. Len quickly fumbled for the air recognition panel, and the tank gun swivelled in search of other targets. The platoon radio crackled to life—it was Big Sunray, AKA Ferguson, asking for a report from Little Sunray, Len, who told his CO the hill was secure. Big Sunray thanked and congratulated Little Sunray for his work, even though the feature was taken without any resistance.

Len's reputation as a man not to be messed with grew by the week. One night a group of men was sitting around the campfire, poring over fresh mail. A private must have received a 'Dear John' for, 'cursing and carrying on a treat', he ripped the letter to shreds. Len told him to pick up the paper but the man ignored him. Len picked up a small tin of petrol and threatened to set the man on fire if he did not do as he was told. 'Apparently he didn't believe me, so I tossed the petrol over him . . . and picked up a burning log.' The digger 'took off at some speed' with Len in hot pursuit, brandishing his blazing stick. 'What he did not realise was that he was moving so fast that the petrol evaporated before we had gone 50 yards. After a short chase, I threw the log at him and returned it to the fire apologising for the altercation. I never found out if he thought I was serious but he did keep looking oddly at me after that time. And he didn't tear any more letters up, at least while I was around.'

The relative lull created a void in which petty squabbles and administrative meddling flourished. Len, the hardened veteran who had almost single-handedly taken a hill, was made D Company quartermaster. 'Apparently some bright spark had learned that I was a clerk in civilian life and therefore would want a clerical job. I pointed out that if I wanted that, I need never have enlisted.' Thankfully for all concerned, Len was in the job for only a short time before returning to 12 Platoon.

Tactics took on a decidedly World War I flavour during this static period; the men spent hours rolling out barbed wire in front of their lines (Len thought it was a waste of time, there being a shortage of metal posts to anchor the wire) and laying mines. Often the minefields were not properly mapped—or even recorded at all—and soon there were casualties. Len and his mates were sunning themselves on a quiet day when they heard an explosion nearby. A patrol was dispatched and it found a dead digger just inside a minefield's perimeter. 'He had a tin of meat in his pocket and had apparently been heading for the Korean Village on the other side,' Len said. 'A little too eager.' For what, Len did not say. Sex or money? Twelve Platoon's newly arrived officer was leading a patrol back to the Australian lines when—perhaps distracted by a radio call—he strayed into a minefield. He and the radio man were seriously wounded. Len was unimpressed. 'The old saying from an officer's confidential report: "The only reason troops would follow this officer is out of a morbid sense of curiosity" comes to mind.'

The battalion was changing. The Kapyong casualties were gradually being replaced and some of the unit's originals were sent home. Men such as Gravener had done their bit, and then some. The official army policy of the time was for men to take leave in Japan before returning to the front, rather than the time-honoured practice of rotating whole battalions in the front line. (Bill Keys missed Kapyong to unsuccessfully contest Eden-Monaro for the Liberal Party in the Federal Election. Battlefront leave to stand for office? These were strange times.) This presented many organisational problems for Ferguson and his staff, so much so that they bent the rules by withholding leave of key personnel before big battles. High command was unimpressed and Ferguson was sacked in June. The diggers were similarly unimpressed—they had grown to respect their CO. In time they would feel the same about his replacement, Frank Hassett.

The tumult sent Reg Bandy to be D Company sergeant major in June, and he and Len became firm friends. Len writes of a morning tea 'ritual' with Bandy and Bill Nimmo, the three of them wondering at the unfolding morning below. 'We used to lie on the ground, drinking the tea and admiring the beauty of the morning. Chosen—Land of the Morning Calm, each one quite lovely—unless it rained.' The Bandy friendship lasted until Len's death. 'We got on very well together,' Bandy said 60 years later. 'I'd been in World War II for three years so we both spoke the same language.' Asked what made Len such a good soldier, Bandy said, 'It was fixed in his mind—kill or be killed. It wasn't that he hated anybody enough to kill them; it was kill or be killed. When he went to Korea he was a very good soldier, very thorough.' But he advised against crossing him. 'If he disliked you, you could go to buggery and he wouldn't talk to you.'

Len's turn for his second leave came in early July, and after a series of nervous flights—including on a plane that lost a long piece of pipe sawn off its engine before take-off, with no explanation from ground or air crew—Len touched down in Tokyo. He headed straight to the model shops, took in all manner of sightseeing, and delighted in long, lazy days at his hotel pool. After a week or so Bandy arrived, and Len spent much of his time with him and one Trixie Fienberg, who he said was secretary to 'the Australian Army Canteens Service's Director' who was also staying at the hotel. His diaries indicate he was quite fond of Trixie, who shared a room with 'some BCOF wife who was a real pain . . . when we wanted an early morning swim or game of tennis we used to gather under Trixie's window and toss gravel against the glass to waken her, much to the disgust of Mrs BCOF'. Trixie appears to be the main reason Len conspired to have his leave extended.

In his last days of leave Len volunteered for a line-up organised to identify a soldier who had strangled a prostitute. Why did he volunteer? He thought it 'would be interesting'. Well he was very interested indeed when three of the five witnesses identified him as the murderer. The other two put him down as their second choice. He asked the policeman when the murder occurred, and was horrified to hear it was on a night when he was wandering the streets alone. Somehow he talked his way out of it. 'I decided never to volunteer again. Never, ever!'

Jack Morrison might have also picked Len out of the line-up. The hard-drinking, hard-smoking and woman-chasing war hero was awarded a DCM and bar and was described by Brigadier Laurie Lewis

as the hardest of the hard. But in his opinion Len was 'a cold-eyed killer
. . . Len made me look like a boy scout'. Morrison also fell foul of the
law on this stretch of leave. The Australians frequently clashed with
the US MPs—who they mockingly called 'snowdrops' because of their
white helmet bands and webbing. On this occasion Morrison stubbed
his cigarette on an MP's face. Another hard-bitten digger made an MP
stand to attention while he finished his drink in an off-limits beer hall.
'It was rumoured that after a few drafts of Australians hit Tokyo on
R and R, some of the American snowdrops requested transfers,' Len
recalled. By some miracle, he and his mates were back to the front line
by the end of July. Len returned to D Company and at the end of the
month was made temporary company sergeant major.

The stalemate continued in their absence but there was ever-
present danger; the skies brought bombs and shells and 'friendly'
napalm but the heavens killed in other ways, too. During a bad storm
word filtered through that men had been hit by lightning. Len raced
off to help and found three casualties. He went to work on the most
serious case, Lawrence 'Larry' Steer. Len didn't mess around. 'I put a
large safety pin through Steer's tongue to stop him from swallowing it,
then looked for something to rock him, eventually finding a plank. My
knowledge of shock treatment was fairly minimal. Anyhow we rocked
him for about an hour before deciding that he was dead, although still
twitching, so we started down with the three casualties. I had tried
to get through on the landline to the MO [medical officer] and all he
could suggest was to administer adrenalin—as if I had any of that!'
Steer's death was mentioned only in passing in the unit war diary and
official history. Perhaps they struggled to explain, to comprehend, how
a digger could come all this way only to be struck by lightning. Steer
was an enthusiast—he joined up as soon as he turned eighteen, but
World War II was over in eighteen months. Korea was an opportunity
to prove his mettle and he had done just that in the string of battles up
and down the country over eleven months, only to be struck down at
age 26 by an act of God. Three weeks later three men from D Company

drowned when their boat capsized on a flooded Imjin River. In his report summarising the month of August, the battalion doctor wrote, 'Our only casualties were two men killed on mines, one man killed by lightning, and three drowned.' The elements were exacting a greater toll than the Chinese. And the fleshpots of Japan were wreaking more havoc than anything—86 men back from their leave presented with venereal disease in August. Most cases cleared up after a course of penicillin. Meanwhile, Len's diary entry of 13 August says so much in so few words: 'I found two small snakes in my weapon pit and dissected them to see if they were venomous. If so, I don't know how I would be sure! Cake from Mum.'

The lack of action was sapping morale, which was hardly helped by some overly officious officers, including the new company commander, Major Jack 'Basil' Hardiman. Len described his new OC as 'tall with perpetually sunburned lips, which he licked continuously'. A few days after Hardiman arrived, Len wrote, 'The new OC has started already charging people for petty offences, with the accent on the petty part.' Len and Hardiman clashed from the start, and relations soured further when the major ordered Korean porters to build an officers' mess. 'And you can have a sergeants' mess, too!' Hardiman said. Len's reply was unsurprising. 'I've got news for you, sir—if you want an officers' mess, the officers can build it themselves; the porters are fully occupied carrying rations, ammunition and water. And there won't be a sergeants' mess while I'm here!'

Hardiman introduced the apparently pointless exercise of ordering the men into the trenches each day to blindly fire into the distance for a minute or two at a predetermined time. One day a group of machine gunners opened up three seconds early and Hardiman went spare. 'Charge the gun crew CSM [Company Sergeant Major]! They were three seconds early!' Len checked with the offenders and returned to explain the men had just returned after being stranded across the river after it flooded, so they were 'fortunate to know the time, let alone be accurate to the second'. Hardiman's response was, 'Well in that case, we will only court martial the corporal in charge of the gun!' Len did nothing of the sort and the matter was soon forgotten. But Hardiman was not stupid—he sought Len's counsel from the start. Despite their clashes he trusted his sergeant major, who tempered the OC's actions and intervened when necessary. Such as the time when a 'loner' was repeatedly charged for sundry offences. Len never subscribed to post-traumatic stress disorder (PTSD)—no such thing, he would say. But he knew this particular man was deeply troubled. One night, Len wrote, 'There was the sound of a rifle shot and when we investigated, we found that [he] had decided to shoot himself in the foot. But, when we took his boot off, we found that the bullet had gone between his big toe and the next one, only grazing the flesh. Basil wanted to charge him again, but I advised against it, as if things got any worse, he might really shoot himself.' Len instead administered 'a bit of friendly persuasion' and a year later the man was a fully functioning corporal in the regular army. The hard-bitten sergeant major, the cold-eyed killer, had a heart when it mattered.

KILL OR BE KILLED

CHAPTER 9

MARYANG SAN

'Their sheer guts is beyond belief.'
Lieutenant Colonel Frank Hassett

The Battle of Maryang San—the last battle of manoeuvre of Australia's Korean War—represented the sum of the Australian infantry experience post 25 April 1915. It had elements of the August offensive at Gallipoli. The long climbs up steep ridges in the dark were reminiscent of the doomed attacks in the wilderness north of Anzac Cove, and the Chinese trenches stormed by the diggers were similar to the pine-roofed bunkers at Lone Pine. There were traces of Pozières, too, as the 3RAR diggers endured their heaviest bombardment of the Korean War. Of course the weight of shelling was nothing like Pozières—no battle involving Australians matches July–August 1916 for sustained, horrific bombardment—so perhaps Frank Hassett's comparison with El Alamein is more apt. The old names roll out because Maryang San was about the past. The action was the glorious culmination of battalion tactics accumulated over 36 years. As such, it was the Australian infantry at the peak of its evolution. That's not to downplay what happened in subsequent wars, it is simply that Maryang San was the army's last battalion-scale fight. And that's not all. The British divisional commander described it as one of the finest battalion attacks against a superior force by a 'British' unit. Former Governor of Australia Major-General Michael Jeffrey said it was 'one of the finest examples of a phased battalion attack in the annals of Australian military history'. If Kapyong showed 3RAR—now known among the UN army as 'Old Faithful'—could defend, Maryang San showed it could attack. And if, as Ben O'Dowd said, Kapyong was won by the man in the ranks, Maryang San was the Australian digger *in excelsis*. D Company was in the thick of it, and its sergeant major was at the heart of the company. At Maryang San the rebel showed he could perform superbly in a senior company position, not just take on the enemy hordes on his own, and win.

The scene in early October 1951 was this: after several months of minor actions, General Van Fleet went on the attack. The newly formed Commonwealth Division, comprising British, Canadian, New Zealand and Australian units, was ordered to advance across the Imjin to seize hills overlooking the river. This would ease the pressure on the UN front and force the enemy back two to three kilometres to the next line of hills. Operation Commando was about creating a 'new forward UN defence line' as the peace talks stopped, started and stopped again. Now part of the 28th Brigade, 3RAR was allotted the right-of-line position in the offensive, the place traditionally given to the best unit. The King's Own Scottish Borderers (KOSB), King's Shropshire Light Infantry (KSLI) and the Royal Northumberland Fusiliers (RNF) advanced on its left flank. The first objective was Hill 355, or, as the Americans called it, Little Gibraltar. Behind it stood the ultimate objective, Hill 317, which was shaped like a pyramid and just as steep. When he handed the front line to the Australians, a US battalion commander told Hassett, 'You won't get it. Hill 355 perhaps, but not 317.' The Americans had briefly held the former but had suffered heavy losses in two attempts at seizing the latter. Hassett noted the Americans had attacked unscientifically; forming up in the valleys in full view of the enemy, before being mown down by Chinese troops deeply entrenched on the heights. The CO, a veteran of Bardia, Tobruk and New Guinea—he was made a lieutenant-colonel at 23—went about his planning.

Hassett carefully studied the terrain from land and air. He decided to 'run the ridges' as Len and his mates had done a decade earlier in New Guinea. Forget about the low ground; the Australians would make the enemy think another frontal attack was coming, but instead hit them hard and fast from the right flank. As he prepared for battle, he drew on wars past for inspiration. Like the Anzacs playing cricket on Shell Green at Gallipoli in 1915, he created a diversion by directing the battalion's trucks be driven back and forth, creating great clouds of dust away from where he would strike. He even led a 'fighting patrol' comprising his company commanders, the intelligence officer and the signals officer—essentially the cream of his leaders—deep behind enemy lines to survey the terrain. All they had was their own small-arms and a couple of snipers for protection. 'We'd move forward and go so far and have a bit of a look and then go a bit further,' A Company CO Jim Shelton said. 'So it was just a normal fighting patrol, moving forward. Then he got us forward to a particular area where we could go up on our stomachs and peer over and look into the enemy area.' Then they'd slither back again, unmolested. Surely no other patrol in Australian history bore so many pips and crowns.

The battalion had farewelled many men who had served their time and welcomed their replacements. Men such as O'Dowd, Beard, Gallaway and Ferguson had gone. Lieutenant Jim Hughes, himself a relatively new arrival, described September as 'the big rotation'. But all the comings and goings had left the battalion grossly under strength. Hughes's B Company, for example, was down to 75 men instead of the full complement of 120. Some of the blame must lie with administrative bungling. At the time of Maryang San, Hughes's elder brother Ron was back in Australia commanding the 1800-strong 2RAR, double the number set down for a fighting battalion. Hassett had barely 750 to capture a seemingly impregnable position. Up on the peaks, rising to 200 metres above the valley floor, 4000 Chinese troops waited in deep bunkers connected to rings of firing trenches. Another 2000 could be called into the fight at any time. Outnumbered, overlooked and seemingly overstretched, the odds were against the diggers as they filed out into the valleys below Maryang San on 2 October 1951.

Moving in single file with 50-metre gaps between soldiers, the companies used folds in the terrain to trick the enemy into thinking the movement was no more than another patrol. Early the following morning B Company stormed an intermediate objective, Hill 199, 3 kilometres north-east of Little Gibraltar. The small Chinese garrison was surprised and quickly overwhelmed, leaving five dead and ten wounded on the summit. The Australian losses totalled three wounded.

Three British tanks rumbled onto the hill to join the Australian Vickers gunners in laying down a long-range barrage to support the KOSBs attacking Little Gibraltar. Piped into battle as in days of yore, the Scots had a tough time of it and by nightfall were still well short of the massif. Enter the Australians. Major Jack Gerke's C Company was ordered to take a feature north-west of Little Gibraltar to ease the pressure on the Scots. Gerke's men did as they were asked—then took Little Gibraltar for good measure.

Setting off at dawn, they crossed a valley and seized a heavily bunkered hill after scaling its steepest slope to overwhelm the enemy in a shower of grenades. Forewarned by the din, the garrison on the next hill fought with grim determination. With the attack momentarily stalled, Lance Corporal James Burnett, a World War II veteran, took the initiative. Creeping forward alone, he hurled grenades into the Chinese posts before racing into the open, firing his Bren from the hip. The enemy replied with mortars, grenades and small-arms fire but Burnett inspired his section to join him in the attack and soon the position was won. The Australians stood on their objective, but Gerke decided to exploit their rapid success and press forward to Little Gibraltar itself. The Chinese had seen enough—they fled down a ridge running to the north-west, chased all the way by shells from the New Zealand gunners. 'It was a moment of triumph for Gerke to stand on the crest of that great, round hill which dominated the battlefield of

4

6

STONE COLD

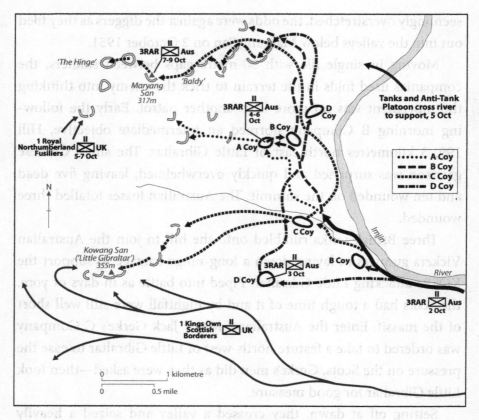

BATTLE OF MARYANG SAN

Operation Commando,' the official historian wrote. The Scots were on the summit within an hour, allowing C Company to return to the battalion the next morning.

Then Len's D Company took the lead. The company was sent to a small hill 700 metres to the north-east of the battalion's base on Hill 199. Dispensing with the convention of leaving a company in reserve, Hassett decided he needed every last man for such a big task. A Company would climb a ridge running north-west to 317, but would only proceed to the top if resistance was weak. Fat chance—A Company was the bait for Hassett's trap. Under his plan, the Chinese would be tricked into thinking this was the main thrust, allowing D and B companies to storm along the crest to surprise the enemy from the east. As company sergeant major, Len was effectively second-in-command of D Company, as the nominal deputy was in the 'left out of battle' group, pulled from the ranks in case the unit suffered crippling casualties. D Company had arguably the hardest task—seizing the final objective. B Company passed through the lines early on the morning of 5 November on its way to clear the slopes below the main ridge. Len and the rest of D Company set off in the dark and visibility was not much better after dawn thanks to a thick fog rising off the Imjin River. 'We started at four in the morning and walked about three miles across to Maryang San,' 12 Platoon's Keith Langdon said. 'It was pretty dark and all that and they said to the skipper: "Where are we?" And he said: "I wouldn't have a clue".' Yes, Major Hardiman was lost. So was B Company. Hassett arrived to find two sheepish company commanders. 'I am lost, sir, I don't know where I am,' B Company's Major Henry 'Wings' Nicholls said. 'And here is Basil and he's lost too.' Len explained how the matter was settled. 'After a short conference, they decided to proceed by compass—due west. B Company headed off—due north.' By veering north, away from the main Chinese positions, Nicholls had effectively handballed D Company the job of clearing the lower slopes and seizing the objective. 'Well, thick as our company commander was, all you have to do to walk up a hill is follow the ridge line,' Len said. 'We were going to the west where their weapons weren't sighted anyway so we just had a fairly easy run up the ridge line.' Hardiman handed Lieutenant Jim Young a map and compass and ordered 12 Platoon to take the lead. 'Not very happily we set off, with a map in one hand, a compass in the other and trepidation over the rest of me,' Young said. 'The fog was still dense and we proceeded slowly and not very happily, as map reading under those conditions wasn't as easy as following a city street guide on a sunny day.'

The mist started to clear, revealing Chinese soldiers scrambling to shift their machine guns to meet this unexpected threat from their open flank. 'They opened up and it was on,' Langdon said. 'The skipper said "fix bayonets, charge!" He was the first one that copped it.' It was Hardiman's first major battle—including during his lengthy service in World War II—and it was all over in an instant when a bullet smashed through his thigh. He might have been the first hit. Others said it was Private Denis 'Snowy' O'Brien, who took a bullet in the head. 'Poor old Denis who had been wounded during World War II in the Middle East; then he had been wounded again seriously in the head at Chongju the previous year,' Len wrote. 'He had been evacuated to Australia and had talked his way back to the battalion and now here he was, our first casualty. We organised a stretcher party and I gave instructions that as soon as he died, the bearers and stretchers should return for further casualties. As it happened, Denis did not make it to the Regimental Aid Post.' Poor O'Brien was strapped to a tank and was swept away as it crossed the Imjin.

Up the diggers charged, bayonets fixed, and down they fell. Stretcher bearers were very much in demand. Jim Johnson was a newly arrived reinforcement who was pressed into service as a bearer. 'OK, we're short of stretcher bearers so you can be a stretcher bearer—thanks very much,' Johnson said when interviewed in 2013. 'So I had a crash course in first aid and off we go. That was that. Stop the bleeding. Treat the shock. Give him a cigarette. Which was the first thing he'd get. As long as he could breathe, of course.' Johnson's A Company was fighting its way up a spur below D Company. Hassett's ruse appeared to be working— the Chinese seemed to think A Company's was the main thrust.

Hardiman remained in command of D Company despite his wound. He ordered 12 Platoon to go to ground while he sent 10 and 11 platoons to its flanks in readiness for a full company attack on the next step in the tiered range. Lieutenant Geoff Leary's 10 Platoon took the lead, the diggers making like their fathers at Gallipoli to grasp at shrubs and saplings to haul themselves up the precipitous slopes. *The Argus* described it in graphic detail: 'The hill loomed high. Its approaches were steep—at times like cliff faces. Well entrenched on the slopes was the fanatical enemy. It was a hillside bristling with firepower.' Upwards and onwards went Leary's men into machine-gun and small-arms fire and grenade blasts. The other two platoons gave covering fire with their small-arms and 2-inch mortars. It was on. As the mist cleared from his forward command post 800 metres below, Hassett watched a seething mass of men swarm over the hills like furious, disturbed ants. Leary soon fell, shot through the thigh like Hardiman. Facing a crisis of command, the company's training and experience kicked in. Young took over from Hardiman and Bill Rowlinson took over 12 Platoon. Len was effectively second-in-charge and would have directed much of the reorganisation. He had to effect this under fire, while overseeing the evacuation of the wounded, the supply of ammunition to the forward troops and the supervision of prisoners. When the ammunition started to run short, he collected magazines and grenades from the headquarters personnel. Captured weapons were smashed or otherwise rendered useless. Len was in his element.

Ten Platoon, now led by Corporal Vincent Brown, fought its way into the enemy's forward trenches where the men went to work with bullets, bayonets and bare fists. Brown was hit in the arm by a round that also smashed his Owen gun. The fight was in the balance until 12 Platoon arrived to turn the tide. The first knoll was in Australian hands. Thirty Chinese lay dead, wounded lay all around, and ten unwounded prisoners were sent down to be dealt with by Sergeant Major Opie. 'These were put to good use carrying the stretcher cases . . . escorted by the walking wounded,' he said. Now the first objective had fallen, Hardiman agreed to be evacuated to the aid post. 'A group of CHQ personnel fell upon the OC, not as he expected, to be bandaged, but to relieve him of his .38 cal pistol,' Len said.

Attention turned to the next objectives in the tiered range—the stepping stones to Maryang San. The newly captured first was christened Brown Knoll, not after the heroic corporal, but because of the soil thrown up from the Chinese digging. The range then dipped to a saddle, before rising to a 210-metre hillock, before another saddle led to another 210-metre hill. Beyond that lay Baldy—so named because it was treeless—and then Maryang San itself. Hassett radioed Young to see if he could press on. Young said yes, as long as he had artillery support now the mist had cleared. The New Zealand gunners and British tanks opened up, pounding all three peaks on the range. Young directed their fire by wireless. 'When a tank scored a direct hit on a bunker, the temporary commander forgot strict protocol,' Norman Bartlett wrote. He sure did. 'Smack in the guts,' Young exclaimed down the line. Eleven Platoon prepared to storm Brown Knoll.

The heavy bombardment had failed to break the defenders' will. The Australians, led by Lieutenant Lawrence 'Algie' Clark, took casualties as soon as they left cover, including from an enterprising Chinese soldier firing a bazooka-type anti-tank rocket launcher into the ranks of advancing infantry. Clark led from the front and the leading section commander, Corporal Ken Black, displayed supreme courage in remaining in charge after taking a machine-gun bullet in his left arm and being bowled over by a grenade blast. Again, the attack was driven home thanks to the diggers' determination, experience and inspirational leadership. 'A Chinese company ceased to exist,' Captain Bill Keys said. 'It was a mighty effort.'

Wasting no time, Young ordered 12 Platoon to leapfrog Clark's men and take the next hill. Eleven Platoon—now down to seventeen men—followed in close support. The enemy, unbalanced by the Australians' furious pace, was again overwhelmed, but inflicted more casualties on the attackers. Rowlinson was wounded but remained in command. He ordered his men on to the next ring of bunkers but as soon as they tumbled over the hill they were immediately pinned down by machine-gun fire. Eleven Platoon—as if it had not done enough already—was ordered to take the lead. Without hesitation or question, Clark's men took the next objective at the point of their bayonets. Thanks to D Company, now only Baldy stood between 3RAR and Maryang San. In seven hours of almost continuous fighting, the company had killed about 70 enemy soldiers and captured another 30. 'What had helped the assaulting platoons was the fact that the Chinese trench system had been dug down the spur from 317,' Len said. 'So as the Chinese tried to withdraw along the trench, the Bren gunners particularly had an easy target. Even if you couldn't shoot very well you just lined up the trench and shot them that way.' Enfiladed is the military term. That is why the old World War I trenches zigzagged through the French and Belgian fields—to avoid being enfiladed.

The Chinese had no idea the hammer blow would fall from the east. Hassett's 'run the ridges' plan had worked. Those of the enemy not caught in the enfilade descended to the floor of the deep trenches to shelter from the fire. But nowhere was safe from the relentless Australians. 'Running along the top, shooting down into the trenches, they inflicted very heavy casualties,' Hassett said. ' "Like shooting rats in a trap" was an expression used. I had seen these sort of results achieved before, against the Italians in Libya, although the Chinese were a far tougher question.'

But the main objective remained, and with B Company still engaged in its own fight off to the north-east, Hassett had a decision to make. D Company had lost three killed and fourteen wounded, and some of the men were fully occupied carrying the wounded to safety down the hill. 'Company strength was now less than 50 . . . there was no guarantee that we would be able to stay where we were,' Len said. 'We settled down, hoping for the best.' Hassett decided Young and his men had done their share, more than their share. Gerke's C Company, depleted after taking Little Gibraltar the previous day but the freshest force at Hassett's disposal, had been following Young's company up the hill. Hassett committed his meagre reserves. Len's mates cheered Gerke's men as they passed through the lines (but probably not Len, as Gerke was a chief Opie adversary) and struck out into no man's land. Speed was of the essence to keep the Chinese off balance. Under the cover of another barrage, Gerke's men quickly took Baldy before pressing on to the summit, 1 kilometre away and 130 metres up. The diggers scaled Maryang San's almost sheer slopes to seize the peak unopposed, apart from ten Chinese soldiers who quickly surrendered.

The battalion had done it. The diggers had taken the 'impregnable' Maryang San. But there was no time for contemplation, let alone celebration. The Chinese lowered their sights and rained mortar bombs and machine-gun fire onto the newly lost ground. All along the range the men retreated to the enemy's bunkers, some three storeys deep. The night passed without major incident. It seemed the Chinese were too exhausted to mount a counterattack. Meanwhile Hassett plotted how to take 3RAR's final objective, the Hinge—a bow-shaped ridge running from Maryang San down to Hill 217, which remained in enemy hands. The Fusiliers had suffered heavily in a succession of attempts to take 217 from the south. If the Australians could get in behind and above the enemy, the Fusiliers might at last succeed.

It was B Company's turn to take the lead. They went in at 8 am on 7 October. After a costly fight—the Chinese were ready and waiting this time—the Hinge fell, making the enemy's positions on 217 untenable. Jim Hughes was one of the heroes of the battle. The newly arrived subaltern was awarded a Military Cross. He had proven himself to the hard-bitten veterans, many of whom demurred at the tactics he had learnt at Duntroon. 'Each platoon had a backbone of people who had served in World War II,' Hughes said. 'They were the corporals and the NCOs that stiffened us up. But we had to get rid of a New Guinea problem.' This 'problem' involved the veterans wanting to fight on one-man fronts as they had against the Japanese almost ten years earlier. But Hughes argued there was room on the bare Korean hills to manoeuvre in sections or even platoons. 'It was hard to make the old blokes accept that. They'd say "in New Guinea we used to do it this way".' For now the offensive battle was over. But not the counterattacks.

The Chinese rained down their most intense and sustained barrage of the war. The men held their nerve, hunkering down. Against a massed charge every bit as big as those at Kapyong, B Company held firm and mowed down 120 of the enemy for good measure. Len was in the forward trenches when the enemy effort swung onto his D Company. 'We had a section of medium machine guns under Corporal Wiltshire with D Company, so we positioned one gun at the top end of our perimeter and two of us held a blanket in front of the gun to shield the muzzle flash. Each time there was an increase in the rate of fire, our gun opened up, hopefully into the flank of the attackers.' Stung by more heavy losses, eventually the Chinese melted away.

Which was just as well. If 3RAR was undermanned going into the battle, it was now a very numerically weak battalion indeed. Hassett walked up and down the parapets, ignoring the enemy shelling. 'Hassett pokes his head into a D Company dugout, asking to see the platoon commander,' Len said. 'Corporal Brown stood forward: "I am, sir!" Hassett was taken aback: "What! A corporal commanding a platoon?" Whereupon Brown replied: "Wait 'til you get to the next platoon, the commander is a lance corporal, sir!"' Len was amused.

Len also delighted in an incident that occurred late in the battle. He was helping carry ammunition up to C Company's posts from D Company's positions on the hillocks below Baldy. He never had much time for Gerke, so the following story was fondly told: 'I reported to Captain Gerke, who was sharing a pit with the CO. There was a certain amount of shellfire and at one stage the CO pulled me into the pit, which was designed for three people, so that I was kneeling on top of Captain Gerke, my first and last opportunity to stand over an officer and I made the most of it.' Back in the D Company lines, a new chaplain had come forward to conduct a service, 'but insisted on standing on the parapet of the trench while we were down in it', Len said. 'After a few random enemy shells flew over, I suggested to him that it would be prudent if he joined us rather than placing too much faith in the Almighty. I am pleased to say he did.'

Len went down the range to check on an aid station set up by C Company's medic, Bob Trotter. 'Now, all the medics in the battalion were first class,' Len said. 'But with Bob Trotter there was one major difference—he was religious. The glade where he had his set-up was virtually unprotected from airbursts and shrapnel and we were not inclined to linger, so, having collected the wounded ready for departure we started to move out, at which juncture he called out to us suggesting that we bow our heads in prayer. At the moment when we were trying to make sense of what he was saying, a shell burst just down the ridge where we would have been had he not called to us.' Len said, 'We'll grant you that one, Trot, now we're off!' Not quite. A shellshock case refused to budge. Len turned to Bill Nimmo and said, 'I'm going to call him every sort of coward who is too gutless to fight or run, but before I start, check the safety catch on his rifle because if I get through to him he may just take a shot at me.' The abuse had the desired effect and they continued down the hill.

Soon everyone was heading down the hill. On 8 October a battered but proud band of survivors climbed out of their bunkers and wended their way through the craters and down past Baldy, Brown Knoll and all the other hard-won features on that bloody ridge. The King's Own Scottish Borderers filed into the line. A month later, despite a heroic stand, the Scots were overrun. Maryang San was back in Chinese hands. It would stay that way for the duration of the war. Many 3RAR men were bitter that the Scots received more decorations in losing the hill than the Australians had in seizing it. 'In Korea, no Victoria Crosses were given to Australians,' Keith Langdon said. 'There were to the English. You work it out.' Still, 3RAR's drum roll of honour was long and strong. Burnett, the Bren gunner who fired from the hip to turn the fight on Little Gibraltar, was awarded a DCM. Like Len's DCM stunt, it was worthy of a VC. Rowlinson received a bar for his Kapyong DCM. Young and Clark received Military Crosses and Brown and Black, Military Medals. Hassett was recommended for a Distinguished Service Order and his men were delighted when it was conferred just two weeks later. All up, the battalion's complement received two DSOs, two DCMs, nine MCs, nine MMs, an MBE and fifteen mentions in despatches. The price was, of course, so very dear. Twenty dead and 89 wounded. The enemy lost perhaps 400 men killed, probably many more. Two Chinese battalions effectively ceased to exist.

Hassett wrote eloquently and with great depth of feeling about the battle many years later. 'There are a number of reasons why Maryang San was so successful, but at the top of the list is the quality of the Australian soldiers involved. These were fit, well-trained and confident men. Confident in themselves, their mates and their leaders. Orders were obeyed without question or hesitation. This was very important at the time because issues hung precariously in the balance and undue hesitation would have been disastrous. Across the battlefield there were numerous incidences of aggressive initiative by individuals turning potential disaster into success. Sadly there were many casualties, inevitable in war. But as one leader went down, another, without hesitation, took his place. Many wounded, where their wounds permitted, ignored them to stay in the fight. These are the soldierly qualities that win battles.

'It is a strange statement, perhaps, to say that there was a wonderful feeling within the battalion after Maryang San. That matters such as death, mutilation, stress, fear, fatigue, hunger, thirst, grief could be thought of, even remotely, as a wonderful, not to be missed experience. It is as hard to understand, I suppose, as are—at a much lesser level— rock climbing, caving or diving amongst sharks. But we go to war to defend our country. Once committed it becomes a case of kill or be killed, and this calls on our inner strengths in a way never experienced in peace time. Certain things happen which a soldier remembers with pride, either in his own actions or the performance of others. Maryang San is my supreme example of this.' Hassett's regard for his men was summed up in his oft-quoted tribute after the battle. 'Their sheer guts is beyond belief.' Many years later Hassett wrote in a letter to Len, 'You are a distinguished man of the battalion and played an important part in Commando and, what is more, saw the operation through from start to finish.'

Lieutenant General John Coates, who, for a time was commandant of Duntroon, described the battle as a 'post World War II classic'. What made Maryang San such a copybook battalion action—not that any

battle is ever really copybook—was that each of its four rifle companies
fought independently towards a single goal. Each delivered when it was
their turn. Yet most accounts heap special praise on D Company for
its drive along the crest of the range. The official historian said it had
performed 'magnificently'. Norman Bartlett wrote that the 'key to the
whole operation . . . was D Company's early rapid progress through
Brown Knoll and other strongpoints guarding the final approach to the
main Chinese defence line'. Another soldier said D Company 'tore the
heart out' of the enemy force.

Hardiman's successor as company commander, Major John
Moloney, had a shorter time in charge than even Hardiman. One day
he went for a walk up to Baldy on his own. 'Half an hour later he stag-
gered back with a gunshot wound in one leg,' Len said. The official
historian said the wound was caused by a booby trap. Len said one
of the 3RAR officers appeared to show little sympathy for Moloney's
suffering. 'Let's go through his gear to see what is worth keeping!' the
officer said. 'This we proceeded to do, with Paddy in a cold sweat from
shock and pain, but still polite, looking on through gritted teeth,' Len
said. 'He was patched up and departed. So far as we could ascertain he
had gone into a Chinese bunker and been shot from outside.' According to Len, years later it emerged that Moloney was accidentally shot by
an RAAF officer who was also wandering through the lines.

Another Len story not in the history books and official records
relates to the opening of the B Company attack on the Hinge. According
to Len, the Chinese soldiers had been wracked with stomach problems,
partly because of a diet that relied chiefly on millet. One of their generals
thought all they needed to do was take their time over their meals. 'Well
after 317 was taken [B Company] moved down towards the Hinge and
they came to a copse of trees and when they tippee-toed up to it, there
were fifteen Chinese sitting around having breakfast,' Len wrote. 'This
was in the middle of a battle. So [the Australians] got all their grenades
and pulled their pins out and did the lot of them. That was because they
were having a leisurely breakfast, they were doing what their general

had told them. If you're told to do something in the Chinese army you do it, you don't query it. And it all gets back to the fact that initially they were having trouble because they were eating their meal too fast and they were obeying his orders in the middle of a battle to sit down and have a long breakfast. It's just the way things were.'

It appeared the Communists charged with progressing the peace talks were under orders, too. The discussions progressed glacially and the north's negotiators were accused of stalling. Coincidentally, the spoil from lines of deep trenches and deeper bunkers appeared all along the line. If the UN wanted the North, it would pay in blood.

Maryang San was the archetypal Australian infantry battle carried upon quick movement. Afterwards the Australian officers might as well have been issued World War I handbooks. Like General Birdwood at Gallipoli 36 years earlier, they now ordered their men to dig, dig, dig, and soon an opposing line of trenches ran from the Yellow Sea to the Sea of Japan.

CHAPTER 10

PRIVATE, TEMPORARY CORPORAL, TEMPORARY WARRANT OFFICER, CLASS TWO

'The Forgotten War: Proud to be a Korean veteran.'
Bumper sticker on Len Opie's last car

Len always said Korea was his best war. But by mid-October 1951, even he needed a break. And he would get one. The morass that masqueraded as the Australian army administration spat out orders saying Len was among a group of veterans who had served their time. They were going home. He was glad, for 3RAR had changed. 'Few of the originals of the battalion were left,' he said. 'The BCOF members had to do only eight months and the reason those of us were still serving was that we were making up the time spent on R and R in Japan, so [we] were understandably anxious to go home.'

Len was put in charge of a batch of 40 troops that entrained on 16 October. But the Australian infantry's most enthusiastic trainspotter had other plans. Entranced by the new model of rail car used in the hospital train to Pusan, somehow he contrived his way onto that train to write an article about it for a trade magazine. He delegated his authority on the troop train to a newly promoted temporary sergeant. What could possibly go wrong? Plenty. The diggers played up from the start—none more so than the temporary sergeant, who was so drunk he fell off the troop train, which fortunately was stationary at the time. When Len caught up with them in Pusan the men had set themselves up in a tent, where the bender continued. Len repaired to inspect the rail yards and upon his return, the transit-camp sergeant major, a British artilleryman, told him of the trouble. 'The sergeant major confided in me that it was the worst draft by far ever to have darkened his doorstep,' Len recorded in his diary. 'Sergeant major, your troops are ruining the discipline of this camp,' the tommy told Len. 'The 2IC and I were on our morning inspection and came across your soldiers, drunk in a tent littered with beer cans. Would you kindly sort things out?' Len went to his men and found the sergeant major was 'right on both counts' so asked for ten minutes grace. 'I then addressed the multitude and informed it that, unless the mess was cleared up, we would not be leaving the camp.' The reply from the drunken rabble was unexpected. 'No worries! Come back in five minutes!' Len went away and duly came back with both the sergeant major and 'a very British major in tow'. The tent was spotless—not a can or even a fag end in sight—to the great surprise of the two Englishmen.

'After their departure, the troops called me back and showed me what they had done,' Len said. 'Simply to lift the flap of their tent and that of the adjoining one and shovel the load in there.' The neighbouring tent was unoccupied or had already been inspected, and by the time the ruse was discovered the men were halfway across the straits to Japan. The incident appears to show the old hands trusted Len enough to include him in the subterfuge.

Down at the docks the men were delighted to be greeted by the Red Cross; lovely ladies doling out donuts and coffee. But wait—GIs only. 'We're American Red Cross,' Len was 'pointedly' told. No matter, despite their state, the men still had plenty of beer, which they traded for donuts and coffee from the US troops. The voyage was uneventful enough, save for a GI who had 'gone berserk' and had to be strapped into his bunk. 'We saw the victim of the night's disturbance being carried down the gangplank and later the stretcher with the poor chap strapped on, laid over the back of two seats in the train, a sad end to a twelve-month "tour" of Korea. I always felt sorry for him . . . he'd done his tour and I suppose he had that PTSD or whatever they call it now', Len recalled. The Australians' reputation appeared to have preceded them, as Len was told of an earlier rowdy bunch of diggers who were harshly dealt with after playing up on a train. The punishment? Their carriage was de-coupled on a stretch of track that 'just happened to be out in the middle of nowhere. After a day or so without food the very subdued carload was attached to a later train.'

Upon his arrival back in Kure, Len made a point of visiting Hardiman and Moloney, who were in the same hospital ward recovering from their Maryang San wounds. After a spot of boating on Japan's Inland Sea—prematurely abandoned after a mini tsunami sped across the previously still waters—Len and the men prepared to head to the RAAF base at Iwakuni for the flight home. Len clashed with an army official who said his luggage was over the 22-pound limit. 'The officer in charge said to me: "Take one shoe out and you will be right." "If I did that I would be as stupid as everyone around here!" After a few heated remarks on either side, I took a pair of shoes out and asked my friend Snow Wiltshire, who was a draft or two behind ours, if he would post them home to me. When we arrived at Iwakuni we had to weigh in again and the aircraft captain said: "You fellows are all travelling light; not one of you has the 22 *kilos* permitted."' Never mind, soon Len was being served lunch aboard his favourite type of airliner, a huge, four prop, Lockheed Super Constellation. At Darwin a customs official asked if Len had anything to declare. Nothing much, just a rifle—his US carbine broken in half to fit in his bag—a few cartons of cigarettes (presumably for his family), some parachute silk, oh, and some leftover syrettes of morphine. The carbine was confiscated at the next stop, in

Sydney, but no one from Customs was interested in the morphine. Then it was all aboard the train for Adelaide, in a sleeper no less, thanks to his rank. He struck up a conversation with a senior intelligence officer, who presciently forecast that Australia's wars would shift from Korea to Indochina. 'I wish I could have met him 15 years later,' Len wrote. Then, home. 'Little old Adelaide . . . never looked better from the hills as we passed through in [the] early morning.' After completing the necessary paperwork at the Keswick barracks, Len was back at Robe Terrace in time for elevenses with his mother and Tarzan the fox terrier. 'A cup of tea, then more and more and a stack of Model Railroaders to read.'

As a volunteer, Len was allowed to apply for a discharge, which would likely be granted given his record of service. But the army was a way of life for him by now; his diaries are full of references to how he found civilian work boring. So he applied for, and received, an instructor's job at Puckapunyal. In the meantime he devoured his backlog of railway magazines, visited friends and coped as best he could with the returned soldier's curse—adjusting to life out of the line. 'In Rundle Street I was accosted by the president of the Norwood RSL who had been at Saints and he asked if I would give a talk "although we all know the war is a joke". I told him that if it was a joke nobody would be interested in anything I had to say, and departed.' *The Advertiser* dispatched a reporter to interview the hero. A very short report appeared on the paper's front page, under the headline 'WO On Apathy Over Korea'. It read:

Australians fighting in Korea felt that much of the apathy towards the Korean war in Australia came from the fact that Australia was not officially at war, and that many people did not agree with tackling the Korean war, WOII LM Opie, of the 3rd Battalion, Royal Australian Regiment, said yesterday. WO Opie returned home to Medindie on 35 days leave after serving for a year in Korea. 'Men in Korea do not like the idea which seems to exist in Australia that they are mercenaries or enlisted because there was something wrong at home,' said WO Opie. As a result of wastage from sickness and battle casualties, many Australian units in Korea were serving much under strength, he added.

The report ran under a lead story describing how the peace talks had again stalled. As if by way of implied threat, the page's main photo was of a mushroom cloud over Nevada from the latest atom-bomb test. Len had to deal with some localised fallout of his own after his story appeared—communist propaganda was stuffed in his Robe Terrace letterbox. News of the hero's return made it as far as Broken Hill, where *The Barrier Miner* ran a photo of a very menacing—or more likely just plain old grumpy—looking Len unpacking his gear at home. Len's quotes in the afternoon Adelaide tabloid *The News* were typical and telling. Acerbically, he noted the men at the front were well aware of the apathy at home. 'The men fighting in Korea have the idea that the public thinks they enlisted to get away from things they did not like at home,' he was reported as saying. 'They resent this attitude. It may be partly true, but it is a man's own business why he enlisted to fight for his country.' He made a public appearance at the department store John Martins, but the public was so seemingly uninterested he left without fielding a single question. His diary indicates he quickly tired of his leave and was glad to head back to Puckapunyal to join 2RAR when it ended.

He must have had second thoughts when he arrived to a frosty welcome. Surely his reputation had preceded him? Or perhaps that was the problem? The name Len Opie was indeed well known at Puckapunyal; the trouble was it was a different Len Opie. Accused of stealing a watch, wrongly as it turned out, Warrant Officer Len Opie had blown the back of his head off in the days before his namesake's arrival. 'Some of the more ghoulish types were going to put me in the same room, but as the ceiling hadn't been repaired and there was still blood and bones adhering, saner counsel prevailed and I was quartered down the passage.' A postscript came a few weeks later when he received a letter meant for his predecessor. 'When I opened it, I found a demand for £5 or threat of legal action from some woman.'

The battalion CO, Ron Hughes, older brother of Jim, sent Len to be sergeant major of a composite company of regular army and K Force recruits. There were problems from the start. Temporary Warrant Officer II Opie replaced a sergeant who had served since World War II. The old digger was unimpressed, as temporary ranks such as Opie's were supposed to be cancelled upon the soldier's return to Australia. As Len said, no one got around to amending—or confirming—his rank. 'I was in a very unusual situation. With a stroke of a pen, I could be reduced to the ranks, but nobody ever got around to doing it. So I held my rank, thus being senior, after a year's service, to sergeants with up to twelve years—or at least since World War II. This didn't always go down too well, although it did not make me lose any sleep.' On one occasion an orderly officer button-holed Len about not wearing any marks of rank. 'Well, actually,' Len replied, 'I am a private, temporary corporal, temporary WOII, but you can put me down as WOII. As I was not—and never made a practice of—wearing rank, he didn't know quite what to believe.'

Len set about winning the respect of a difficult band of men. Two regular army corporals who lived in nearby Seymour asked Len for permission to knock off early on Fridays so they could head home. Len created two enemies when he refused. There were ramifications on the parade ground when the whole company pretended not to hear one of his barked orders, leaving him to 'make like a sheepdog' lest the marching columns disappear in the direction of the rifle range. 'I soon found that being in a recruit company was not to my liking,' he recalled. 'The young pups in the [regular army] thought they could run things to suit themselves and did not take well to discipline.' After a few weeks he asked the battalion second-in-charge, who he knew through his Adelaide Steamship contacts, to be transferred. He was given a choice of five different postings and opted for a holding platoon of soldiers waiting embarkation to Korea.

At this point Len's diary is replete with word pictures of the battalion's many characters. He wrote of a sergeant so unpopular that when he broke his leg in a football match no one helped him—a first-aid party had to be ordered to remove him from the field; a quartermaster who ribbed a comrade for being taken prisoner in World War II—and copped a broken nose for his trouble; a company commander who for 'some reason affected an American accent'; and a 'panty raider'—believed to be an MP—who terrorised the married quarters and hospital nurses. Anzac legends? Bronzed diggers are hard to find in the pages of Len's diary.

One morning Sergeant Harry Gleeson, a 'real old bushy', returned from the grenade range, walked into the orderly room, and tossed a bag into the corner in disgust. 'Damn grenades,' he said to a puzzled Len. 'Not one of them went off. I collected them and there they are.' Len quickly identified the problem. Len: 'Harry, did you clean them before you primed them?' Gleeson: 'No, there wasn't time.' Len: 'Well, when you went out to the range it was nearly freezing and the grease was stiff. Now it's 0900, the sun has been up for a couple of hours and the grease has probably melted. When the pins were pulled, the almost solid grease stopped the pins from going down. But now, Harry, the heat will have softened the grease and they are likely to go any time, so pick up the bag and very gently walk away and keep going.' Gleeson gingerly picked up the deadly cargo, albeit while complaining that he had left some unexploded mortar bombs on the range because he thought 'they'd be dangerous', and tiptoed out of the room. Len told him to keep walking until he was a safe distance from the huts, whereupon he would gently put the bag down so the grenades could be detonated by rifle fire. At that moment the company commander arrived to carpet Len, his affected American accent fuelled with rage. 'Goddamn, sergeant major! You aren't in Korea now! If someone gets hurt, imagine the paperwork!' Len reacted in typical fashion. 'I lost interest, passing the problem to others as I had done my best.'

So after surviving New Guinea, Balikpapan, Hill 614, Kapyong and Maryang San, our hero was very nearly blown to bits in a hut in rural Victoria. Bill Rowlinson was not so lucky in an incident some months later. Newly commissioned (or as Len deliciously described it, he had graduated from a 'knife and fork course'), Rowlinson decided to enliven an exercise by tossing sticks of dynamite as his men picked their way through barbed wire. 'Not the brightest of ideas and even less bright when he held on to one too long and it blew his hand off', Len said. Len heard the bang and rushed to help. They patched up Rowlinson the best they could and bundled him into a truck, where patient and first-aiders all stood on the drive to the camp hospital. 'The sister on duty didn't endear us to her when she announced that "we can do without the spectators", so we departed.' Rowlinson recovered sufficiently to make captain.

Rowlinson was one of a sprinkling of Korean veterans in camp. Major Darcy Laughlin—he who took an aperitif in his command tent as the Chinese swarmed down the Kapyong Valley—was Len's commander at one stage. Len had a curious respect for 'The Master', as he called him, even though his accounts of Laughlin depict a somewhat enigmatic character. Major and sergeant major developed a good working relationship, even if Len would probably take credit for 'training' his boss to be putty in his hand. 'As I had found early on in the army, the way to get on was to do the job, be polite and stand up to authority', Len said. At a conference with his platoon commanders ahead of a move to Ingleburn camp, Darcy demanded to know how many troops were in each platoon. His temper grew darker as each commander said they did not know, which was understandable given all the comings and goings. Then he came to Len. Darcy: 'Do you know how many troops you have sergeant major?' Len: 'Yes, sir.' Darcy: 'At last we have someone who knows! How many?' Len didn't miss a beat. 'Twenty-eight or 29, sir.' Darcy: 'What! You said you knew your strength!' Len: 'Yes, sir, 28 or 29.' Laughlin gathered himself before saying, 'How can you say you know, then give us two figures?' Len: 'Well, sir, I had 29, but one man has applied to transfer to [the regular army], in which case, if he is accepted, he won't be going to Ingleburn. So, depending on your decision, the figure is 28 or 29.' 'The Master' gave up. '[He] had not earned his nickname for nothing and he never gave an inch, but he was scrupulously fair,' Len recalled.

'I had not looked forward to serving with him, but from that day on we understood each other and got on well.'

Laughlin was partial to more than the occasional aperitif and was regularly driven into town for a decent session. He was also an accomplished pianist who played jazz or classics, 'depending on his mood'. Len liked to go to town, too, in his case because the camp cook was 'absolutely the worst I had ever known'—which was saying something. After his meal Len would sit outside the hotel with Laughlin's driver and listen to the major play. 'Eventually Darcy would come out. On seeing me he would demand to know what I was doing and when I told him I was hoping for a ride back to camp, he would tell me to get in and away we would go. One night, when we arrived back, I got out, said goodnight and started to walk away. Darcy called me back: "Sergeant major!" "Yes, sir?" "You bastard!" "Yes, sir!" "Goodnight!" "Goodnight, sir!" And we went our separate ways.' On the morning after one of Laughlin's benders the battalion CO turned up to inspect a full-company parade—a parade minus its hungover commander. The colonel thumped on Laughlin's door with his cane, eliciting a torrent of abuse from within. Laughlin might have had his faults, but his service record was outstanding. A 39er, he served the duration of World War II, much of it in one of the nation's finest fighting units, the 2/3rd Infantry Battalion, before his heroism in Korea. A hairdresser by trade, he must have been some character and sadly died young, in 1967, aged fifty.

The various characters leap off the pages of Len's diary. A grizzled assault pioneer sergeant was fed up with soldiers relieving themselves against the wire of the stockade. The old digger's solution? 'He had some steel plates placed on the ground at the bottom of the barbed wire and these were wired up to a power point—presumably something less than 240 volts,' Len said. 'Whatever it was, the effect was to put a sudden stop to the practice.'

Practical jokes and characters aside, Puckapunyal was a 'drag', Len said. Ingleburn, on the outskirts of Sydney, was better. The unit travelled to its new camp by train, with Len brandishing a .303 and fixed bayonet—he pretended to be a sentry so he could stretch his legs when the train stopped. Once he sized up the new camp, he became similarly adept at stealing into town to go to the movies or get a square meal. Familiar faces abounded, such as his old friend Tom Muggleton. Bruce Ferguson was here, too. When a member of Len's platoon trailed past Ferguson with a billy swinging from his belt, Ferguson sent Muggleton after the column to find out who was in charge of the 'bunch of swagmen'. When Muggleton returned to report that it was Len's platoon, Ferguson exclaimed, 'I might have known!'

Discipline was a problem at Puckapunyal and matters barely improved at Ingleburn and its attendant camp at Glenfield, a spartan outpost comprising a few motley huts and tents. Len's men were forever trying it on; pushing him, testing him. Len usually prevailed, but not always. After the morning parade some of the troops occasionally hid to dodge work details. 'One of my villains told me years later of one episode when some of my platoon were missing,' Len said. 'This particular morning I had dashed into the huts looking behind doors, but, as Brownie pointed out, not into cupboards, where he had parked himself with some of his companions.' The climax came on a field exercise when the rankers went on strike when they should have been striking their camp. Len had a decision to make about this bunch of 'bush lawyers', as he called them: turn a blind eye or confront the men. He chose the latter, of course. 'I went over, lined everyone up and informed them that in the morning I would be going back to camp and reporting that they were unmanageable, as . . . they were obviously not ready to go to Korea,' he said. 'They were on their own and could do what they pleased. So saying, we went back to our area to pack up. A few moments later, a deputation arrived with the request that we give them ten minutes, then come back and start again. When we arrived back, the fire was out, everyone was lined up, quiet as mice and very subdued. I told them that I would make no promises but I was prepared to complete the week as per schedule and then would decide what to do. Needless to say the rest of the week went off without a hitch with everyone behaving. Also needless to say,

I was not invited to their "end of course" party, which apparently most of the platoons held, not that I was ever invited to one.'

The men were preparing for a route march one morning when there was a disturbance in the lines. 'When I went to see what was going on, I found a couple of foreigners drinking with some of my platoon,' Len wrote. 'I handed them over to Ron Watts. The CSM lined the platoon up and found a few coincidentally under the weather so I announced that, instead of the customary ten-minute halt in the hour, we would march for two hours before halting and if anyone had any complaints, to blame the drinkers.' A harsh penalty indeed, but turning the main body against the drinkers seemed to work. The trouble was, one of the drunks could not keep up. When he fell out vomiting, Len gave instructions for him to be left behind, to make his own way to camp when he felt better. When the patrol marched back into camp four days later there was no sign of the miscreant, alive or dead. (Len wrote 'no body' was found.) A jeep was scrambled to where he was last seen, but he had vanished. The mystery remained until the following week when he wandered back into camp. His story was amazing. He remembered lying in the roadside grass and the next thing he knew he was on a platform at Spencer St Station in Melbourne—some 800 kilometres away. He was quizzed by a brace of MPs before somehow arranging passage back to Ingleburn. 'Knowing him, I could believe his story, incredible as it sounded,' Len said. 'He was wheeled up and fined about £5 for the time he was away. He bore no grudge.'

When the offences were considered too egregious to be ignored, Muggleton brought them before the battalion CO, Lieutenant Colonel John 'Black Jack' McCaffrey. 'One time . . . the CO ordered the room cleared except for the prisoner, so everyone departed and waited outside, and waited and waited until eventually Muggo opened the door and there was the prisoner facing the CO who was asleep at his desk,' Len said. 'On another occasion the CO began to rant and rave about what he was going to do with the prisoner, shaking his finger and thumping the desk, until Muggo pointed out that he was shouting at one of the escorts.'

Romantic liaisons with the camp nurses were common. One nurse was stringing two diggers along at once, including a sergeant who had spent much of World War II as a POW. Len was unimpressed. 'Poor old Bob imagined that the lady was keen on him, although his mate was the front runner,' Len said. 'They provided the mess with plenty of gossip until it was found that the lady was already married but had neglected to tell the authorities, so she departed overnight with a bad discharge.' Other lovestruck diggers sought Len's unlikely counsel. 'A sergeant . . . came to me and asked my advice,' he said. 'It appeared that he had been going with this female and getting up to some hanky panky and she announced that she was pregnant and that he was the father. What should he do? Firstly, was he the father? He was sure he was not. Well, fairly sure.' Len's advice? Run her over in the car. 'Yes, I thought of that, but too many people knew where we had gone!' the sergeant said. 'Then bluff it out,' Len said. 'She doesn't have any proof and even if you call her bluff and have a blood test, it won't prove anything.'

Another soldier bravely told the sergeant major he was about to desert because he had got a girl pregnant. 'No need to do that,' Len told him. 'The army isn't very fussy about these things. Go and see the padre, tell him she is your fiancée and ask his advice.' The man replied, 'I can't do that! I've already got my fiancée pregnant!' Len told him to go ahead and desert. 'But make sure your gear is packed or it won't be here if you come back!'

While Len was at Glenfield he had a bed reserved at Ingleburn on weekends. 'One Friday, after spending the evening in the mess with the crowd . . . I left for bed but when I arrived at my room, the door opened a fraction then jammed.' He forced it open and there in his bed lay two soldiers—with their boots on, no less. Len raced back to the mess to report the incident to the duty officer, who was three-quarters drunk and not interested. Len was clearly disgusted. One of the men deserted immediately. The other man was later charged with a civil offence in Japan, although Len did not specify the crime. 'Perhaps justice was finally catching up with him,' Len said. He 'hoped that justice would also catch up with' his Ingleburn lover. Len's open homophobia was curious. Reflecting the times, aspects of homosexuality were illegal in Australia during the 1950s. So Len was merely in step with the rules. And he was mostly a stickler for the rules. For duty. Doing the right thing.

Hidden and forbidden homosexuality and undiagnosed post-traumatic stress disorder no doubt contributed to the suicides recorded in Len's diary. 'One morning a crowd was standing around outside one of the huts when a shot was heard from inside,' Len wrote. 'Jack Morrison went in to investigate and was inside for about ten minutes. When he came out he was asked what had happened. "Chap shot himself," Jack said. "Is he dead?" "He is now!"' Morrison, you will recall, was the same man who stubbed his cigarette out in an American MP's face in Japan. He was a great soldier and a close mate of Len's—they shared a certain detachment when the going got tough. No doubt he did all he could for the poor man, who killed himself in a lonely hut a long way from home.

After a few months at camp Len was longing to be back in the line. If he couldn't go back he might as well leave the army altogether. His personal papers include an unsigned application for discharge in which he wrote his instructor's post 'could be filled satisfactorily by an NCO without Korean service . . . . I feel that my period of useful-ness to the army is at an end.' His applications to return to Korea or for discharge were routinely dismissed by his superiors. Eventually McCaffrey relented. 'If you really want to go back to Korea, you will have to revert to sergeant,' the CO said, to which Len replied, 'That is no problem since I am only a private, temporary corporal, temporary WO2.' His application was accepted, and he filled in the time before his embarkation making models of Soviet T-34 tanks and SU-76 self-propelled guns in the intelligence section's office. He flew out of Sydney on 22 October 1952. It was a different war now, one that suited Len down to the ground. The legend was about to grow even greater.

CHAPTER 11

EYES LIKE A CAT AND NO NERVES AT ALL

'Death was part of the game.'
Len Opie

Jaded by war just seven years after the greatest conflict in the planet's history, the public was not much interested in the deeds of a few thousand troops, in a country far, far away, so war correspondents pushed the envelope in their despatches from the front. In this *Courier-Mail* report, which ran midway through Len's second tour of Korea, the florid journalism of the era hints at how Korea was perceived on the home front. The writer has wrought every last ounce of colour out of his subject, but he had plenty of raw material with which to work.

> Meeting Len Opie, you'd wonder how he got his reputation up here as probably the deadliest fighter in Korea. Opie is 30, thin and small boned. He's fair with blue-grey eyes and doesn't smoke or drink. He looks, in fact, as inoffensive as a shipping clerk on leave for a while from his firm in Adelaide—which is just what he is. But he's become a legend up here. As company sergeant major, he doesn't need to go out looking for trouble on patrols now—but he still comes along each day to volunteer. Often he cooks up some plan and asks permission to go out at night alone. He's done more than 50 patrol missions; made one-man swings deep into

enemy territory 'hunting' with an Owen gun; has eyes like a cat and no nerves at all. His individual score: more than 50 Chinese. Opie is one of a brand of Australian fighters whose deeds in this war should be stirring the nation's pride.

After writing similarly purple prose about Len's mate Jack Morrison—'the happy-go-lucky extrovert with a score of 120 enemy'— the *Courier-Mail* writer signed off, 'They're night fighters—as good as any we've ever sent away. They're tough, resourceful, and skilled—many of the Chinese they scored were killed the hard way, in hand-to-hand night fighting on frozen hillsides. We dips our lid to them.'

Len was honoured in a more formal manner soon after he flew to Japan from Australia. He received his Distinguished Conduct Medal at a parade in Kure on 28 October. Jim Hughes received a Military Cross for his Maryang San heroics. He was also there as an aid to the brigadier handing out the gongs. They pulled up in a staff car and the brigadier said, 'Out you get Jim, you first.' Hughes remembers a beautiful bright sunny day and a ceremony that was over in an instant. 'We didn't even have a cup of tea afterwards.' Len must have been disappointed. When word of the decoration reached home, the Adelaide Steamship Company secretary sent Len a letter of congratulations that informed him the news would be added to the agenda for the next board meeting.

The army's bureaucratic cogs were not turning any faster; Len learned he had been awarded the medal only two days before it was pinned on his chest—twenty months after the action for which it was given. He had just been dressed down for having a crumpled uniform— after a long flight of course—by his old adversary Gerke, when he was handed a telegram from his old section-mate Bill Nimmo that read, 'Congratulations on decoration. Keep your head down. Bill.'

'While I was digesting this, there was another summons to the Great One,' as Len referred to Gerke. 'What had happened was this: The postal sergeant; one of Gerke's lackeys, had read the cable and run to Gerke with the news. Gerke had contacted HQ British Commonwealth

Forces Korea to verify it, then called for me. When I went in he congratulated me and pinned the ribbon on my still creased battle dress with a few mumbled comments.' The humbling of Gerke came after he had ordered Len to remain in Japan as an instructor. 'Don't tell me where you're going . . . do you realise there are people getting killed in Korea?' Len was unmoved. 'There were people getting killed the last time I was there and I am going back to 3RAR and nowhere else!' Gerke was in a mood to disagree with everything Len said, which worked in the latter's favour when he told Gerke he was supposed to surrender his warrant officer's rank upon arriving in Japan. 'Give me your paybook! Nothing in it about reversion. As far as I'm concerned you're still a warrant officer!' So Len kept his rank, but lost his fight to rejoin the battalion. But first he would escort a detachment of reinforcements to the front. Len's gear included a gross of condoms. He protested, saying the men had no use for condoms at the front but was told it was 'standard operating procedure'.

The static war that greeted Len upon his arrival back at the front in November 1952 provided a stage for him to reach his zenith as a soldier. Opposing lines of trenches separated by a broad expanse of no man's land enabled Len to do what he did best—operate alone, with no one else to look after; no one to push out of the way after they were shot. He drew on his supreme fieldcraft, ingenuity and, of course, courage, to build on the Opie legend by becoming known as the master of no man's land.

Len and his draft of reinforcements sailed for Korea on 3 November. They docked at Pusan the next day and boarded a train to the front. It was unseasonably hot and all the troops had to drink was two jerry cans of water between them. In the spirit of Anzac, Len handed the first can to the Kiwis, which was empty by the time it had circulated back to Len. 'The next time we sent the jerry can around the other way.' Well that didn't help—again it returned empty. 'So much for Allied cooperation,' Len wrote. He was getting thirsty when the train slowly passed some Korean boys waving bags of oranges for sale.

Thinking quickly, he passed the box of condoms to a boy in exchange for a bag. Never mind any moral issues of giving a minor condoms, the youngster had just made the deal of his life. 'I learned later that the going price for a condom was $10, which must have made the lad very happy and made my oranges probably the most expensive fruit in the country.'

When he arrived at 3RAR HQ Len was button-holed by the latest CO, Lieutenant Colonel Ron Hughes, the former commander of Len's old training battalion and older brother of Jim. The CO asked what he was doing there. Len said he had brought a draft of reinforcements, and was leaving the next day for a training posting in Japan. Hughes was having none of it. 'I'm short a CSM and you're it. Don't get back on the truck—you're going to Support Company!' Len was exultant. 'I had escaped Gerke's clutches once again!' Support Company included the mortar, anti-tank and machine-gun platoons, so the posting gave Len a plethora of new toys to play with. And he did not have to waste time breaking in a new officer—Captain Les 'Bronco' Hatfield had briefly been Len's commander at Puckapunyal. Happy days! Len's arrival coincided with the battalion being pulled out of the line for a rest, so he made the most of the lull to catch up with a host of old mates, including A Company OC, Captain Colin 'Dolly' Brown, who Len knew from the St Peter's school cadets.

The situation upon Len's return was this: Maryang San, seized so audaciously by the Australians the previous year, had been retaken by the Chinese a month later, to the obvious despair of the diggers who had lost so many mates on its slopes. The front line had stabilised and now ran in a north-easterly direction in the valley below Maryang San. There was a no man's land of about 2 kilometres between the opposing lines, and the lowlands were heavily mined and wired and equally heavily contested by patrols sent out by both sides. As in the Great War, artillery was king of the battlefield, forcing the opposing armies to dig deep bunkers and tunnels; some of the Chinese fortifications were three-storeys deep. They needed to be, for shells were not the only danger: the UN had wrested air superiority from the enemy, whose MiGs were outclassed by UN Sabres flown by well-trained US pilots. This cleared the way for ancient World War II bombers to bomb the front and supply lines. Suddenly it was all about the past. Wire coiled on pickets, machine guns and blanket barrages—add gas and this could have been Flanders circa 1917. But didn't tanks make trench warfare obsolete? Partly, but the terrain was too mountainous for massed armour. Tanks were instead dug into the UN trench lines to supplement the artillery. Faced with the politically unpalatable prospect of sustaining heavy losses while trying to seize the heavily fortified enemy lines, the UN armies mostly limited their operations to patrols in strength and the very unpopular—but all too common— raids to try to get prisoners, mostly without success.

The US commanders were constantly ordering raids to snatch prisoners, but the mass surrender days of Kapyong were long gone; by this stage of the war the Chinese were less inclined to pack it in. The deep fortifications further complicated matters, as the Chinese bunker networks were so complex that raiding parties sometimes leapt into enemy trenches only to find them vacant. Worse than that, on the rare occasions Australians did manage to snare a prisoner he was invariably a ranker and so of little or no intelligence value. After a host of failed attempts to get a prisoner, Hughes called on Len to have a go. Len had a left-field idea. He asked for a Chinese burp gun so if there was any trouble the enemy would hear only their 'own' gunfire. Hughes agreed and a burp gun was duly found and delivered to the battalion, where a curious soldier decided to test the unfamiliar weapon—and used all the available ammunition. So much for that idea. Fortified with a cup of tea, Len went through the wire at 7 pm on 31 December. Len's small patrol, notionally led by Lieutenant Brian Bousfield, made its way via a series of outposts—including 'Alice Springs' and 'Cloncurry'—into no man's land, whereupon the main group stopped to deploy from a 'firm base' for the snatch raid. Len, Private Adrian Lord and an unnamed signaller continued on into the murk. They crept over a paddy bund and into a valley directly below the enemy's trenches. There Len came across a signal wire and promptly cut it. He wanted the enemy to send out a party to investigate. Len's orders were to act as bait: be seen by the enemy, then race back to the firm base, where the main party would grab its prisoner. Presently an enemy soldier was seen about 40 metres away so Len told the signaller to radio the code word, 'hunted', back to Bousfield's party. 'After the radio operator had given the code word several times he woke to the fact that he had lost his radio aerial.' Patrol aborted.

Len documented misadventure in and behind the lines as much as he did battlefield bungles. In one such incident Len displayed as much courage as he had in any action in both of his two wars. Two soldiers—probably drunk and smoking in bed—set their tent on fire. They escaped the flames, but that was not the end of the matter. They had left a cache of high explosive and phosphorous grenades behind, as well as their personal ammunition. Len unhesitatingly plunged into the blazing tent, found the grenades, and threw them out of harm's way. 'At the subsequent inquiry the occupants denied vehemently that they had been drunk . . . so I asked them to challenge my version,' Len said. 'When they questioned me, my reply was: "Well, if you were drunk when the fire started, you were certainly sober by the time I arrived!" Panic certainly has a sobering effect!'

Len's diary of his second Korean tour is populated with the names of many friends. Some were friends on their way to high places. And some did it the hard way. Lieutenant William 'Digger' James's patrol strayed into a minefield where a man was killed and four wounded, including James, who lost his left foot and broke his right leg. After the war he graduated from medicine, rose to major general, and was national president of the RSL. He was a great friend and ally to Len over many decades. Lieutenant John Kelly was a platoon commander in Len's company. They went on at least one long-ranging patrol into no man's land. Len seemed to greatly respect Kelly, who no doubt learned much from his sergeant major. Kelly also rose to major general and was appointed commandant of the Royal Military College, otherwise known as Duntroon. Len had no time for lefties, but it appears he was impressed by future Labor premier of South Australia Des Corcoran for leading a rescue party when a patrol was mired in a minefield. Sergeant Corcoran was wounded in the action. Many others rose through the military through the next twenty or so years, and became invaluable contacts when Len was in a bind.

While the infantry fighting was limited to patrol actions, the front line in the so-called 'static war' was a more dangerous place than ever. The Chinese artillery—while not very accurate—was incessant. In December, Len noted the Chinese fired 924 shells and 1340 mortar bombs at the Australians, a daily average of 31 and 45 respectively. These were probably official figures but it would not surprise if Len kept count himself (although by this stage of his military career he was known to sleep through the heaviest bombardments). The Australians were well dug in but anyone in the open was in mortal danger. As Support Company's sergeant major, Len spent more time in the open than most. 'The platoons were scattered throughout the area, the machine guns split between the rifle companies, the mortar platoon in its own location to the rear, the assault pioneers in their own area on the perimeter and the anti-tank platoon combined in a two-platoon company on Anti-Tank Spur facing Hill 227, so there was a fair amount of movement just visiting the various elements,' he recalled. Daily ablutions were a risky business. 'The Chinese, either having put an observer in the paddy field . . . or out of pure guesswork, had a habit of lobbing the odd mortar round over . . . when we were showering,' Len said. 'We had a primitive bucket shower rigged up outside the command post and it was embarrassing—not to say downright dangerous—to be caught outside when the bombs were dropping, and the only protection was a towel plus a fast pair of feet.' All the while the men had to be on their guard against Chinese attack. A Canadian unit made the mistake of holding a formal officer's mess one bitterly cold night. The Chinese somehow knew there were no officers in the forward trenches.

They crept forward to drop grenades down the metal flues marking each deep bunker. Those Canadians not killed were quickly driven out of the positions.

Len might have seemed hard-hearted at times but his diary has glimpses of his sadness at his mates' deaths. Corporal Bernie Cocks and Private Adrian 'Laddy' Lord were able and trusted comrades of Len's on several raids. One day Len returned to the line from a conference to learn Cocks had been wounded by a mortar blast. 'True to form, Bernie had been out tending casualties,' Len said. 'Unfortunately when he called in to see me I was asleep and, again, being Bernie, he did not want to disturb me, so I missed him and he returned to the line after treatment of his wound.' The next day's diary entry reads, 'To battalion command post for breakfast to learn that Bernie, again helping with wounded overnight, was himself killed.' Lord was the victim of another catastrophic stuff-up when a green officer decided to test whether their patrol's 'tail-end Charlie' was on his guard. The officer took Lord with him on a wide sweep from the front to the rear of the column, where, Len wrote, 'the tail-end Charlie was indeed alert and killed them both'. Lord survived three years fighting the Japanese in the islands to be killed by an Australian bullet in Korea. Such a stupid waste.

On one patrol Len's Owen magazine fell off without him noticing, so if there was a fight he would have had to 'beat the enemy over the head with the butt'. On another sortie, he roamed deep into no man's land but when he returned he was in trouble with Hughes, who was irate that Len had gone out—alone—without his permission. Later in the tour he was barred from patrolling by a new company commander who believed that a sergeant major's role was organising the troops rather than embarking on solo patrols of no man's land. But Len's diaries provide scant detail of his solo patrols. They are barely mentioned.

So how do we reconcile this with the man who had 'done more than 50 patrol missions' and who had 'made one-man swings deep into enemy territory "hunting" with an Owen gun'? Why does Len's diary have so little about his after-dark forays into no man's land when they were common knowledge among his comrades? Kapyong and Maryang San veteran Keith Langdon said Len was a 'terrific bloke' who would 'go out on patrols on his own'. Mick Mummery, a Vietnam veteran and close friend of Len's, said, 'His reason for going out by himself was because he found it much easier if he only had Len to look after and not someone who might be a liability.' Mummery and Brigadier Laurie Lewis said the stories of Len's 'sharpened shovel'—tailored for hand-to-hand combat—were well known among the ranks of old soldiers. Just as well known were yarns about how Len garrotted enemy sentries with piano wire. Colonel Peter Byrne said his friend and comrade 'had a reputation for being very effective after dark'. Len wowed his young nieces with stories of the piano wire, but of course he might have been making it up for effect. In opening a Len Opie display in the Army Museum of South Australia, Colonel Bill Denny, who knew his subject well, said, 'Len was utterly fearless and was credited with 50 night patrols all of which he did on his own.' Denny paraphrased Len, saying, 'If you are on your own you don't have to trust or worry about anyone else. [And] if you get knocked off then, likewise, there is still no one to worry about!' There was nary an old digger of the regiment who hadn't heard of Len's proficiency with the piano wire. So where does the truth lie? Perhaps Len simply did not mention the patrols in his diary. Especially if he was acting without orders. Other sources show he certainly glossed over many incidents in his diary. As ever with such matters, there is, no doubt, more than a nub of truth to the stories. The truth is usually somewhere in the middle, stuck out in no man's land. That's what makes it so hard to find.

John Hartley was posted to train at Canungra during one of Len's stints as an instructor. The young subaltern was immediately drawn to Len's strong personality. 'He was different and was very well worth listening to because he saw things from a slightly different perspective,' Hartley said. Asked about the Opie legend, Hartley said much of it was true but it was fanned by Len's personality and dry, droll humour. 'I think there is some truth. And a good deal of myth. His personality was one that attracted that kind of comment. He would just drop a few words.'

Another good mate and hardened veteran Tony Mogridge was in no doubt—the solo patrols happened. Mogridge said Len told him about his no-man's-land forays but Mogridge, quite understandably, was reluctant to elaborate on them third hand. 'You'd talk to Len about his one man patrols in Korea,' Mogridge said. 'He was an honest man. He didn't bullshit. Out on operations he was icy cold. He was very good at reconnaissance and he had no hesitation in hand-to-hand combat.' Mogridge's account reinforces the theory that the one-man patrols really did happen. It appears Len just chose to censor his diary.

One matter was certain by the northern winter of 1952–53: the Opie legend was here to stay. In his book on the 'static war', Captain Colin Brown included a short passage titled 'Two sergeant majors' in which he paid tribute to Len and Jack Morrison, while juxtaposing their different personalities. 'Born to be a soldier . . . [Len] was dour, a man of few words, every one of which was measured precisely,' Brown wrote. 'He was a fearless man who put a chill up many a young soldier's spine. He had rather severe features, and did not smile readily.' That is a shame, as Len had a more than agreeable smile.

Len suffered his two most serious war wounds during the static war. The first came when he cut his hand slicing into a ration carton with a knife. Whoever filed the requisite report about the incident must not have known Len very well—they convened an inquiry into whether it was a so-called 'self-inflicted wound' to escape the fighting. One can only imagine the looks on the inquiring officers' faces when the charge sheet was read out. Fortunately Len only found out about the charge many years later thanks to a freedom of information request. His other, more serious, 'wound' was a bad case of frostbite. He was hospitalised but was only out of the line for a week. Its effects, however, troubled him for the rest of his life.

Len saw a lot of killing in Korea. Men's brains blown out right next to him. The diggers cooked in napalm at Kapyong. Unspeakable cruelty.

But nothing so cruel, he wrote, as an incident while he was in hospital in January 1953. 'The food was British and poor and the water used was heavily chlorinated to the point that the tea was almost undrinkable,' he said. 'After each meal the various orphanages took turns to collect the remnants of our meals from the garbage bins; this constituting their principal diet. After lunch, when we were emptying our mess tins with the orphans looking on, waiting for the bin to fill, I saw two British soldiers deliberately washing their mess tins with the tea into the bins and making a joke of it, despite the protests of the crowd.'

When Len's eight months were up he was happy to leave. The war was nearing its end—for the Australians, at least. Finally the peace negotiations were starting to achieve results. The timing of prisoner exchanges had been a sticking point, but in Len's final weeks the North had agreed to release 25,000 Korean POWs. But the fighting continued until the armistice in late July. Five 2RAR diggers were killed in heavy clashes on 24–26 July. The valley below was carpeted with hundreds of Chinese dead. No doubt their generals were trying to exact one last concession at the bargaining table. These were the days seized upon by Hollywood in *Pork Chop Hill*, where Gregory Peck, Rip Torn, George Peppard and co. played GIs left to die because they were nothing more than a chip on the peace talks bargaining table.

All that was behind Len now. He flew home via Guam and Port Moresby—where the men breakfasted on tea and buns served by the Ladies Auxiliary and Len gave a speech in reply—before landing in Sydney. There, a lieutenant colonel from the army's public relations department asked Len to talk again—to the press. It did not go well. 'There were two correspondents, one the aviation writer for *The Sydney Morning Herald*,' he said. 'Since most of the draft were a bunch of ruffians who, I was sure, could produce more than enough horror stories, I was told that I was to be the one to answer questions.'

'Did you use your bayonets?' one asked. 'Of course,' Len replied. 'Really?' asked the reporter, sniffing an angle. 'How often?' Len replied, 'Depending on whether we had can openers, mostly for digging holes.'

The pressmen pushed on gamely. 'If you didn't use bayonets for fighting, what did you use?' 'The usual weapon was the Owen gun, but most of the people here didn't get to see a Chinaman,' Len replied. Press conference over.

The next day the papers carried the story of the warrior's triumphant homecoming. 'A sergeant major who arrived in Sydney last night said that the war in Korea had become boring,' one lead paragraph read. Len was quoted as saying, 'The war has become static. Some of the chaps who have been in Korea for twelve months have never seen a Chinese. Most engagements are fought with automatic weapons at a distance. Close in hand-to-hand fighting occurs only when either side is out to get prisoners.' Another article reported him as saying, 'I didn't even get a glimpse of the Chinese during these last eight months. Even on night patrols I saw nothing. If we thought we saw something in the darkness we usually let them have it full blast from our automatic weapons.'

Len was discharged on the day the armistice was declared: 27 July 1953.

CHAPTER 12

BELLES AND BULLIES

'I didn't worry about girls. I've got two loves in my life,
war and railways.'
Len Opie

Len never married, but his niece, Jill Marton, thinks he preferred
the company of women to men—out of uniform anyway. But here is
another Len Opie paradox. At times he appeared shy and awkward
around women; at other times he was described as debonair and a
perfect gentleman. Jill's sister Lee accompanied Len on an overseas trip
when he was an older man. 'I always assumed Len was socially inept.
But when we went to Kashmir I was blown away. He was lighting cigarettes for women, he was so urbane. He was two different people.'

Elvia Johnson was an attractive, spirited and outgoing young
woman. She had many suitors. It must have taken some effort for the
shy and skinny young bloke from the Adelaide Steamship office to ask
her out. Well, Len did not exactly ask her out. They never really went
out, as such. Rather, he would ride his bike down the hill from his
parents' home to the Johnsons' place at Woodville. They didn't go to
the pictures like other couples. Instead Len would spend hours at the
Johnsons, cradling weak cups of tea and not saying much. But Elvia—
everyone called her Ellie—didn't seem to mind. She saw something in
Len that others missed. She liked him.

'Len didn't have competition,' Ellie's brother Ross Johnson said. His sister was entertaining and vivacious. The life of the party. 'The exact opposite of Len. He would keep turning up at our place for meals. He would never take Ellie out. He wouldn't say anything at the dinner table. Len never contributed much to the scene; he was the last guy you thought would be a war hero. He just sat like a log and wouldn't say anything. But if you got onto the army he would open up and blossom.' Gretta McDonough speculated why her sister was so sweet on Len. 'I thought, he's enthusiastic,' Gretta said. '[But] he never took her anywhere. He didn't know how to treat a girlfriend. He never took any advantages and that was the boring part—he wasn't a male.' More friend than boyfriend, Gretta said. Ross contemplated the same question. 'Perhaps he was a good listener to her stories. Maybe it was nice to have a fella around.' Whatever, Len and Ellie were close from about 1947 until he enlisted for Korea. Ross and Gretta said he was a big part of their lives during that time. And Ellie was a big part of the Opies' lives. She got on well with Len's mother and was very friendly with his sister Pat.

But Ellie was a feisty type and all hell broke loose when Len arrived home from his second tour. Why hadn't he called earlier? Ross remembers them having 'a barney and that was that'. They eventually made up and some years later Len plucked up enough courage to propose. Ellie blew up again. No one can be sure why. Perhaps Ellie simply wasn't the marrying type. Whatever the reason, apparently she told him 'never to darken my door again'. Ross played cupid. He invited each of them to his house separately to conspire a reconciliation. 'When Ellie saw Len's car drive in our back driveway, she raced out our front door and drove herself off,' Ross's daughter Anne said. 'She was furious—and she was a scary woman. She never changed her mind and never backed down, although the rest of our family remained friendly with Len.'

Ellie never married either, perhaps because she was self-conscious about a serious lung condition. 'She had lots of opportunities (to marry),' Ross said. 'She had a chronic cough . . . and she was a bit nervous about her future.' Len's three nieces all have fond memories of Ellie. 'He did have a series of friendships with women,' Lee said. 'Ellie was the best of all. Ellie was gorgeous. Absolutely stunning. She was lovely to us.'

Len's diary is chiefly about his military life but it tosses up occasional tidbits about his attitude to women. He wrote with some warmth about a US Marine he met during the Vietnam War, Captain Vera Jones. She and a female master sergeant arrived at Vung Tau for a spot of swimming. After meeting them at the airstrip, Len showed them the crowded and polluted local beach before taking them to his camp with its beach of 'clear, white sand' and adjacent air-conditioned facilities. 'They enjoyed themselves so much that they asked to come again. Captain Jones was a very pleasant lady and the master sergeant was also, but I suspect that she had achieved her rank without much trouble.' It appears Len's credo of expecting the same standards of others that he set for himself extended further than his fellow combat soldiers.

Len returned to the Steamship, as Adelaide people called his old firm, in August 1953, after he was discharged from the army. He lived with his parents and sister Pat—Molly married in 1943—at the Robe Terrace house on a sprawling block planted with typical trees of the era: figs, pomegranates and the like. There was a fern house and a shed for Len's model train tracks. 'We were not allowed in there,' niece Carolyn, one of Molly's three daughters, said. The house was a place of wonder for young children. There was a pianola and an ancient mangle, the kind of oddities children love. 'It was a very interesting house,' Lee said. 'It had a huge back garden. It was the most imaginative place for a child.' Len's mother was very caring and considerate to her grandchildren even if the house was a tightly run ship. Dinner was always in the dining room and Tuesday was clock-winding day—every main room had a chiming clock. Len would pedal off to the Steamship each day and would often return with treats for the girls—whole boxes of Violet Crumbles and Polly Waffles. As to his own tastes post Korea, well, Mrs Opie was handed a bottle of something called soy sauce and taught how to cook fried rice. Mother and son were very close and Len's nieces felt he inherited her 'caring and kind' qualities, even if he didn't always show it. These qualities were on show each Christmas when the girls— and later their own children—received gifts of cash or David Jones vouchers from Uncle Len.

Were Len and Molly close? 'I wouldn't have thought so,' Carolyn said. 'They were entirely different. She was an extrovert. He was an introvert.' Lee: 'She enjoyed a drink and a smoke and a gamble. They were entirely different. But they did have a connection. At the end of the day she would've been very loyal to him and he to her. She was spoilt rotten. And she was very attractive and very precocious, our mother, let's face it.' Jill said Molly was a 'social butterfly' and 'the queen bee' but according to Lee 'along came Len and she was really usurped as the star performer'.

Out of uniform Len's primary interests were trains, reading— especially military history—model-making and pets. He always had dogs. Jill remembers an Australian terrier called Roxy at the Robe Terrace house. Len lived with his parents well into his thirties. Why move out when all he needed was a base to head to his next war? The army was never far away. The DCM came with certain benefits and honours. In March 1954 he was presented with his DCM ribbon by the Queen at Government House in Adelaide. According to *The Advertiser*, Her Majesty wore a pink floral flock with a pleated skirt, three-quarter-length bell sleeves and two long strands of pearls. Len wore khaki. This grand occasion must have been especially thrilling given Len had sent off letter after letter—and called in a few favours—while in Korea in a failed bid to be part of the army's coronation contingent the year before. Later, in 1954, Len was invited to a civic ceremony for Korean veterans at the Adelaide Town Hall hosted by the lord mayor, Sir Arthur Rymill. One of the diggers persuaded Len to present Rymill with his only Kapyong Presidential Citation emblem. 'It probably ended up in the bottom drawer in his office,' Len lamented.

But Len missed the army. So much so that he was back in uniform only six months after his discharge. He joined the Citizen Military

Force, the forerunner of the Army Reserve. He was drawn by the lure of whipping a 'bunch of eager volunteers' into shape. Although Len also said he was talked into the job by his one-time platoon commander in Korea, Peter Johnston, who was the 27th Battalion's adjutant. Len was promised CSM of Support Company—his old and favourite role in Korea—but instead was sent to Headquarters Company. 'There was nothing but administration and, as a form of National Service was in being, many people did their best to avoid their duty,' Len said. He railed against the favouritism shown by one of the unit's officers, who allowed one man to skip some of the 27th's parades to work at a city department stone, but fined another for doing the same thing—even though the poor man risked the sack if he did not work. So much for his expectations of eager volunteers. Worse than that, the 27th was known as the 'Scottish' battalion for its historical links, which meant the men had to wear kilts on parade. Len hated it. 'The idea of wearing Scottish dress went very much against the grain. I used to park alongside the Torrens Parade Ground just before parade and dash back to the car immediately afterwards. I do not think I ever went into the sergeants' mess.' He quit after six months. As usual, there was a final clash with officialdom. Len asked the quartermaster if he could keep a unit shoulder flash as a souvenir. Sure, the man said, as long as you pay for it. 'There was a pile a foot high on the floor of the Q Store and I told the gentleman that he must surely be joking,' Len said. 'He insisted, so I gave him mine, then picked another from the pile and defied him to do anything about it. He didn't.' Wise man. And with that, a 'veil was drawn on the whole sorry episode' of Warrant Officer II Len Opie and the 27th Battalion.

In 1958 Len decided it was time to get 'back in the game'. He weighed up his options. The 27th was out, for obvious reasons. He was unable to get into the prestigious 10th Battalion, so settled for the 'poor relation of the three South Australian infantry units', the 43rd/48th Battalion based at Beulah Park in Adelaide's eastern suburbs. He asked for, and this time received, his plum posting—CSM of Support Company.

This time he stayed. Thus began a happy time of field exercises in the Flinders Ranges and the El Alamein base near Whyalla—even a 'covert' amphibious landing to seize the town of Ardrossan on Yorke Peninsula. He was in a volunteer/conscript army training in peacetime, but there was still danger. In its wisdom, the local brass decided all soldiers must be able to shoot a rifle, no matter their army role. So cooks, drivers and batmen were sent to a rifle range at Port Adelaide, where one day Len was trying to herd an unruly mob of naval reservists. 'I have had periods of nervousness during my years in the army but nothing to approach that day. Apparently these people had never handled weapons before and certainly had never learned range discipline. The result was that they waved their weapons around [and] every time they had a query they turned around to talk to their coaches'. Presumably inadvertently pointing their rifles at the instructors as they did so. 'In the end, everyone managed to fire without accidental discharges.'

Nervousness? Len seemed to be fearless when he should have been scared, and scared when he should have been fearless. He was terrified of heights, for example. So what did he do? He applied to be trained as a parachute soldier. That meant an interview with an army psychiatrist who asked, 'Why do you want to jump out of aeroplanes?' Len replied, 'I don't want to jump out of aeroplanes—I'm terrified of heights!' Somehow he passed the test and was flown to Williamtown RAAF base in NSW for his parachute training. He was greeted with a very pleasant surprise; a host of old mates and comrades from previous campaigns. Paddy Brennan, a friend from Korea, was now a regular with 4RAR and, like Len, had flown across for the course. The chief instructor, Major John Church, was another Korean comrade, and Buck Buchanan, Len's old 11 Platoon sergeant, was a principal instructor. Brennan was the perfect bunkmate. 'Paddy Brennan just could not put up with dirty equipment, so he cleaned mine as well as his own and on the Monday morning, we SHONE!' It was a happy time. The RAAF mess was about the best Len encountered in the forces.

The students' initial training was confined to towers and large hoists. Len found a 20-metre drop more terrifying than falling 200 metres from a plane. 'I had to drag myself up the stairs even to get to the top so the rest was something of an anti-climax but the terror was still there,' he said. When they were 'ready'—Len would argue he never was truly ready—they filed into a Dakota and headed for the drop zone. Then the instructor's barked instructions started. 'Stand up! Hook up! Red light! Stand in the door! Green light! Go!' Out they jumped, trying to impress their instructors by unfurling a perfect star dive. Len's technique was described as more 'praying mantis'. The callow recruits were told it was impossible to hit the plane but the dents outside the exit door suggested otherwise. The door and tail safely avoided, the students fell 30 metres before the static line ran out, triggering their hopefully incident-free descent and safe landing. Len somehow emerged intact so it was on to the 'honeymoon jump'—two jumps before breakfast. After a while they progressed to a night jump, which Len said 'wasn't too bad, as . . . the feeling of committing suicide was not so strong'. One of the other classes lost a student—an SAS man no less—on a night jump. 'Once every one of the stick was on the ground, the jumpmaster called the numbers to ensure everyone was down all right,' Len said. 'When he called: "Number four—OK?" The reply was: "No! I've got a broken leg!" "How do you know your leg is broken?" "Because I'm a *@"?! doctor!"'

Len feared he would fail the course. His technique was apparently so bad one of the senior RAAF instructors hid in a hangar every time he was due to jump. When it was all done Len sheepishly presented to Major Church. 'When I said that perhaps I shouldn't qualify, his reply was that having completed the jumps (however poorly) I did qualify, but don't come back!' Len later joined a parachuting club and inspired niece Carolyn to take up the sport at age seventeen—making her the youngest Australian girl to jump. 'Carolyn Shaughnessy is a pretty blonde school-girl with a wide friendly grin,' the *Women's Weekly* of 28 February 1962 reported. 'It is a simply marvellous feeling,' Carolyn told the magazine. 'Frankly I was far more nervous at the thought of this interview than at jumping 1500 feet.' Fifty years later, Carolyn recalled that Len was a far more confident parachutist than he had been at Williamtown. 'He would climb out on the wing and they'd say "jump" and he'd just stay there.' He wasn't scared; he was showing off, making like a daredevil in a 1920s newsreel. He would also tell first-timers who had second thoughts 'oh all right, you don't have to' before pushing them out the door. How very Len.

Len was commissioned lieutenant in October 1958, and when the Australian infantry was restructured in 1960, and the three South Australian Citizen Military Forces (CMF) battalions were folded into the Royal South Australian Regiment, he was appointed a platoon commander in 1 Battalion. The field exercises continued, including an expedition to One Tree Hill in the Mount Lofty Ranges. He hurt his knee on manoeuvres, so was borne past the mess queue shoulder high on a stretcher like a 'Viking warrior'.

On an exercise at El Alamein camp a twig brushed across his eye and he was hospitalised with a corneal ulcer. 'I found myself next to my old friend Don Moss, a regular army sergeant on the staff. Don had a stomach ulcer and we were in adjoining beds. An orderly marched up with a dose of antacid—for me! When I asked him what it was, his reply was: "You've got an ulcer and here is your medication!" My response that it was for the wrong type of ulcer just did not register until I refused to take the stuff and he went off to get the MO who sorted the matter out.'

Len came across still more characters during his CMF years. Lieutenant Joe Love must have been a fiery customer. After a long day marching in the Flinders Ranges, Len and Love were approaching the camp when they were 'ambushed' by a group of enthusiasts. It was not part of the sanctioned exercise and Love was in no mood for games. He reached for his flare gun. 'We were hot and tired and Love threatened to let fly at the leader of the push with a Very pistol if he did not let us pass,' Len said. 'You wouldn't dare,' came the reply. 'Blam went Joe's pistol, missing the fellow's head by a few inches. The language that followed could not be repeated, but suffice to say we continued on our way.' Len and Love sound like kindred spirits. Love was also interested in military history, and tracked down Mao Tse-tung's book on guerrilla warfare in an Adelaide bookshop. 'Joe went in and bought a copy—and was photographed by ASIO on the way out, with the necessary Please Explain to follow.'

Back in Adelaide there were more ceremonial duties, occasions Len approached with relish. Jill remembers Uncle Len looking neat as a pin during a big turnout at Torrens Parade Ground. For a time he was appointed to the Government House Guard, for which he was required to wear a sword. They marched from the parade grounds, up King William Street to the Government House gates where they were inspected by the governor. 'There wasn't a lot of room outside the gates and as I fronted His Excellency, he said "Watch out, Mr Opie, that you don't stick me with your sword."'

When the Queen returned in 1963, Len was part of the guard at an investiture at Government House. It fell to him to signal the band to stop playing background music and break into 'God Save the Queen'. The trouble was, the bandmaster was facing the other way and Len had no way of making his signal. 'I began to make frantic efforts to attract his—or anybody's attention by miming throat-cutting motions together with saluting. I have wondered what HM thought as we were facing each other at opposite ends of the ballroom and I was behaving like someone gone crazy. Eventually, one of the band saw my gestures and pointed them out to the bandmaster who took his cue, stopped the piece the band was playing and swung into the national anthem. So disaster was averted and the audience did not stand to the strains of "The Blue Danube"!'

Meanwhile, Len was studying hard for his captain's exams and in September 1964 he passed, albeit after getting only 51/100 for the 'administration' subject. Len was no fan of paperwork. Local tradition dictated that newly promoted captains must down a beer in the officers' mess. Len was allowed to down a glass of milk instead. He was of course never one for the army's boyish shenanigans as expressed in its drinking culture. 'I remember someone saying that one third of an officer's pay was expected to be spent drinking in the mess, but I never went along with this . . . all sorts of stupid penalties were enacted. At 3RAR after it became a parachute battalion, one trick was to coat the mess tables with beer and the participants were expected to take a running jump, slide along the table and land on the floor at the other end without breaking their fall. The fall wasn't the only thing some of them broke.'

After his promotion Len was made second-in-command of his company. About this time his mother suffered a second stroke, forcing him to miss some Monday-night parades so he could be by her side. He told his company commander, who complained to the battalion commander about Len's ongoing absences. Len was summoned to the CO's office in the city. 'Your company commander has complained that you are missing from parades, which I find very disturbing,' the CO said. 'Well, sir, it's my mother,' Len said. 'She is dying and is not expected to last more than a week, so, after I have fulfilled my duties at the depot, I dash up to the hospital to see her for perhaps the last time. I am sure if she knew the OC's concern, she would be concerned too, but I have made a promise to the OC that if my mother dies on a Monday, I will not miss the parade.' The CO was aghast. 'Oh no! You take all the time you require! I was not aware of the circumstances!' When Gertrude died four months later Len confronted the company commander. 'I have some good news for you—my mother died this morning and I won't be absent from any parades in future, sir.' According to Len, when the man started to express his sympathies, Len said, 'Forget that, I made a bargain and I have kept it!'

Len made an impression on the striplings of his CMF unit. He was successful in grafting his ideas about fairness onto his young comrades. 'We asked why he went to so many wars and he said "because I didn't like bullies",' Brian Kilford said. 'He used to say as long as we had a big stick we'd be OK. He was the sort of bloke that if you had to go into conflict you'd be confident if Len was there.' Kilford never fired a shot in anger—'my marble never came out'—but Len's lessons remained with him always. Rob Thornton, who served with Len in Vietnam, said he would not have made it into the SAS without Len's help. 'He rarely raised his voice, even when he was angry,' Thornton said. 'His eyes and actions said it all. He was very forgiving when junior rankers screwed up, but woe betide anyone above corporal. At least two WOIIs quietly got transferred for professional errors during my time. He was also very generous in giving credit for good work when it was due, and he would spend hours teaching me weaponry, communications, map reading and navigation.'

Soldiering might have been his main interest, but it was part-time soldiering so it didn't pay the bills. His managers at the Steamship tolerated Len's many absences but the times were changing. He received a letter from the company in March 1961 that read, 'It is with much regret that consequent on a reduction in the volume of the company's business, it was found necessary to terminate your services on 31st March next.' He was paid a tidy sum from the provident fund and in accrued long service and annual leave. What to do? He liked reading, so he bought a bookshop in Adelaide's Da Costa Arcade.

About this time he struck up a friendship with Heather Woods, who worked around the corner at Wigg & Son stationers. They had much in common: a love of dogs, the military—Helen had served in World War II—and a need for companionship. But they were opposites in many other ways; Heather was a commanding, outgoing woman who liked a drink and a smoke. Later Heather lived in one of Len's two houses. 'He put on his jacket and tie and went up there every morning at 7.30 and left every night at nine,' Lee Waye said.

His three nieces remembered helping at stocktake time and being told by Uncle Len that they could pick a book off the shelves for their trouble. Jill tells a lovely story that speaks so much about Len's finely honed sense of justice. Jill was in grade six or seven when she was made to stay at school while her class went on an excursion to hear a talk by a young and emerging British naturalist called David Attenborough. Her crime? She wore a sports uniform to school. The punishment? Sit in a room, alone, all day. Len was livid when he found out about it although he didn't make a fuss. A few days later Molly gave Jill a book. It was Attenborough's latest, about an expedition to Madagascar or Borneo or suchlike, signed by the author. Len must have tracked the man down or called in some contacts in the publishing industry. Len had seen an injustice and acted accordingly. 'My mother said I could take it to school and when you're in year seven that's pretty good,' Jill said. 'I thought that was terrific. Actually I thought it was terrific that I could have a book. And he never made a fuss about it. It wasn't about him. He saw an injustice. It was a way of getting back at someone for that injustice. He always said he didn't like bullies. There were probably lots of times that we haven't heard of that he stood up to bullies. Ways in which he didn't need a rifle in his hand. But that warm feeling that someone had done something for me stayed with me. And for a young girl, it was a pretty bloody long day alone in a classroom I can tell you.

'When he came back to Adelaide I think he was just waiting for his next . . .' Her sisters didn't give her a chance to finish the sentence. 'War,' they said, in unison. He would soon have it. He was keeping a close eye on what he saw was another bully sneaking down through South Asia.

CHAPTER 13

VIETNAM

'There's nothing like combat. You can't equate it with
anything else really.'
Len Opie

There was never any doubt in Len's mind that he was going to Vietnam.
He might have been in his early forties and starting to suffer the effects
of his two previous wars—his frostbitten foot was causing him bother—
but he was going, no doubt about it. He had done his bit—and then
some—but that did not stop him. His diary does not contain a single
line of contemplation about whether he should fight. Quite the
opposite. In mid-1965 he wrote, 'The US forces were building up and
we were hoping that just perhaps the CMF might get a guernsey.' His
hopes were fanned by an escalation in commitment from the US and
then Australia, which was mobilising 1RAR for the war. Australia's
involvement started in 1962 with the almost token contribution of 30
'advisors'—officers and warrant officers sent to train South Vietnamese
units. The Australians had something the Americans wanted—experience in jungle fighting taught by veterans of New Guinea and honed in
the Malayan Emergency. By 1965 the Australian Army Training Team
Vietnam (AATTV) was 100-strong and getting stronger. The new
members arrived to a worsening picture on the ground. The Vietcong
dominated the rural areas of South Vietnam and had gained footholds

in many of the cities and towns. Plainly, the South was losing the war. When Colonel Oliver Jackson arrived to assume command of the team in early 1965, he wrote, 'The Vietcong were thoroughly on top from a military point of view . . . it was just a matter of weeks or months before the war militarily was lost in South Vietnam.' So the US, which until then had provided the South with only limited support, ratcheted up its effort, first by scrambling B-52s to carpet-bomb North Vietnam and then sending in the Marines, who ostentatiously waded ashore in March. The lead elements of 1RAR started arriving in May and the team sent for reinforcements.

Len wanted in. He didn't have to wait long. The US dispatched a general on a 'hearts and minds' tour to recruit potential AATTV members. Flanked by Special Forces master sergeants in battle fatigues, Major General Charles Timmes was preaching to a converted Captain Opie when he gave his 'briefing' at Keswick later that year. The Training Team was ideal for someone with his experience and pedigree.

There was a problem, however: his age. The upper age limit for the team was 35 and Len was 41. Then there was the psych test. Len had that sorted. When a selection board convened at Keswick in June he pulled a few strings. The Psych Corps Regimental Sergeant Major (RSM) was a comrade from World War II. 'I knew where the bodies were buried, particularly among the hierarchy of the corps,' Len wrote somewhat cryptically in his diary. Len's confidence in being chosen was underlined by his audacious questioning of the length of training set down by the army. Len asked Colonel Russell McNamara, who was to assume command of the Training Team later that year, why men who had already served needed twelve months' training in Australia. 'We are the selection board [so] you mean if you are selected, not when,' McNamara told Len. 'I'm going,' Len said. 'I have more service than anyone else, so I would hope that I would be selected.' McNamara's reply is unknown. Once again, Len's extensive network of contacts came to the rescue. Another old comrade, a lieutenant colonel, told him, 'I hope you're fit, because I've pulled some strings to get you on the list and you are six years over age.' Another scare came when his medical revealed a mysterious rash, marking his card as unfit for tropical service. That was crossed out when Len said the army doctors made the same diagnosis when he joined up in World War II and he had spent a bit of time in the tropics since then. He safely negotiated the series of tests and signed for full-time duty on 29 September 1965. While he was waiting to head to Ingleburn for pre-Vietnam training, a regular army officer tried to take the impudent and part-time Captain Opie down a peg. He ordered Len to do a stocktake of the officers' mess silver. That, as you might imagine, did not go down well. 'I don't think so,' Len told his superior. 'I won't be here.' The regular officer was undeterred. 'You will do it, and to make sure I will have the silverware laid out on the floor of the mess.' And there it stayed. 'I don't know how long it remained there,' Len said. It was probably still on the mess floor when Len boarded the train to Sydney.

Len was one of 58 recruits sent to the Infantry Training Centre at Ingleburn commanded by Lieutenant Colonel Ron 'Judy' Garland, who had been awarded an MC and Bar in the commandos in World War II. It would be hard to find anyone better to instruct the men in jungle training. Captain Barry Sullivan, ex-3RAR, was chief instructor and Captain Barry Petersen MC was a tactics instructor. Lieutenant Colonel Peter Smeaton, Len's platoon sergeant for a time in Korea, was another senior instructor, as was one of his old 3RAR platoon commanders, Chapman 'Chappie' Walsh. Major Peter Badcoe, who was to find death and a VC in Vietnam, was head of research and development. Len translated the army jargon to mean Badcoe instructed in the use of 'various exotic weapons'. (Len covered himself in glory by accidentally discharging an unfamiliar Spanish automatic rifle after Badcoe told the trainees such a discharge was impossible.) There was a leavening of old Korean comrades, including Digger James, who was the unit's medical officer, making the camp a gathering of the finest soldiering horseflesh in the nation.

Len had made the cut of 58 but still had to pass the training course. The bar was set high; especially so for a man much older than the others. 'There was constant emphasis on fitness,' Captain Mike Wells said. The recruits were subjected to 'Tarzan' course rope work, route marches, 'speed marching' in full battle order, defensive position exercises, 'attack, ambush, plus later in the course, long exercises in very hilly country for weeks at a time'. It was tough for commandos such as Wells; it was a stern test indeed for Len. 'For some reason we linked with Len and "mentored" him with the physical stuff,' Wells said. 'He was an aggressive bastard and on runs we would carry his pack and weapon quite often, give him tips and close support on rope work (we were all roping instructors), and generally cajole him to get through. I think Barry Sullivan turned a blind eye to all this, plus we had no doubt that with his DCM from Korea, there was no way Len would not be selected!' The fact the younger men helped Len through the course did not mean Len was a 'quitter', Wells said. 'The complete opposite actually. It was his dogged determination to keep going that prompted us to intervene—much to his bellowing—so that he didn't collapse with a heart attack.'

Only five men passed the course. Wells, three other commandos . . . and Len. Or as Wells put it, 'Four commandos and one DCM winner!' Len had cleared every hurdle through a combination of his own determination, help from his fellow candidates, and favours from old comrades. 'Fortunately I had enough friends in the business, people that I'd served with in Korea were then becoming generals, and head of the army and adjutant generals.' From there it was back to Canungra for six weeks of jungle training, where Len's four younger mates also helped him on rope climbs and training runs. At the end of it all he flew home for seven days of pre-embarkation leave—a luxury not experienced on any of his previous departures for the front. He arrived in time for Kapyong Day—the 23 April commemoration of the battle at Woodside Barracks—but it did not look as though he would be able to attend as he was due back at Ingleburn to ready for embarkation. 'Lieutenant Colonel Mick Bryant . . . made two phone calls: One to 3RAR CO Lieutenant Colonel Leary to tell him to expect me and the other to the Commandant Infantry Centre to tell them I would be a bit late arriving back. It is nice to have friends in power.' He attended the ceremony.

Upon his return to Ingleburn Len learned he and Wells would fly to Vietnam together. 'We were the only two remaining of the original group,' Len wrote. He also learned that, because of his age, he had been recommended for an instructor's posting. A friend in a high place intervened. 'Again, perhaps because COs do not like to be told what they should do, that didn't happen either. Thanks be!' Len and Wells left in early May 1966. No cramped troopship for members of the Training Team: Len and Wells flew Qantas to Manila where they caught a connecting Pan Am flight to Saigon. They feasted on free chicken and champagne (of course Len confined himself to the chicken) lavished upon them by the hostesses in first class. Wells said they landed in a very happy mood indeed. That didn't last long. No one was there to meet them and they had no idea where to go or what to do. 'We were half expecting to be shot or have a grenade thrown at us,' Len said.

The confused scene was an apt metaphor for Len's role in this war. What was he to do? At first he was told he would be posted to the Combined Studies Division (CSD), one of the many units in Vietnam whose benign name belied its real role. The CSD was not, as it sounded, some sort of back-office records department of the army. Quite the opposite. It wasn't even army. Or Australian. The incongruous name was a cover for the Covert Action Branch (CAB)—Len also referred to a Covert Activities Bureau—a highly secretive, counter-insurgency arm of the CIA. Australians posted to the CSD and its sister sub-branches set up by the CIA were at the bottom of a chain of command that led to Washington, not Canberra. The Training Team's CO, Lieu-tenant Colonel Milner, told Len, 'I've only got three things to tell you: You will be wearing civilian clothes, don't get caught in Cambodia and I'll see you in twelve months—or sooner if necessary.' Len makes no comment in his diary about his apparent secondment to a US para-military organisation. While he regularly railed at officialdom, he was first and foremost a man of duty. If that duty meant working for the US, then so be it. Although at the outset he didn't even know he was with the CIA. 'I ran into some American Marines and the fellows said: "You're CIA." And I said: "CI what?" "CIA!" And I said: "No, I'm in the Training Team." And when I got back I said [to his US boss]: "This fellow accused me of being CIA." He said: "Do you know who we are?" If I'd known earlier I'd have run screaming into the night.'

Len reported to the CSD's headquarters in Saigon, where he was introduced to 'Ace' Ellis, 'the American top man'. A communications expert, Lieutenant Alger Ellis was head of the Covert Activities Bureau. Its Saigon headquarters, Training Team historian Ian McNeill wrote, was a plain whitewashed building devoid of any signs and filled with officials in civvies who 'stood about talking to one another or scurried between openings delivering papers'. The Americans were wary of the Australians. According to Len, whenever Australians arrived at a US headquarters the officials would 'dive on [folders] marked NOFORN (No Foreign Information) and hang on to it until we left'. When Len, inevitably, stole a look inside one of the folders, he came upon top-secret information such as 'Christmas Day will be held on December 25' and Buddha's birthdate. Such were the secrets being kept from the Third Country Nationals, as the Australians were classified by the US command.

Len's first few weeks in Vietnam did not reflect well on the level of organisation on the ground. It appeared the authorities had no idea what to do with this ageing captain from Down Under. After a few days he was flown to a quiet fishing village on the Gulf of Thailand coast. An air of foreboding hung over the settlement. His quarters were in a hut next to the airstrip. The windows were covered with wire grilles as protection against grenades, and he was issued with an automatic shotgun 'just in case' there was trouble. 'Needless to say, I did not sleep well.' He was taken on a tour of the surrounding villages before being flown to Vung Tau, where he was deposited in a fully furnished—but deserted—two-storey villa with nothing but Coke in the fridge. He arrived after dark and as there was no one to talk to and nothing to do except drink Coke, he went to bed. 'Early next morning an American arrived and asked why I was there. Apparently it was his house and when I told him that I didn't know what was happening, he relented and told me he would drop me at the Revolutionary Development National Training Centre where I was to undergo some days of briefings.' Another agency to add to the 'alphabet soup', as Len described it, of Vietnam acronyms. At the RD centre, teams of Vietnamese were trained to infiltrate villages where they would try to win the hearts and minds of the locals. They would do this by 'assisting people', Len wrote. 'There were medics, labourers . . . and engineering members plus a protection element. Students were taught communism, democracy and how to meld with the locals but, as we found out in the countryside, it was hard to convince the Revolutionary Development team members to move out where the Vietcong would target them.'

Len did not stay long at the RD centre. The Americans were still having trouble finding him a job. This account of a trip from Saigon on the CIA-funded Air America airline is typical: 'I was dropped at Air America with my bag but no explanation. The officer asked where I was bound and when I told him I didn't know, he looked at a manifest and put me on a Beechcraft twelve-seater aircraft and we took off, although there were no other passengers. An hour later we arrived at Nha Trang, Vietnam's premier tourist attraction on the China Sea. I was collected in a Jeepster and taken to the embassy compound, again without explanation. In fact, the two chaps who came to pick me up asked why I was there.' Next he was deposited alone and unloved at Tam Ky, a coastal town at about the country's midpoint. 'The aircraft turned and took off, leaving me alone and bereft. If anything, I felt lonelier than I had when we arrived at [Saigon]. At least there were people in the city. I had hand-me-down clothes and was without a weapon.' The silence was broken by a motorbike. The teenage rider, a local, stopped, introduced himself and told Len he was there to take him to the local headquarters. Boy and man puttered off along a former railway track—sans

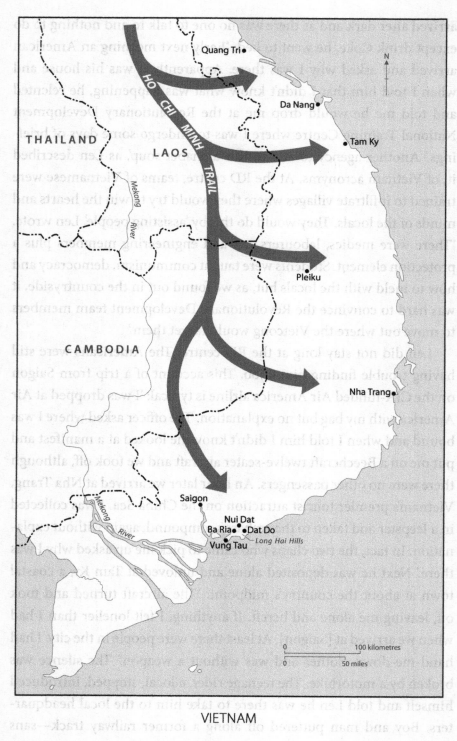

Quang Tri

Da Nang

Tam Ky

THAILAND

LAOS

HO CHI MINH TRAIL

Mekong

River

CAMBODIA

Pleiku

Nha Trang

Mekong

River

Saigon

Nui Dat

Ba Ria   Dat Do

Long Hai Hills

Vung Tau

0   100 kilometres

0   50 miles

VIETNAM

sleepers scrounged for firewood—and past a bombed-out locomotive. Welcome to Tam Ky. He was taken to the local HQ, then to his quarters, a villa next door. Superstitious locals donated the house to the Americans after its owner, a local official, 'stopped a rocket-propelled grenade round' while he was standing on the verandah 'admiring the sunset'. This was to be Len's home for seven months.

Tam Ky was a dangerous place. Early one morning Len was woken by a massive explosion. Someone had bombed a meeting of the Vietnamese National Party, killing 69 people. Len said the Vietcong was blamed, 'but it could well have been one of the nine opposition parties'. The Vietcong dominated the central Vietnam hinterland with the support of tens of thousands of sympathisers. Len's predecessor, Captain Ian Teague, who was based in the neighbouring Quang Ngai province, had given sterling service in a role that was five parts manager, four parts diplomat and one part soldier. The People's Action Teams he created—units of 40 Vietnamese who spent most of their time in the villages helping with various menial tasks while trying to win local hearts and minds—were so successful, his model was expanded under the auspices of the CSD in Vung Tau. Widening the program, however, had the effect of diluting its effectiveness; and at the end of his tour, in December 1965, he left Vietnam with a 'feeling of unease', McNeill wrote. By the time Len arrived, Tam Ky was organised in a manner befitting the general disorganisation he had encountered in his short time in the country. The 'headman', as Len called his American boss, gave the impression of being somewhat uninterested in the role. Len's other colleague was a suave European who was ex-Special Forces but whose counter-terror team in Tam Ky was essentially unemployed. 'I never saw them conduct an operation.'

Gradually Len's job description became clearer. It was to 'keep the communists out', he said, when asked about his role many years later. 'You're just sent as an advisor and it's on-the-job training and when you get there you find out what you're supposed to do. Well the fellow from whom I took over [Teague] had left two months earlier so I didn't know what he was supposed to do, so I just learnt as I went along. There weren't too many NVA [North Vietnamese Army] coming down at that stage and it was just a counter-guerrilla war.' Learning on the job meant grappling with new technology and methods—such as how to evacuate the wounded. When a man was hit on an early operation, Len co-opted a hammock for a stretcher, had the man carried to a river, commandeered a sampan and finally hailed down a bus to get him to hospital. Upon their arrival an orderly said, 'Why didn't you request a Dustoff?' Len didn't know he was allowed to call for a chopper evacuation. He soon became very familiar indeed with the aerial war in Vietnam.

Len set about getting the lie of the land. For someone who was afraid of heights he spent a lot of time in the air. He was forever flying to the various bases, outposts and villages. When there was no room in the chopper Len gave the co-pilot a stack of *Playboy*s to keep him occupied on the ground while he slipped into his seat. Many of his trips were resupply missions or to oversee movements of troops to and from training schools. His apparent newfound love of flight unsated, he started hitching a ride with a Bird Dog spotter plane on many of its daily reconnaissance flights over the province. The US pilot needed a spotter, and Len was it. 'So almost every day if I had no business with the Revolutionary Development teams, I flew with him.' It is easy to see why Len liked this job so much. The tiny, open-windowed Cessna spotter plane was also charged with directing air strikes on Vietcong units. They would mark the target with smoke then US Phantom jets would zoom in to drop their 500-pound bombs or napalm canisters. Len directed taxi ranks of as many as four flights of jets waiting their turn to strike. But he had another problem as well as his fear of heights: air sickness. 'If we were marking a ground target for the strike aircraft, the pilot would throttle back, lift the nose of the aircraft, then dive on the target and fire a white phosphorus rocket. Almost every time, as we went over the top and reached zero g-force, I would be sick, which was embarrassing, especially when we had three or four layers of strike aircraft stacked up and each strike required a new marker. I overcame this by using the big folded map of the province, covered with plastic, which I carried. I would use this as a windbreak and be quietly sick over the side. Problem solved.'

He suffered his first Vietnam wound on one of these missions. 'After one strike, I was showering back at the house when I noticed a glint of metal reflecting from my cheek in the mirror. It brushed off without any trouble and I realised that a fragment of the white phosphorous rocket had hit me as it fired under the wing. I thought no more about it as the mark disappeared in a day or so, but some years later it reappeared. It is at least a lasting souvenir of my time in Vietnam.' Len downplayed the injury, but the splinter had missed his right eye by millimetres. He had a scar for the rest of his life.

Len soon grew to love flying. He thrived on the adrenaline hit and the fact he was doing something useful. The map-reading and sightseeing appealed to his slightly obsessive and adventurous sides in equal measure. He mostly flew in the day but wondered at the spectacle of night flights where the sky was decorated with flares, artillery duels and tracer—the green and white of the Vietcong and the 'friendly' red. But after a while his previously uninterested boss became interested enough to make the Bird Dog off-limits. Len was livid and sought a higher ruling. 'I caught the first available flight down to Saigon and fronted Lieutenant Colonel Milner, explaining that with nineteen Revolutionary Development teams in the province, I wasn't exactly joy riding, but was familiarising myself with the territory. It sounded convincing or at least I thought so.' He threw in that his commander was withholding 'daily reports about projected attacks, with numbers, names, even weapons carried by the enemy parties' because Len was a 'third country national'. Milner said he would deal with the dispute personally as he was scheduled to fly to Tam Ky the next week. He was true to his word; Len had freer access to information after Milner's intervention.

The disparate nature of the nationalists' varying units and their quality was illustrated in an attack on the outskirts of Tam Ky. The

People's Front outpost drove the enemy off, while the Revolutionary Development team on the other side of the road 'abandoned their positions and took to the bush leaving their weapons and gear, which the VC collected'. The Vietcong were driven off after the men on the ground called in 'Puff the Magic Dragon' or 'Spooky'—a Dakota fitted with multiple machine guns fired by the pilot, who would bank the plane in the required direction and blaze away with three rapid-fire miniguns. One of Len's comrades described Spooky thus: 'The pilot would set the co-ordinates, put the aircraft on auto pilot and sit back drinking coffee and reading *Playboy* while spraying the perimeter at the rate of 6000 rounds per minute.' Spooky's intervention turned the fight at Tam Ky, and, a few days later one of the RD men appeared out of the jungle asking for a ride back to base. Len told him to walk and 'if he moved as fast as he had the night of the attack, he would probably beat us back'.

As the weeks passed Len settled comfortably into his job, which of course was very different to leading a section or running a company in Korea. He had a very unconventional role in a very unconventional war. All up, he was responsible—'logistics operator' he called it—for about 3000 nationals, organised into 40 Revolutionary Development teams each of about twenty soldiers backed by medical units and a 'self-protection' squad. Len was responsible for payroll, which arrived in US C ration boxes of about two million piastres per box. 'On one memorable occasion, the Air America pilot dropped off a number of boxes and flew away,' Len said. 'The problem was the case officer on the ground did not check the number of boxes before the aircraft left and came up one short. I believe he was still paying $250 per week when he left for home.' In keeping with his punctilious nature, Len made no such mistakes, and soon became very unpopular with the Vietnamese troops for paying only on presentation of ID to foil the 'ghosting of payrolls for dead or non-existent members'. At one stage he was threatened with arrest by the local police for not paying the funeral benefits of three dead soldiers. 'I'm a third country national so you can't arrest me,' he told them. He suggested the police instead charge one of the local commanders for being a troublemaker. So they did.

A month into his Tam Ky posting, Len was ordered to Danang to meet Brigadier Ted Serong, the Training Team's first CO. Serong was an enigmatic man who Australian war historian Paul Ham described as 'almost a character of his own imagination'. Len's first meeting with Serong ended unhappily. 'During the evening at Australia House, he invited anyone who wanted a ride to Saigon to be at the airfield the following morning. I told him I had to go down as we did a monthly trip to collect our allowances. So I turned up at the airport and he said: "Sorry, old boy, I'm full up with fuel and we can't fit you in. Better luck next time!" He didn't pay my wages so I wasn't interested in him but he was a bit too arrogant for my liking.' Len's diary mentions a social function arranged by Serong in which each member of the unit had to contribute seven dollars—even those who were absent on a mission.

Yet another of the host of acronyms that categorised the paramilitary campaign was set up by Serong in early 1966. The National Police Field Force's (NPFF) role was to 'maintain control throughout areas cleared by the regular forces, and to operate in support of those forces'. The NPFF's training centre was in the temperate highlands near Dalat, 'a picturesque town of rose gardens and stately French villas'. There was even a golf course there, but the players were 'wise to carry a carbine among their clubs'. Serong brought two stalwarts out of retirement to train the locals. Brigadier George Warfe DSO MC was a former Canungra CO who used to take jungle-centre trainees out into the bush, where he would explain how the jungle had everything a soldier needed to survive. Hey presto—he would then pull a planted bottle of whisky out of a bush. When Len visited Dalat the pair sat in the lounge 'while he put away vast quantities of liquor [and] at two in the morning I excused myself, saying I had to be up early'. Warfe replied: 'OK, young fellow, if you want an early night, go ahead.'

In a gruesome example of Vietnamese tradition intersecting with wartime practicality, the Revolutionary Teams were in the habit of cutting the ears off their Vietcong 'kills'. The locals believed that a soul could only rest if the corpse was intact, so cutting off the ears condemned the enemy soldier to wander the earth for eternity. And, under CIA policy, the men were paid for each kill, as verified by the ears. Len first came across the sanctioned mutilation when he saw a string of apricots drying on a fence. 'On closer inspection they turned out to be ears,' he said. After one action Len stopped a man busily hacking off ears as he had arrived after the fight so had no right to the bounty, which was paid by Len. 'When one of our people appeared with four ears and requested payment and I was prepared to pay for two lots, the claimant referred me back to the ears, which, on closer inspection proved that they were all left ears. I have no doubt somebody else on the advisory side paid for the right ears.'

One commonly told Len Opie story has its genesis in the 'ears as bounty' practice. It goes something like this: Len is eating his dinner alone in a mess somewhere in Vietnam. In come a bunch of newly arrived subalterns, somewhat wet behind the ears but aware of Len's reputation, who take seats at the other end of the table. Gesturing in Len's direction, one says to his fellow diners something along the lines of: 'Do you think it's true that they cut off the enemy's ears?' Between chews Len fires back: 'Well their heads are too heavy to carry in the jungle.' Surely it was another of Len's enigmatic one-liners, but consider this diary entry from his final Vietnam tour: 'For Vietnamese a soul may not rest in peace if it or any part of the body is missing, and the soul must wander the Earth forever unless it is whole . . . this is basically the reason ears and/or heads are cut off.'

Len seemed to enjoy putting people off their food. In Australia a few years later the chatter at a dinner party turned to an airline crash where the survivors had resorted to cannibalism to survive. One of the women at the table, possibly the hostess, pondered what human flesh tasted like. 'Salty,' Len replied. 'It certainly was a party stopper,' Laurie Lewis said.

The brutality of the Vietnam War manifested itself in many ways. When a Vietcong fighter was killed it was common practice to hang the corpse outside his home. This helped Len and his men identify Vietcong households, but many families had sons fighting on either side so it was an inexact science. The villages were dangerous places. On one patrol a Vietcong prisoner became agitated as Len's column filed into a village. Presently Len noticed an artillery shell poking out of the ground. A booby trap. Len and his men tiptoed out of the village. The prisoner was right to be jumpy; he was shot dead later that day, although Len's diary is hazy about which side did the deed.

All manner of cultural issues had to be overcome by the US and Australian instructors. The irregular soldiers decided they were not bound to their regular army's rules regarding disciplinary measures. 'It was common in irregular units for soldiers being forced to kneel, sometimes on rocks in the sun, with arms outstretched holding hand grenades from which the pins had been removed,' Len said. Then there was the 'tiger cage'—cut-off star pickets and barbed wire constructed in the shape of a coffin. The offender slid inside and remained there until his superiors decided he had done his time. 'On one occasion I saw a soldier in the cage with a poncho draped over the top,' Len said. 'Whether it was to protect him from the sun or to make it hotter I couldn't be sure.' Some cages would not have presented Houdini or Hilts with much of a challenge. One rainy night Len noticed a prisoner wriggle out; he was back in the cage in the morning when the storm had passed by. Many years later Len elaborated on his views of the Vietnamese and their culture. 'We found if you told them that the sun wasn't coming up tomorrow and it came, that's your fault. You never promised them anything until you had it in your hand and put it in their hand. If you promised them anything they lost faith. They don't think that we lose face, [rather it is] "you made me lose face".

There were almost as many cultural issues to negotiate with the Americans. Len was fascinated by their quirks, foibles and customs, and recorded all manner of American curiosities in his diary. Such as the time he presented at a US army dentist to have a lost filling replaced. 'The dentist, I was surprised to learn, was not an officer, but a Spec 4—a

Specialist Private Soldier,' he said. 'When I told him that, in our army, a dentist would be at least a captain, he said: "Perhaps I'm in the wrong army!" I then pointed out that my pay, as a captain was $90 a fortnight, so he wasn't so sure. I remember hearing about a major and his wife (a nurse) who, between them, were making $US1000 a month.'

The fighting intensified. On one patrol there were, according to Len, some 'light contacts'. Light contacts in which a US colonel standing next to Len was hit in the leg from a burst of machine-gun fire. Len patched him up and called in a Dustoff using his code name, the very incongruous 'Glitter'. It was only a flesh wound and the colonel cheered up considerably when he found a Vietnamese go-go girl in his quarters back at base. 'The colonel limped in to pick up his gear, opened the door—and there was Sam, who really made his day,' Len said. Female company was scarce, apparently. Len's boss went on a diet of tinned oysters and stout ahead of his 'amorous activities' during a week in the US. When he returned he 'complained bitterly that his ex-wife expected him to stay with her for the whole of his leave'.

Presently intelligence reports indicated two Vietcong battalions had moved into the area and Tam Ky itself was imperilled. The US command responded by airlifting a large force of Marines into the town. Soon the fields in front of the HQ were full of choppers, tents and artillery pieces. The enemy had its own artillery. One night it moved a 75-millimetre gun into range and fired a single shell that killed a Marine major at the front of Len's quarters. 'A member of the team should also have been killed, as his bed place was next to the major's,' Len said. 'But he had taken an extra day off in Danang.'

As the fighting continued, Len was spending more time in the air. After a while the veteran flyer was even trusted with the controls while the pilots did their paperwork. One day he was aloft for almost eight hours with three different pilots, including a stint helping direct F4 fighter/bomber strikes on the 72nd Vietcong Battalion. 'Our last strike was just on last light, when we caught a large group moving from one hamlet to another and set a flight of F4s on to them with

In Vietnam, Len worked with the kind of CIA hired guns that set in train President Nixon's downfall at Watergate. Here the former vice president and future president is snapped by Len at Ban Me Thuot in 1967.

Len's personal arsenal, Embassy House, Tam Ky, 1966. His armoury stocktake reads (from left): M1 folding stock carbine .30 calibre, AR-15 .223 calibre, M79 grenade launcher, Swedish 'K' 9mm and (holding) M72 rocket launcher.

'Poor old B827.' Len's plane after being hit by ground fire as it landed at Pleiku in the Vietnam central highlands in 1967.

That Len was prepared to put aside his abstemious ways illustrates his respect for local cultures. Here he receives rice wine from a hamlet chief at a sacrificial ceremony in 1967. His comrades clearly appreciated Len's own sacrifice of his teetotal principles.

Len with a Montagnard elder in April 1967. He was interested in their customs and did his best to overcome the significant cultural barriers.

Len captioned this April 1967 photo, 'Sometimes I sit and think and sometimes I just sit.'

Marching on his stomach: King prawns, rice, chow mein and salad. Len's diaries are so full of food references it is a wonder he remained so thin.

Saddling up for Operation Applecart, aimed at hitting the enemy on the Ho Chi Minh trail, in June 1967.

Len did his best to disappear into the battlefield. Here he is in the black pyjamas worn by Vietnamese villagers, with matching black face-paint, pistol holster and rifle.

'If I'd have been a Vietcong, you'd be dead,' Len told a patrol that filed past an old man sitting cross-legged under a paddy hat, AKA Captain Opie.

The master of unarmed combat imparting his skills to his students in Vietnam. He even let his opponent get the upper hand—briefly—on occasions.

Len headed for the beach as often as he could in Vietnam. He sometimes swam in the nude, which a comrade said must have startled the local sniper into inaction.

Len loved animals as much as he did the army and trains. Woe betide anyone who mistreated an animal in his presence.

Taking five on a patrol. 'Eating peanuts,' Len wrote on the back.

Len and his Phoenix instructors with George, Fred and an unnamed puppy. The puppy's father, Suzy, is absent. The CIA agent charged with naming the dogs had difficulty distinguishing between genders.

These five AATTV men are wearing two US Unit citations—one from Kapyong and a second newly earned with the Training Team. Pictured at Vung Tau in September 1970 are (from left): Brian Lawrance, Ray Deed, Bill Eade, Len and Reg Bandy. As usual, Len appears to be the centre of attention. (AWM FAI/70/0749/VN)

'When Len's got all his medals on you've got a row from here to here,' Korean veteran Reg Anock said, stretching his arms as if describing the one that got away.

The generational links remained strong until the end: Len returns to the 3RAR fold at Holsworthy Barracks on Kapyong Day, 2007. He has just attached the ceremonial Kapyong streamer to the Colours.

good results,' Len wrote. It was not all one-way. Several South Viet-namese outposts were over-run and one garrison was wiped out when it left its defensive positions to have breakfast in a hamlet. Training Team member WOII Jim Stephens was awarded a Military Medal for his role in extricating his unit from a tight spot during this period of heavy fighting.

Len escaped the battle zone—if anyone was ever really out of harm's way in Vietnam—when his CIA boss sent him to a Revolu-tionary Development conference in Quang Ngai. The meeting was chaired by Robert 'Blowtorch' Komer, a leading figure in the 'other war' in Vietnam. With the lofty title of US Presidential Assistant in Vietnam, Komer was in charge of the CIA's operations and carried a reputation for being 'brash, abrasive, statistics crazy, and aggressively optimistic'. No wonder Len's boss sent him to the conference in his stead. Each province representative had to provide a situation report to the meeting. When Len's turn came he was characteristically frank. After a while Komer interrupted. 'Just a minute! What you are saying doesn't agree with any of the other speakers! They seem much more upbeat than you!' Len, of course, spoke his mind whether it be to a green private or a presidential assistant. 'Sir, it depends whether you want a briefing or a rosy picture and I can't give you both in the one talk!' Komer was impressed: 'I want a briefing—carry on!' Len thought he had changed Komer's mind about the 'pictures of sweetness and light' painted by the other speakers.

And all the while Len kept flying. One day he was puzzled by his pilot's repeated sweeps over the Tam Ky strip. When they landed he asked the pilot why they had made so many low-level passes. The pilot replied, 'I was trying to provoke the resident sniper to have a shot at us, but he must have taken the day off.' Sniper bait, great. 'The theory wide-spread in Vietnam was that every airstrip had its resident sniper, but that they should be left alone because the replacement might be a better shot,' Len said. 'Well, a little while later, he was a better shot, because the C46 carrying the major general in charge of the RD program and his staff was hit and crashed in flames alongside the runway. By the time we arrived the aircraft was well on fire, with fuel from ruptured tanks running into a ditch, which we widened and diverted away from the wreck.' No one was hurt but the sniper remained at large. The Americans converted the plane's burnt-out fuselage into a hamburger stand, as you do.

The ready availability of flights for often trivial purposes was a manifestation of the US might—and overwhelming air superiority—in Vietnam. Booking a chopper was like hailing a taxi. 'All we had to do was say we wanted to fly and they would fly you anywhere, no questions asked,' Len recalled. Witness the time Len's boss ordered 20,000 sandbags be airlifted to Tam Ky. When they arrived he proclaimed they were the wrong type, so back they went to Saigon. 'Just another example of the massive waste to the American taxpayer,' Len said.

On another occasion, Len's Saigon-bound Dakota was diverted to make an unscheduled stop at Quang Ngai. This was a curious order as the short strip was unlit and this particular night was dark as pitch. A couple of trucks were driven to its edges and their lights were somehow sufficient for Len's pilot to land safely after a few dummy runs. The reason for the diversion? A packet of documents was passed through a hatch and they were off again. What was in the documents? The Gettysburg Address? Len never found out. 'We got to Saigon around midnight, half-frozen because there was only a heating element in the roof of the C47 and we spent the time holding it to keep our hands warm,' he said. Risking a plane, its crew and passengers, such as Len, in this manner was typical of the authorities' cavalier attitude, Len said. When an Air America plane was reported missing south of Tam Ky, all available aircraft were scrambled for the search. There was not a plane to spare—except for the one seconded by Tam Ky's Police Special Branch (PSB) representative, who all of a sudden decided he had urgent business in Danang. 'Some hours later the missing aircraft was found, having flown into a mountain, but the important thing was that the PSB adviser made his conference.' More earnest searches were mounted when a surveillance drone—yes, the US had drones in 1966—went down. 'The Americans were paranoid about them, flying in special teams to secure the area when one crashed or was shot down.'

Illuminating strips with trucks' headlights was safer than the method employed at another air base. There, a bright-spark officer ordered that a truck circumnavigate the strip with petrol trailing from a drum on the back. 'His idea was to light the petrol and illuminate the strip,' Len said. 'But the scheme came unstuck when some eager beaver struck a match before the truck left the area. Result: the flames raced around the strip and caught up with the truck, which was destroyed.' Whether the fuel drums were labelled ACME and the bright-spark officer was a Wile E. Coyote devotee are unrecorded. One airstrip hacked out of the jungle was so narrow and short it was known as the 'Aircraft Carrier'. It might as well have been called the widow-maker, judging by the wreckage lining the runway. 'Once the aircraft touched down, the pilot stood on his brakes while crossing his fingers. Landing was not a pleasant experience as both ends and sides dropped away to the jungle floor.'

There was a silver lining to some of the flying mishaps. One day Len deposited a bag of groceries on his scheduled China Airlines flight to Tam Ky from Saigon, then went to the airport café to kill the time before departure. He got chatting with a few chopper pilots and duly missed his flight. No matter, his new friends were going his way and he was welcome to hitch a ride. 'It was a very interesting trip, taking eight hours, flying along the coast and stopping in at Tuy Hoa, Nha Trang and Quy Nhon to refuel,' Len said. 'As we flew up the coast the weather closed in and the pilot decided to follow Highway 1, which was all right until we met a [Sikorsky helicopter] coming the other way and there was almost a collision, but both pilots' reactions saved the day. Eventually in the late afternoon we arrived at Danang and there waiting for me was my paper bag of groceries.'

Len was glad to miss the China Airlines flight, as he had little faith in the type of plane flown—the C123—and precisely no faith in its Taiwanese pilots. The C123 was a beast of a plane that had only two engines when it needed four, Len recalled. Some C123s were fitted with booster rockets in an admission they were underpowered for take-offs on short strips. Len said the pilots routinely described landings as a 'controlled crash'. Some crashes were not controlled. Eighty-five passengers and crew had been killed when a C123 clipped a tree line in December 1965. The US commander-in-chief, General William Westmoreland, used a C123 as his personal plane. It was called the 'White Whale', inviting delicious comparisons with Captain Ahab and his quarry, in this case the elusive Vietcong. As for the Taiwanese pilots, Len said they had a 'devil-may-care attitude to life in general, and flying in particular, and seldom seemed to know where they were . . . on one occasion we took off from Tan San Nhut in bad weather and flew for two hours in what seemed to me to be due west, which would have put us in either Thailand or Cambodia, but we eventually landed at Ban Me Thuot in the highlands'. Once, when the flying gear refused to lower, the pilot wound it down manually and said: 'Let's keep our fingers crossed.' Len was on good terms with the Air America pilots, most of whom had left the United States Air Force (USAF) for the better money on offer with the CIA's airline. As they told Len, 'Why should I stay in the air force after my time when I can earn three times as much flying for the company?'

Len's airborne exploits were rewarded with a foreign honour—the USA Air Medal. 'He was subjected to hostile small-arms and automatic-weapons fire while airborne but always maintained the highest degree of air discipline,' the US officer making the recommendation wrote. 'His meritorious performance of duty on the ground and in the air is a credit upon himself and the Australian army.'

A truce was called for Christmas 1966, leading Len to complain that it only allowed the Vietcong to roam the countryside unmolested. Chinese New Year in January—Tet—was a louder affair. 'Seemingly everyone in the country with a weapon fired it off and the night air was

filled with tracer and flares.' The new year brought a fresh challenge for
Len. He was bound for the mountainous interior to tackle a problem
that had defied all the bombs and napalm and Agent Orange the Americans could muster—how to block the flow of men and matériel flowing
south on the Ho Chi Minh trail.

south on the Ho Chi Minh trail.

CHAPTER 14

ON THE TRAIL

'Len was a soldier above soldiers.'
Keith Payne VC

Snaking down through the neutral Laos and Cambodia, the Ho Chi
Minh trail was North Vietnam's back door to the war. Not so much
a single trail as a grid of parallel and connecting roads, tracks and
footpads, the trail was the North's artery, pumping men and supplies
into battle. 'Stations were set up as supply dumps and rest areas with
anti-aircraft batteries deployed,' Len said. 'Initially, supplies were
carried on porters' backs, then using bicycles, which could carry up to
400 pounds, using a pole attached to the handlebars.'

By 1965 the US was growing increasingly concerned about fighting
the war with one hand tied behind its back, so it violated Laos's neutral-
ity by bombing the trail. Australians flying US Phantom jets zoomed
into the fray, but as one pilot explained, a supersonic Phantom was not
much use against a Vietcong soldier on a bicycle in the jungle. The US
generals thought again: they needed to attack the trail from the ground.
And for that they needed an army that could fight in Laos.

Enter the Montagnards. Since early in the war the US had recruited
the tribes of the central highlands to its cause. Montagnards—French
for 'mountain people' but also known as the Degar—is the collective

name for the dozens of indigenous groups straddling the borders of Vietnam, Laos and Cambodia. Even shorter than the diminutive Vietnamese, with a matriarchal system ensuring a family's wealth was divested in their women, the Montagnards were far removed from western 'civilisation', but the US turned to them to deal with the thorny problem of the Ho Chi Minh trail. Enter Len, who was appointed to train the new Montagnard units under the classified Trail Watch program. 'Len was sent to organise them,' Don Beard said. 'He was sort of commander, teacher, organiser, father figure.' In late January 1967 Len was sent to Pleiku in the Central Highlands to recruit men for the Montagnard units.

But before he got too settled, the heads decided it would be less disruptive if he took his owed leave immediately. Len wasn't complaining; he loved travel and his subsequent break in Hong Kong seemed to rate highly in his many out-of-combat adventures. Len alighted in Hong Kong, where he was spirited through Customs and driven to the Hotel Astor. There he and his companions were treated to free drinks and lavished with freebies such as vouchers for suits from the hotel manager's tailor. That Len had an earlier night than his main travelling companion was apparent when Len called on his room the next morning. 'When I looked in, the bare bottom I saw protruding from the sheets certainly did not belong to him, so I left things undisturbed.' Len instead hooked up with a pair of US Marine officers for a 'very upmarket' lunch at the Hilton, before he peeled off for a spot of sightseeing. Coming across a British ship, HMS *Fearless*, at dock, he invited himself aboard for a tour. 'My name is Opie and I am a captain on R and R from Vietnam. I would like to see over the ship if possible.' The gangway sentry replied, 'Come aboard and I'll take you to the captain.' He was introduced to the captain, who apologised for being too busy to show Len around, so delegated the task to his second-in-command. After a most interesting walk through the 12,000-ton ship—'which had its own dock holding landing craft [so] by lowering the stern, these could be floated in and out of the ship'—he stopped at the captain's cabin to thank him for his hospitality. 'I mentioned to the captain that perhaps one day he might join the fun in Vietnam,' Len said. 'Good God, no! I wouldn't want to be involved in that shemozzle! By the way, what is your ship?' Len: 'Ah! Well, I don't have a ship, I'm actually an army captain!' Captain: 'Haw! Haw! The laugh is on us! But I hope you enjoyed your visit!' With that, Captain Opie departed. He was not piped down the gangway.

Len's busy and happy holiday included a train trip to the interior to have a peek into China. He also took up the manager's offer and was fitted for two suits. He visited a Chinese department store where 'on every floor' were 'large dioramas showing poor peasants being subjugated by the ruthless landlords—it was total overkill'.

While he was in Hong Kong news arrived that more than 100 had been killed in a surprise rocket attack on Danang. It was time to go back. Upon his arrival Len was met by Training Team comrade Major Ross Buchan, who took him to the site of the rocket launchings. Len's attention to detail is apparent in his diary entry: 'Fifty-one rounds of Russian 140 mm rockets landed at the SE corner of the air base, hitting barracks, communication centre, aircraft and the village of Ap Hai nearer Danang. Casualties: 100 Vietnamese civilians and 17 US killed. Destroyed; six aircraft, barracks, houses and 1 ammo trailer. The rounds were fired from dismantled launchers of Soviet 16-barrelled track mounted launchers at a range of 9000 metres. There were 134 firing positions. The rockets weighed 85 pounds, had Soviet and Chinese markings and were manufactured in 1962.'

Returning to the highlands, Len selected Lac Thien, a remote village outside Pleiku, for his training base. He chose it deliberately: it was extremely isolated, so the Montagnards could not easily desert. He set about recruiting the first draft of Montagnards and spent much of his time touring the country to get the lie of the land. In somewhat of a cultural role reversal, Len would, on occasion, ride shotgun with an M16 while his American companions would drink beer in the front of the jeep. Len again crossed paths with Ted Serong, who told him,

'You're lucky—I can't get down to Lac Thien.' As usual, Len was unconcerned with matters of rank or reputation. 'I told him that it was a
restricted area anyway and we parted.'

The training began in earnest. Len's Montagnards were schooled
in weapons, photography, river crossings and—of all things—tree
climbing. As usual Len wasn't getting on with one member of the group,
the medic/interpreter, who was forever skiving off and complaining
that Len was too hard on the trainees. The interpreter routinely started
parades by telling the Montagnards not to laugh at Len. Len knew
enough of the local language to make sense of what was going on, so
one can imagine how that went down. No hex was cast, but when the
interpreter was stuck in a tree during an exercise, Len told his diary
'perhaps I should have left him up there to starve or fall and break
his neck'.

The Montagnards were generally keen but had moments of what
a westerner might describe as indolence. 'Training started with daily
PT, then after breakfast minor tactics and route marches to toughen
the troops, because their previous lifestyle consisted largely of lying
around doing nothing.' Once when Len returned from a few days out
of camp he ordered them to run three laps of the base to catch up on
their PT. 'After one lap they refused to do any more as they considered
it punishment,' Len said. Managing the Montagnards was a matter
of delicate diplomacy. 'From the start, it was hard to get the recruits
out of bed and doing anything physical,' he said. 'So that every day
there were a couple of casualties, really just slackers and of course
with the so-called interpreter—who was next to useless because of his
lack of English—being the medic, we had a hard row to hoe. He took
off to the village for cigarettes without permission leaving us to sign
language.'

Len might have had his issues with the recruits, but he got on well
with the local civilians. He was interested in their customs and did his
best to break down the towering cultural barriers. 'There was an old
Montagnard couple who came out every day across the road from us

to scratch around, apparently digging charcoal, and I used to chat with them. None of us understanding a word the other was saying, but we got on quite well and they were fascinated by our binoculars. The old boy wore only a loincloth while his wife had a longer skirt but was bare breasted as were a lot of the womenfolk in the area.'

Soon the Montagnards were ready to go out on patrols. Len, of course, revelled in getting out into the jungle. He wondered at the elephants roaming the bush and the delights of nature. And he thrived on being close to danger. There was no shortage of that. The Vietcong attacked local bases, prompting the American and Vietnamese mortar crews to regularly fire a few desultory rounds into the jungle in case they hit someone. The jungle was laced with Vietcong booby traps, including the terrifying punji pits. These were hidden holes filled with bamboo sharpened to a point and often dipped in poison or smeared with faeces. They were designed not to kill, but to slow up a unit that had to stop and painstakingly extricate the unfortunate comrades. Horror of horrors, Len trod in a punji pit on one of these early patrols. 'Fortunately the sharpened stakes had rotted, so no damage was done.' Hidden danger abounded. After a long patrol in which the men had to wade through a swamp, Len plunged into a fast-flowing stream to wash off the mud. For some reason the Montagnards were reluctant to follow. 'I found out a little while later when they produced a small alligator a couple of feet long, but quite capable of giving a nasty nip. Fools rush in!'

The Allied camps' fortifications of barbed wire and Claymore mines did not deter the Vietcong from launching harassing raids. There was danger within as well: there were periodic outbreaks of cholera, that most cruel and virulent disease caused by poor sanitation and dirty water that literally drains the life out of a person. 'Living conditions were rather sparse,' Len wrote. 'There was a kerosene refrigerator and a stove, but the most important acquisition was a water filter, because we had stark warnings about water quality and, until it arrived, we had to boil all our drinking water. We existed on C rations and Vietnamese

Long-Range Reconnaissance Patrol rations, which were mostly rice and dried fish in plastic sachets to which hot water was added. These were not popular with the Montagnards.'

The Montagnard units were themselves unpopular with the Vietnamese troops, who lorded it over the mountain people. Brigadier Pat Beale also commanded Montagnards and said the Vietnamese called them 'moi'—'slave' in Vietnamese. 'The Vietnamese—North and South—have no time for the Montagnards at all; there's a great deal of animosity between the two groups,' Beale said. Len noted how his troops were treated when they visited other bases. Before one joint patrol, a water buffalo was slaughtered to provide rations for the Vietnamese and Montagnard troops to share. 'But by the time the [Vietnamese] troops had taken their share, all that was left was the skeleton. Talk about spare ribs.'

Food was scarce and usually bland, but the booze could be lethal—Len wrote of 25 soldiers dying after drinking rice wine poisoned by the Vietcong. Len was safe on this score; he was still, and remained, teetotal. The drinking binges that kept him awake throughout his army life continued unabated in Vietnam. '[They] lasted all night, so sleep was a precious commodity,' he said.

He wrote fondly of leave taken in coastal towns such as Nha Trang, where on one trip he was taken in a landing craft to a small island for a spot of snorkelling. No doubt he was treated to myriad marine delights but Len instead chose to write about the island's 'battery of Hawk surface to air anti-aircraft missiles'. Back on the beach a small girl peddling hats approached Len's companion, Paul Anderson. 'She did not make a sale, but sat with us, stroking his arm,' Len said. 'Vietnamese are fascinated by westerners' hair, and she eventually left—with Paul's watch, which she had seen him place in his shoe when he went into the water.' On another trip to the beach Len was left forlornly standing in his swimming trunks when his clothes, wallet and car keys were stolen. He suspected the thief was a local child, who compounded the indignity by alerting his schoolmates to the near-naked 'roundeye'. He was hooted and jeered by the school children as he strode half-naked into the town.

When in Saigon, westerners were well advised not to hang their arms out of car windows. A favourite trick was for the pillion passengers on the 'multitude of Hondas on the roads to snatch the wristwatches of Americans dangling their hands out of the vehicles'. Len was forever taking photos, so was livid when his camera was stolen in Saigon. 'I made the mistake of leaving the camera hanging from the jeep's choke knob when I left for about five minutes. That was just enough for one of the locals to help himself.' He cursed his stupidity when US Defence Secretary Robert McNamara's big black limo with its entourage of secret-service agents running alongside glided through Saigon's streets. 'At each set of red traffic lights these characters jumped from the jeep and ran alongside the car, then as the lights changed, they piled back on board,' Len recalled. It would have made a nice shot. 'Never again was I caught without a camera.' The Len Opie collection includes photos of former US Vice President Richard Nixon's visit to the highlands. 'The crowd of photographers and reporters clustered around, but for some reason he headed across the strip towards us, perhaps because a civilian aircraft—Air America—with Stars and Stripes displayed, on a military airfield in Vietnam, was a rarity. But, whatever the reason, his minders surrounded him and directed him back to the limousine leading the VIP convoy and he was whisked off to see the province chief et al.' Thieving was rife throughout Len's time on the tour. A May 1967 diary entry was typical. 'I washed my socks, which were promptly stolen.'

As the training continued it was clear the Montagnards were not happy. Or, more precisely, the medic/interpreter was not happy; and Len was in his sights. In early April he led a delegation of students, who demanded a hearing with Len's CIA boss to air their grievances. The CIA man was not in camp, so the issue blew over, although it was clear some soldiers wanted out because, they said, Len's methods were too harsh. The unrest boiled over a few weeks later when Len's CIA boss was in the camp. Len was again accused of working the men too hard. Fearing he would be sacked, Len demanded to see the next man up the command chain, Ernie Sparks, in Nha Trang. Sparks asked for Len's version of events and after some thought, Sparks said, 'Are you prepared to take over the whole training program?' Len replied, 'Of course. That is what I have been doing since we started.'

At a practical level, nothing much changed as Len had been effectively in charge in any case. Most of his time was taken up with training in and around the camp, with an occasional patrol. Most of the patrols were merely glorified exercises for the trainees; they were of little value otherwise. The Vietcong were active in the area, but there were few contacts and fewer firefights. That didn't stop a reporter beating up a benign patrol, turning it into a tale of terror. 'We had taken a stroll through the village with its longhouses, and in the door of one was a girl wearing a sarong and a white bra, whereas most of the women were topless,' Len said. 'From memory we just exchanged greetings, but the story came out something like this: "As we moved through the village, we could feel eyes on us from all sides and we knew that if we halted it would probably be our last. We approached this lovely young Montagnard lass and spoke to her. She said: 'Keep going! Keep going! I am an outcast and am marked for death because I have had contact with the roundeyes.'" As it was siesta time, I doubt any of the villagers were awake—apart from the girl—but the story read well.'

If the reporter had only waited a week or two he would have had his story. A true story, too, about two warriors: two of Australia's greatest diggers fighting side by side in Vietnam. In May Warrant Officer II Ray Simpson was appointed as Len's second-in-command. Simpson was a larrikin-type cast in the Anzac mould. Serving alongside Len in Korea, Simpson had distinguished and disgraced himself in the same action. When a US tank was knocked out by shelling, Simpson bravely rescued some of its wounded crew. 'Apparently he did such a good job he was recommended for a DCM [Distinguished Conduct Medal],' Len said. 'But there was an abandoned .50 calibre MG on the turret of the tank, so Simmo helped himself to it. That almost got him a DCM (District

Court Martial) too, but when the authorities weighed one against the other, they decided to call it square.' On another occasion Simpson got hold of a bottle of whisky and tore into it with relish while a hurried battlefield funeral was held for his and Len's friend Bernie Cocks. 'He was three sheets in the wind and the fourth one flapping, and he tore into Big Jim Norrie, the A Company OC,' Len said. 'For some reason, he blamed Jim for Bernie's death and in front of the crowd stated: "He's the bastard who should be on the stretcher—not Bernie!" I managed to get him to one side and had someone tip the rest of the whisky into him, then went back to the service.'

Simpson arrived in Vietnam with the first batch of the Training Team in 1962. After returning home for commando training, he was badly wounded in an action for which he was again recommended for—and was awarded—the DCM. Len said he was in Vietnam illegally, but somehow managed to talk his way out of trouble and into regular service. In 1969 Simpson fought in an action for which he was awarded the Victoria Cross. Len was glad to have him, of course. Soon after Simpson arrived the pair led a Montagnard patrol through thick, leech-infested jungle. It was tough going. Stricken with heat exhaustion and salt deficiency, Simpson wanted Len to leave him in the jungle. Len dispensed some tough love. 'Wouldn't it be great if I turned up without you?' Len said. 'Get going!' They made it back by nightfall, both dotted with leech bites that bled through the night.

Len's former boss had been a more frequent visitor since being ticked off by Sparks. In late May he had his revenge, flying in to order Len to conduct his next Montagnard course from Pleiku rather than his camp at Lac Thien in the jungle. Len had chosen Lac Thien because it was out of the way; the Trail Watch program was, after all, supposed to be top secret. According to Len, if his antagonist could not have him sacked he would make his life as difficult as possible. 'It is apparent that, having lost the argument with Ernie Sparks over the camp issue, he is going to get his way by shoving me off to Pleiku,' Len said. The shift meant Len and his men were under far greater scrutiny at the bigger base, indeed the biggest and most important camp in the Central Highlands. It also meant their program became subsumed by the wider Montagnard training program at the Pleiku Montagnard Training Centre. Still, by now the first intake of recruits was sufficiently trained to go on patrols of up to six days on their own. But a bigger base was a bigger target. The Vietcong struck on the night of 9–10 June, softening up the defences with a mortar barrage then charging in to hurl satchel charges over the wire. At least one recoilless rifle—essentially a descendant of the bazooka—also took a heavy toll. As many as 38 men were killed and three times that number were wounded. The enemy's casualties were unknown. It was that kind of war. Len was off the base collecting supplies at the time. His frenetic flying schedule was continuing unabated—he must have made close to 100 flights in his tour so far, many over country crawling with the enemy. His luck was going to run out eventually.

The day after the battle Len flew north to Dak To in a plane carrying men killed in the attack. There was a short graveside ceremony with a guard of honour provided by the Montagnards, before Len was in the air for the flight back to the base. It was an uneventful flight until the final approach when there was a loud 'thunk' or 'thwack' as Len variously described it. The Dakota B827 had been hit by a burst of small-arms fire and soon the starboard engine was trailing flame. It was looking grim for Len, but the American pilot coolly set his plane down on the strip, where it promptly burst into flames. 'By the time we touched down and managed partly to clear the runway, flames were running down the floorboards,' Len recalled. 'We unloaded, the crew not having time to collect their belongings from the cockpit. There were a few Montagnards escorting the coffins and they took off for parts unknown. We grabbed an extinguisher on the way out and on the tarmac was a wheeled extinguisher of about 40-gallon capacity, which we lined up on the burning motor. But just as we started, there was a woof as a tank blew and that knocked the extinguisher over, and the fire just engulfed the aircraft. The Sunday crowd had gathered and eventually a Huskie firefighting helicopter arrived from Chu Lai with foam which was dumped without much effect and the fire continued to burn. A fat little character in a camouflage suit was whirling around trying to keep us away and he asked me which way did we come in. "From the west." "Oh! You shouldn't have come that way; there is a sniper out there!" "Thanks for that gem of information!" Poor old B827. I had a photo in a book of Laos with her being loaded in the background. She had been a real old workhorse and we were all sorry to see her go.' The reason they came in from the west was Len wanted to avoid ground-fire from a reported enemy force to the east. 'I ignored the deadly glares of the pilots,' Len said of the frosty mood. Still, the pilots posed behind gritted teeth for a photo with their passenger as the blaze raged in the background.

Death narrowly avoided, two of Len's American comrades decided it was time to live a little on a night off at a US base. 'After dark, three of the local ladies appeared,' Len noted in his diary in his typical dry hand. 'One not required—presumably for yours truly—and paid appearance money of 2000 Piastre. We drove her back to her establishment, but as we approached, a police vehicle was parked outside, so we doused the headlights and parked in the dark until they left. Back to the pre-fab, where the lads disappeared into their respective rooms for an hour or so. To top the evening off, I was offered either of the participants. Having dumped the ladies, the boys retired to the bar until midnight.'

After safely negotiating Operation Call Girl, Len moved on to Operation Applecart, the code name for an insertion of his Montagnards on the Ho Chi Minh trail. After a few false starts, it began in late June. Guided by a Bird Dog light plane, the men flew to the trail in two helicopter gunships. Len was responsible for identifying the landing zone; a fraught task given the thick jungle and lack of landmarks. This was illustrated earlier in the war when two US transports put down in Cambodia after mistaking clearings for strips in Vietnam. 'The Cambodians, fearing an invasion, took off, allowing the somewhat embarrassed pilots to take off unscathed,' Len said of that incident. If US pilots could make such a grave mistake, what hope was there for an Australian infantryman? 'My map reading has never been good, but I could pick out two areas of bare ground in the middle of the jungle, so I told the pilot to keep going north along the highway until the bare patches appeared, then we turned west and let down.' The Montagnards ran into the bush and soon the choppers were back in the air; the horse was well and truly before the cart. The extraction went just as smoothly, so score one for the Trail Watch program and Captain Len Opie. It was a rare victory.

■ ■ ■

Author Lee Child once wrote that plans go to hell as soon as the first shot is fired. Chaos is the abiding impression Len gives of Vietnam in his diary. A war where a largely unseen enemy fights on a shifting battlefield; no set-piece battles here. The war devolved into platoon and company actions and endless patrols; American generals so befuddled they drenched the landscape with millions of litres of defoliant to expose the Vietcong; a dysfunctional command structure; a divided local population; foreign footsloggers wondering why they were there. Len believed Vietnam was a just war but was scathing about how badly it was waged. His war was the Vietnam War in miniature. He was forever in the air, shunted from base to base, and at times felt like a supernumerary. Indeed, he later found out he was transferred to Pleiku because a South Vietnamese colonel thought this 'American' in mufti was part of a civilian movement committed to gaining the Montagnards their independence. Len was a mystery to many in Vietnam. A US general once asked Len why, given he had such responsibility and moved in such high echelons, he was only a captain. 'I explained to him that I am the equivalent to their National Guard and not eligible for promotion,' Len said. He might have been in civvies, but Len still proudly wore the badge of the infantry, not of the team or any other unit, metaphorically at least.

After his training camp was closed Len led a nomadic existence for a few months before settling in an instructor's job at the Pleiku Montagnard Training Centre—although it appeared he would not be there long, as his CIA boss had arranged to have him replaced with another Training Team member. 'It is obvious that I have been written off and they are waiting for a more subservient replacement,' Len said. In the meantime, bizarrely, he was sent to Singapore to deliver an attaché case; all very cloak and dagger. Under the US system, officers chose their own hotels and Len selected one that sounded 'rather classy' but turned out to be less so. One phone call and he was booked into an upmarket hotel in the centre of town. The Americans' lack of military organisation did not always extend to R and R, it appeared. He delivered his case to Colonel Peter Seddon, and this is where the plot thickens. According to the official Australian nominal roll, Seddon was not attached to any outfit; his unit is tantalisingly listed as 'Official Duty'. Len said Seddon gave him a 'briefing', but did not elaborate. Was he being sounded out for something clandestine by this mysterious colonel with no unit?

Upon his return to Vietnam Len hosted the Training Team's Australian CO, Lieutenant Colonel Martin Tripp, on a tour of the various bases. Once aboard the C47, Len asked permission to sit in the cockpit as he usually did. Permission granted, an astonished Tripp said. They flew from Saigon to Pleiku and then on to Dak To where they found a dishevelled Simpson camped under a tent fly and subsisting on C rations. 'Poor old Ray was living like a dog,' Len said. Tripp was unsympathetic. 'You haven't shaved this morning, sergeant major?' he said. Len was having none of that. 'Fair go, sir. Ray is supposed to be a civilian, he doesn't even have a vehicle and look at his living conditions.' Tripp murmured something and they were on their way. The weather set in on the flight back, prompting the pilot to say they would have to bypass Pleiku and instead land at Nha Trang. No way—there was a movie Len wanted to see in Pleiku. According to Len, most of the Air America pilots would fly 'anywhere, anytime and had usually completed combat tours of Vietnam . . . but once in a while . . . perhaps it was PTSD', they needed some encouragement. 'We saw the movie, although I think the pilot lost a couple of pints of sweat.' Back in Saigon the CO asked Len how he was able to conjure a plane or a jeep whenever he wanted, when Tripp often had to wait hours. 'Well sir, as someone once said: Life wasn't meant to be easy.' Len and Tripp were oil and water. 'We parted on less than friendly terms,' Len said.

Len had, however, made an impression on the Americans. Tripp called him in one day and asked what he would do at the end of his tour. 'When I told him I would be applying to come back, his response was: "Colonel Redel, head of the PRU [Provincial Reconnaissance Unit] program, has requested that you be assigned to him, so how about taking 30 days' leave and you can come back still with the team?" "Would I ever!"' A week later Redel briefed him about 'the expansion of the PRU program'. He was talking about the Phoenix program, the CIA's campaign of black ops rolled out with the aim of destroying the Vietcong in their home villages.

CHAPTER 15

'SNEAKY WORK': THE PHOENIX PROGRAM

'Well I really am a mercenary because I do it for money,
tax-free money, nothing like it. See the sights and get
tax-free money.'
Len Opie

Phoenix rose from another of those accursed Vietnam acronyms, ICEX, or Intelligence Coordination and Exploitation Program. They were essentially one and the same beast; perhaps someone in high command felt catchier nomenclature might turn the tide. Phoenix is not as well known as the usual Vietnam lightning rods—Agent Orange, conscription lotteries and *that* photo of the naked girl running down a road as her napalmed village burns—but it is from the same family as those infamies. Designed to unravel the Vietcong's support network by targeting civilian communists, the program has been labelled by some as the US's final solution in Vietnam. Its agents—the Provincial Reconnaissance Unit (PRU) teams and their CIA leaders—killed between 20,000 and 40,000 Vietnamese, almost invariably without trial and often after torturing them. The program was cloaked in the usual military jargon. Targets were not killed, they were surgically removed. Pacified. Neutralised. It wasn't about people, it was about infrastructure; winning hearts and minds. Well, Phoenix

broke hearts—literally—and as for minds, one of the torture tech-
niques involved inserting a six-inch piece of dowel into a victim's ear.
They either talked or the wood was tapped into their brain.

Len joined the program in October 1967. Redel, a veteran of World
War II and Korea, who still wore his Marine uniform, had much in
common with Len, and it appeared he held Len in high regard. Len
had also struck up an unlikely friendship with Major General Charles
Timmes, whom he had met at Keswick when Timmes had visited on his
recruiting drive in 1965. Timmes was a counterinsurgency expert who
joined the CIA in 1967. The pair lunched several times in Vietnam. 'He
is a nice old boy,' Len wrote. It is easy to see why they clicked, as Timmes
commanded a parachute battalion on D-Day and later fought in the
Battle of the Bulge. So the deal Len struck with the authorities went like
this: Len could stay in Vietnam—his tour had technically expired—if
he joined Redel's staff. In return, Len exacted a promise that he would
spend half his time on operations—active service—and the other half
training recruits. He was duly appointed Phoenix's head of training—
and thus became immersed in a world populated by Special Forces,
Navy SEALs, Rangers, Green Berets, Seawolves and CIA spooks.

It seems the Training Team's then CO, Lieutenant Colonel Ray
Burnard, played a central part in sending Len to Phoenix. In *The Men
Who Persevered*, authors Bruce Davies and Gary McKay wrote that
Burnard 'was keen to see the experience and expertise of team members
spread as widely as possible and he seized every worthwhile opportunity
to deploy team members where Australians could get greater recognition for their national presence'. In a letter to the authors, Burnard
wrote, 'I was especially pleased to see Captain Len Opie approved as
the chief of training at the Vung Tau centre.' Burnard was another Len
ally from Korea.

Len started with scant details of how Phoenix would work and
what it was supposed to achieve. It was, of course, highly classified,
but that did not stop a segment about the program being telecast on
Armed Forces TV. Len and his new comrades sat down to watch.

Phoenix took the paramilitary role of the PRUs to another level. While CIA and Training Team advisors were attached to the PRUs, ultimately the units were under local Vietnamese command. Under Phoenix, they were under direct CIA command (although notionally Phoenix came under the overarching CORDS—Civil Operations and Revolutionary Development Support—program in what might have been an early manifestation of the plausible deniability doctrine). Phoenix represented a dramatic escalation in the counterinsurgency campaign in Vietnam. The program's more contentious aspects—challenging, catching and often killing Vietnamese civilians—soon became apparent. Like a World War I general tallying the numbers in a war of attrition, 'Blowtorch' Komer set Phoenix a target of 'neutralising' 1800 communists a month. Phoenix was all about the numbers.

After a few months Komer read out the tally at a briefing in Saigon. Len recorded the results in his diary in a detailed table that showed there had been 12,891 operations in 1967. Precisely 3497 of the 'enemy' had been killed, and 1183 wounded. This had been achieved at a cost of 218 killed and 425 wounded. Komer even listed the unit cost of each loss—$200 for every operative killed, $75 for a wounded man and $170 for each one captured. Len wrote, 'The above figures were typical of the computer approach of "Blowtorch" Komer and have little relation to reality.' Later, two VIPs arrived from Washington to frame an appraisal for President Lyndon Johnson. According to Len, 'One of them asked: "How does this fit in with winning hearts and minds?" I pointed out that we weren't in the business of winning hearts and minds.' Indeed. Phoenix was the antithesis of a public-relations campaign. It was machine-gun diplomacy.

When asked many years later if he had any pangs of conscience about Phoenix, Len said, 'I didn't really have a conscience. I was doing a job.' The interviewer tried again: 'Nevertheless you were confronted with decisions that were affecting other people's lives. How did you maintain some moral balance in all this?' Len replied, 'Well, I did what I thought was right. The same reason I went to Vietnam. People said we were wrong going to Vietnam but I think I was right going to Vietnam.'

Brigadier Pat Beale commanded a chopper-borne cavalry battalion in Vietnam and was awarded a DSO for his work with Montagnard troops. Asked about Phoenix, Beale said, 'I was well aware of it.' And the controversy around it? 'Yes, but it was a very effective program. Unfortunately you've got to get down and dirty in wars like that.' Beale is referring to how the North routinely targeted civilians throughout the war. Another team man described Len's Phoenix posting as 'sneaky work'. American journalist Zalin Grant summed it up neatly when he wrote: 'The idea behind Phoenix was to bring all the intelligence units together at province and district levels in an attempt to identify and eliminate the political and administrative organisations of the Vietcong.' Grant wrote it was all about targeting the officials who bought the rice, who recruited the soldiers, who preached communism. He argued that the language used by Komer and his apparatchiks—that is, the weasel words such as 'neutralisation' and 'infrastructure'—made it sound worse than it really was. It was the locals who did most of the killing, even though the CIA and its Australian helpers often pinpointed who was to be killed.

After 30 days' leave in Australia, Len returned to take up his appointment as Phoenix's head of training at Vung Tau. He was one of only six Australians in the highly classified program. He set about writing a training syllabus ahead of the first intake of recruits. His staff included a CIA operative, who Len described as a 'three-time loser' who had fought at the Bay of Pigs and in the jungles of Laos. Then there was a US ex-master sergeant who claimed to have been bayoneted in the Six Day War (he must have made a quick recovery as the war had been earlier that year). Len's CIA boss had some spurious claims to have been in the US unit next in line to 3RAR at Kapyong. Len decided he was a vain man—he had recently had a facelift. They were the kind of anti-communist soldiers of fortune who broke into the Democratic National Committee headquarters in 1972. As such, it could be argued that Phoenix was a stepping stone to Nixon's downfall.

Completing the motley crew was a PRU leader Len suspected of being a Vietcong agent and a shadowy province chief who had six fingers on one hand. When the recruits marched in Len looked them up and down and decided they were 'thieves, murderers and rapists and everything else, we had the dregs'. These cutthroats—American spooks and Vietnamese gangsters—were the men charged with turning the war for the US. It seems Len was chosen under a 'takes one to know one' philosophy of management. If anyone could keep them at heel it was Len.

He must have wondered what he had got himself into. Less than two weeks into the job Len decided to test his men by setting an ambush on a known Vietcong track. The team moved into position but the ambush had to be abandoned because his band of deadly warriors was followed all the way—by children from the local village. A few days later a PRU sea patrol's barge was blown up by a Vietcong underwater demolition team. Five were missing, presumed killed, and eighteen were wounded. Worse was to come. On the morning of 7 December the students filed into a building for a lecture. Their Vietnamese instructors were late, as usual. A bomb exploded, killing three outright and wounding twenty. A local hospital refused to take the wounded—probably fearing reprisals or another bomb—so the most seriously wounded were taken by ambulance to another hospital. On the way the ambulance hit a mine, killing one of the wounded aboard and wounding all the others for a second time. One later died of his wounds. The magnitude of Len's task was apparent: could he trust the instructors who had turned up late? What about the four students absent that day? Len already had his suspicions about the PRU chief, who had been seen near the classroom the previous day. To top it all off, a woman running a lemonade stand near the bombing was a Vietcong widow. Talk about punching at shadows. 'In our estimation the province chief was [also] highly suspect,' Len wrote. 'Not a conspicuous start for the new-look PRU!'

Len quickly set about framing a course based on the Canungra Jungle Training Centre syllabus. 'As at Canungra there are no passengers—everyone must complete the course to graduate and be awarded the PRU insignia,' Len said. The recruits were drilled in field-craft, hand-to-hand combat, demolition, communications, sniping and all manner of weapons, including the SLR—the standard Australian infantry rifle of the time. Len noted that when it was first adopted by the Australian army, the SLR's range was given as 600 yards. However, when the brass realised the enemy's AK-47 had a range of 650 yards, the SLR's gazetted range was upgraded to 700 yards. 'The only reason was to outgun the opposition.' The specifics of a course in 'special operations' is a window into Phoenix; its elements were 'Capture, Raid, Ambush, Rescue, Deception, Maritime'.

Unsurprisingly Len's strict regime soon led to conflict. When Len dressed down his instructors for dismissing a class halfway through a working day, they sent a delegation to his quarters in Embassy House to demand details of his qualifications. The meeting did not end well. Later, they were so enraged word filtered back that they were about to attack Len's barracks. Len's response was Eastwood-esque. 'I sent word back that if they did and the raid was successful, I would pay them a bonus as it would be the first time ever that they had done something right. Needless to say, they didn't take me up on my offer.' Another problem to be overcome was the White Mice—the South Vietnamese police—rounding up and arresting his students, meaning Len had to leave his post to bail them out. Working out who was enemy and who was friend was an enduring problem.

A new year ticked over and while his American comrades were sleeping off their hangovers Len went down to the beach for a swim. He was helping the locals haul in their fishing nets when the extreme heat prompted him to shed his briefs so he could use them to shade his head. Presently a utility approached along the beach. He thought nothing of it until it came close enough for him to see one of his colleagues had brought his wife along for a bit of sightseeing. 'Rapid rearrangement of apparel with me being the only embarrassed one,' Len said. It appeared Len was not always so shy. A similar incident occurred a week later, when he stubbed his toe on a nail. 'So I took off my briefs and wrapped my foot, then walked back to camp past the whole domestic staff and half the students. I was in no mood to be embarrassed but I'm sure the Vietnamese if they did not consider me eccentric beforehand certainly did after this day.' Fellow team member Rob Thornton had a similar tale from later in the war. 'The sea was only 50 metres away on a great stretch of beach, so we swam at least twice a day,' Thornton said. 'There was a sniper up in the hills who took every opportunity to shoot at us in the water, but he never hit any of our guys so we never shot back at him. Len said that if we shot the bugger they might find someone who could really shoot so best we leave him to his fun! I don't know if Len was a "naturist" or not. But he used to strip off after walking a few metres away from HQ company and wander stark bollock naked most of the way up the beach and back! Now, those of you that know Len know that he was tall and lean of build, with slightly stooped shoulders. What you will not know (but many shocked and intimidated Vietnamese will know) is that he was abnormally "well hung" by any man's standards.' Thornton said the locals were astounded by Len's behaviour and the local CO asked Thornton if he would suggest that Len be more modest. 'I told them not to worry and that this was part of Captain Opie's religion that had to be practised several times a week. I never did have the nerve to bring this to Len's attention. All I know is that whenever Len went for his nature walk it was safe to go swimming. Because the sniper up in the hills was too stunned or just plain fascinated to shoot at anything so long as Len had his clothes off!'

All was relatively quiet in the lead-up to Tet, Vietnam's sacred festival marking the start of spring. The North declared a seven-day ceasefire from 27 January, and the South responded with its own, shorter armistice. Len was in Pleiku for the previous Tet, when the locals celebrated by firing tracers indiscriminately into the sky like Middle Eastern revolutionaries. Strangely, this year there was no firing. All was quiet, too quiet, in the manner of the Western movie cliché. The American tanks might as well have been circled wagons and the Vietcong the Indians.

To stretch the allusion, Len's quarters at the training camp were nick-named the Ponderosa.

When the attack fell it fell hard; 70,000 Vietcong struck almost every city and major town in the South. Not even central Saigon was safe. The US Embassy's walls were breached by commandos who then briefly seized the building. 'The US Embassy in Saigon was attacked with nineteen VC killed,' Len said. 'A platoon of 101 Airborne Division had landed on the roof and fought their way down to retake the building with four troops and one US Marine killed and five WIA [wounded in action].' Len's old 3RAR CO, Arthur MacDonald, now a major general, arrived to assume command of the Australians in Vietnam only to land in the middle of bitter street-fighting. He watched from his quarters as the Presidential Palace was attacked.

US firepower meant the Tet Offensive was doomed to fail. But the tactical defeat was a strategic victory, as Tet marked the turn of the tide on the home front—in Australia as well as in the US. Unusually for Len, he missed the fight. Vung Tau was about the only place in the South not attacked by the Vietcong. 'The Vung Tau Peninsula was probably the most peaceful area in the whole country,' he said. So Len and his CIA colleagues watched it on TV.

The training continued and the instructors' grumbling mounted. Len seemed to thrive on the complaints. When a standoff over pay seemed set to escalate Len drew his pistol and told his colleagues to leave the room. Sorted. When a man was found pilfering from the camp stores Len sent him packing. 'Down the beach a way, he started to scream abuse so I had the guard fire a couple of shots in his general direction to smarten his footwork.' Still, the training seemed to be progressing satisfactorily and soon the first intake graduated and another marched in. Len continued to modify the syllabus, still using the Canungra methods as his main guide. Eventually he developed a program that won praise from on high. 'Captain Opie reduced the length of training, allowing the students more direct field experience and knowledge in fighting the infrastructure by capture, elimination and special operations,' a US superior wrote. His reorganisation led to a 40 per cent increase in output at the training centre. 'Due to Captain Opie's superior organisational ability, outstanding tact and leadership, he accomplished all missions in an exemplary manner and earned a well-deserved reputation as an exceptionally competent and resourceful individual.' The same document mentioned his 'highly professional skills in unconventional warfare'.

As he said all those years later, he never had any trouble killing humans. On the other hand, Len loved animals. He donated large sums to animal charities throughout his adult life. He railed against animal cruelty in all his wars. In April he wrote with great warmth about a particularly happy day when the camp dog, Fred, had seven puppies. Apparently one of the more hapless CIA agents had made a mess of the names. 'The father was Suzy,' Len said. A few days later Len investigated a disturbance outside, where he found the camp cook and maid digging in the sand. They had saved one of the pups from a horrible fate. Fred, or perhaps Suzy, had decided 'six were as many as she could handle and this poor little pooch was to be left to die'. It was the second time she had buried the seventh pup. 'He was as healthy as all the rest and the only difference was in the colour of his paws— pink while the others were white. We pointed this out to Suzy and had no more trouble.' The cook and maid lavished attention on the pups, which were all sent to homes handpicked by Len. Heaven help anyone who mistreated the dogs. One of the CIA agents was a card-carrying Ku Klux Klansman who wanted to train one of the dogs 'to be savage'. No dog for you, Len said. Another dog, George, accompanied Len on his rounds. One day he went missing from the back of the pick-up but turned up much later at the home camp, 'limping a bit but pleased to see me . . . he never explained how he found his way home'.

While he spent most of his time with CIA agents, there were opportunities for Len to catch up with his Australian comrades. He spent much of Anzac Day 1968 with Ray Simpson and another well-known member of the Training Team, Ernest 'Ossie' Ostara, a kindred spirit who fought in World War II and Korea and was awarded a DCM for his heroism in a sharp fight in 1965. Len had regular meetings with Redel and other senior officers, usually in Saigon. He would fly to the Tan Son Nhut base then catch a cab to a hotel in the city. One cab driver who tried to rip him off really lucked out; Len not only refused to pay, he had the man arrested and possibly hexed. One conference at Nui Dat was a veritable *This is Your Life* parade of diggers from Len's past. Present were Brigadier Ron Hughes (Jim's brother, ex-3RAR, now commanding the Australian task force in Vietnam), Colonel John Kelly (ex-3RAR), Colonel Phil Bennett (an acquaintance from Len's commando training, now CO of 1RAR) and 'Digger' James, who was now with 8 Field Ambulance. When the assembled brass had an audience with Prime Minister John Gorton, Len, whose CIA-issue jungle greens had faded to a nondescript off-white, was told to stand at the back and if anyone asked any questions to say he was a reporter. Well, someone did ask questions—a reporter. When Len muttered something about working in revolutionary development, the reporter said, 'Oh, I want to do a story on that.' Len made his excuses before sneaking off to the sergeants' mess, where he had a chat with the Australians' supreme commander in Vietnam, Major General MacDonald. Len also often met Don 'Doc' Beard, 3RAR's medical officer in the early days of Korea and now a colonel in the Medical Corps. Many years later Beard said Len was comfortable with his lot in Vietnam. He was confident in his abilities and at home in his skin. 'At that stage he was a very happy man, unlike what he eventually became.'

But what about the deal for a 50/50 split in training and combat operations? It seems Len's American bosses were happy to let him off the leash once the training program was bedded down. From the middle of 1968 he was in the field as much as he was in camp, and he revelled in it. From here on he wore the black pyjamas of the PRU soldiers as much as he did his washed-out and faded uniform. For five days in July he planned and directed operations to capture six

Vietcong cadres. Every operation was an adventure for a soldier at his peak. Len was on one of three gunboats—part of the South Vietnamese Junk Force, essentially PRU teams on the water—that slipped out of a base near Vung Tau to raid Vietcong camps on the coast. Leaving at 3.30 am, the little force attacked at dawn, only to find the camps deserted—but with their breakfast fires burning. Len reported that his PRU men 'moved well initially but became separated and voice contact gave away their locations'. After blowing up two bunkers and torching the camp's huts, the men withdrew when their Bird Dog reported movement in the jungle. On the way back Len fell asleep on the sun-bathed deck. Oh what a lovely war! A subsequent boat ride for lunch at a coastal hotel was more eventful. The boat broke down so Len organised a tow from the locals. The weather turned and the rescuers, fearing both boats would be swamped, made to cut the towline. But Len drew his pistol and all safely made landfall. 'Altogether it was like an episode from *McHale's Navy*,' Len said.

Len was always comfortable in and on the water. In uniform, at least. He bought a boat in his retirement but his nieces said he wasn't much of a sailor, in spite of his undoubted enthusiasm. At Vung Tau he once paddled an air mattress across the bay to explore a World War II Japanese gun emplacement, just for fun. He was fond of fishing and especially crabbing, but with mixed results. A US SEAL had more success in the waters off Vung Tau—he used grenades. Len also liked to take a boat trip to the Peter Badcoe Club—named in honour of Badcoe, who was killed in action in April—where he would swan in from the beach to funny looks from diggers wondering who the hell was this bloke dressed in black pyjamas. Any swim, fishing expedition or boating trip was dangerous in this war without defined front lines. The sporadic attacks on land—commonly from Vietcong teams firing rocket, mortar or RPG rounds from the jungle—were supplemented by intrepid enemy parties bombarding the shore from islands opposite the base. One rocket attack on Vung Tau airfield destroyed a Caribou cargo plane and killed a US serviceman.

Len commanded an operation to snatch 'suspects' from a monastery on a tributary of the Mekong River. He coordinated the artillery support and briefed the Seawolves—helicopter gunships crewed with volunteers expert in covert operations—the day before the mission. Setting off at 1 am, they sloshed through paddy fields to their objective, where they waited for the 5 am dawn. Seventeen suspects were seized without a shot being fired, but the column came under attack from a company-sized Vietcong unit on the way back. Len's preparation might have saved the day, for he quickly called in a barrage and summoned the Seawolves, who raked the enemy with rockets and machine-gun fire for almost half an hour. Len's men made it out without a casualty.

Len collected SEAL and PRU teams for his next mission. The objective? Capture two Vietcong from separate houses in Cho Van village. Amazingly, illustrating how the confounded conflict pitched friend against friend, Len prepared for the snatch in the village chief's house. Len was given the headman's bedroom, where he had trouble sleeping on a bed he described as a 'plank'. They crept into the paddy fields soon after midnight and deployed around the two houses. 'We lay up while the snatch team captured one suspect, then a blocking force was set up while the second house was raided without result,' Len wrote. 'We did however have the hot tea, which the captive had prepared for an early breakfast.' Discipline in the PRU teams appeared to be improving but it was coming off a low base: on the way back the men came upon a Vietcong flag, which they set about shooting from its pole in a hail of M16 and machine-gun bullets and even twelve rounds from a grenade launcher. The flag fluttered on. Eventually one of the men climbed up and tore it down. Len was back in time for breakfast.

Len was making up for his long time in camp. The missions were coming thick and fast—he was on the move again two days later. He was flown to a village, then another, where he was driven to a mooring of two speedboats and a large, whaling-type rowboat. The force of SEALs and a PRU team would head up the Bassac River to the Mekong, where they would continue upstream to the Cambodian border, then disembark and set up an ambush inland. Upon reaching the Mekong they rendezvoused with a patrol boat sent to guide them to the border. 'We motored silently upstream with no word from the patrol boat so we called him up to be told that his radar was out, but that he was showing a light to guide us,' Len wrote. 'As we could see no light upstream, we informed him, but he replied that he had been showing the light for nearly half an hour so we asked him to move it about a bit. To our consternation a tiny pinpoint of light showed about a mile *downstream* from us, so we surmised that we were the best part of a couple of miles inside Cambodia. I remembered Colonel Milner's warning: "Don't get caught in Cambodia!" So we turned around and very quietly retraced our steps (or wakes).'

Eventually they came ashore and set the ambush. The SEALs were disconcerted by Len's off-white dress, fearing he would be seen in the jungle. 'So I of course was to be relegated to the back of the ambush, under a bush where I couldn't be seen. As it turned out (and I already knew), as soon as night fell I became invisible.' The SEALs gave him a 'stay-awake' pill, which worked but not in the intended fashion—it gave him a splitting headache. Other than some tracer fire seen in the distance, the ambush was a non-event, and they returned to base without incident the following day. The next ambush, a day later, was set in a graveyard on the Cambodian border. Len and his PRU team were mortared but the enemy mostly stayed out of reach over the border. The mortar crew was supposedly firing from a pagoda but when Len and his men investigated they found only a blind monk. Len claimed the monk had served breakfast to two Vietcong fifteen minutes earlier. Len's war was starting to resemble *Apocalypse Now*.

Understandably, given the nature of the work, Len included almost no details of the assassination missions. There are clues in his diary entries, as we have seen. The hardest evidence of his 'sneaky work' is found in his citation for the US Bronze Star Medal, which reads: 'Captain Opie participated or led many operations into Vietcong territory after targeted Vietcong infrastructure and repeatedly demon-strated his highly professional skills in unconventional warfare.' As well as the Bronze Star, Len was awarded a Vietnamese medal for his sustained gallantry in 1968. The recommending Vietnamese major wrote, 'He has participated in more than 40 small as well as big opera-tions in the country, and conducted capture operations of a number of VC sub-infrastructure cadres.'

After another night mission—in which Len and his team were fired upon but escaped unscathed—he was mysteriously and immediately recalled to Saigon. There he had a brief argument with the team's senior officer in the Mekong Delta, Major Graham 'Curly' Templeton, who asked why Len had never reported to him. 'I pointed out that I had no connection with the team, therefore no time to waste on idle chit chat, and that didn't seem to please him either!' Then it was off to see Redel, who dropped a bombshell: Len was off to Kashmir.

Kashmir? Australia had been providing observers to the UN peace-keeping force in Kashmir since 1952. But why Len? Well, it is hard to be certain about the exact circumstances; perhaps one of his many enemies had been active behind his back? Whatever the reason, Len was to be granted no more extensions to his—until this time—very fluid tour arrangements in Vietnam. 'They said I had to have a holiday,' Len said. 'And I said: "I thought I was having a holiday in Vietnam?" They said: "No, you can have twelve months in Kashmir and then you can come back." So I was ordered out of Vietnam . . . I didn't want to go to Kashmir at that stage because I was just getting my feet wet in Vietnam, you know, I was just getting the hang of things. And they said: "Oh no, you go to Kashmir." They didn't have anybody to go, so that's why I went there.' A diary entry some six months earlier sheds more light on the matter. Len wrote, 'Interview with Assistant Military Secretary, who advised that my extension will probably be granted and he noted my request for a UN mission party.' It appears Len knew he wouldn't be granted an extension so even then was trying to wrangle another overseas posting.

He pleaded his case to Brigadier John 'Freddie' Whitelaw. 'I told the brigadier I didn't want to leave Vietnam and that if I had to, I wanted to go to the Middle East. His reply was: "I can't get you to the Middle East until 1972; in the meantime, have a holiday in Kashmir and when you come back you can either go to the Jungle Training Centre as an instructor or come back to the team."' So that was that. Kashmir. Just as he was having so much fun in the field. Instead he had to pack his gear and learn yet another acronym—UNMOGIP (United Nations Military Observer Group India and Pakistan). His last two months in Vietnam featured a string of lunches with his high-ranking friends—Timmes, MacDonald, Redel—before he flew out on 15 October. But it was not goodbye, only so long. Len was determined to return to Vietnam.

CHAPTER 16

KASHMIR INTERLUDE

'I haven't seen anyone else in the military in the niche that
he was.'
Major General John Hartley

Len returned home briefly before his Kashmir posting. As usual he
went via Sydney, and as usual he had an argument with Customs. How
dare the desk clerk object to his Montagnard crossbow! The situation
threatened to escalate when the Customs officer asked if the weapon
was for Len's personal use, and Len, in his usual uncompromising
way, said of course it was. As often happened in such situations, an old
comrade—this time a Korean War–vintage warrant officer—intervened
and Len was allowed to keep it. He headed back to Adelaide for ten
days' leave.

If someone did want Len out of the way they could scarcely have
picked a better posting than Kashmir. Sharing borders with Afghanistan, China and the belligerents whose competing designs were the
reason for the UN presence, India and Pakistan, Kashmir seemed a
long way from anywhere. It had been disputed ground since the English
left after World War II, leading to a major war in 1947 and a minor one
in 1965. Of course the North-West Frontier had been contested territory since Alexander the Great, Genghis Khan and the British Empire's
skirmishes with the impudent tribesmen in and around the Khyber

Pass. It was somehow appropriate that Len was sent to the place where a young subaltern called Winston Churchill got a taste for blood— and for whisky in the officers' mess—in the previous century. Len was no longer a young man—he would turn 45 soon after starting his Kashmir assignment. But he was fit. 'Observers had to be fit and tough,' the Australian War Memorial says of the handpicked Kashmir peace-keepers. 'Patrols might involve climbing on foot through the snow to positions more than 3000 metres above sea level.'

Flying via Singapore, Bangkok and Karachi, Len landed in Rawalpindi in northern Pakistan on 7 November 1968. 'The overrid-ing impression which immediately struck me was a persistent haze in the atmosphere and everything looked washed out and faded, even the brick road,' Len wrote. Vultures circled endlessly, tear gas hung in the air after a recent riot, and 'cars full of screaming youths waving rebel flags' sped past as he was taken to his hotel. The schools were closed and civilians had been ordered to stay indoors.

Len longed to go back to Vietnam. He counted down the days like a prisoner scratching notches on a wall. 'Only 10 months to go, then back to Vietnam!' he wrote in mid-January. His diary is strewn with snippets of news from Vietnam; the latest offensive, Australian troop movements and casualty lists.

Len's role was straightforward when compared with his various positions in Vietnam. The Indian and Pakistani armies were sepa-rated by a ceasefire line. No side was allowed to enter no man's land or fire within 500 metres of the border. Improving fortifications was forbidden, as were incursions into opposing air space. UN peacekeep-ers in posts along both sides of the border were charged with settling disputes and ruling on alleged infractions. It seemed simple but there were problems. First, the official map was a relic of British rule. Drawn in 1896 and updated in 1923, the map was small in scale, so that when the ceasefire line was drawn in felt pen it showed the demarcation zone to be several kilometres wide. Also, the dispute-resolution process was problematic, as the UN representatives tended to rule in favour of the force they were stationed with, which was human nature as their host soldiers cooked their meals. A third issue was that goatherds often turned their flocks loose in the fertile and overgrown no man's land. 'So far as the Pakistanis were concerned, the local farmers could go where they liked to graze their goats, whereas the Indians stuck rigidly to the terms of the agreement and fired at any violators,' Len wrote. 'The result was that any firing had to be investigated and it usually turned out to be some poor farmer, taking advantage of the good grazing and getting himself shot. The Pakistanis would then register a complaint (not about the farmer being killed, but the violation of the agreement about the Indians firing within 500 yards of the CFL). This entailed an investigation by UNMOGIP with a written report on the incident.'

His comrades on the peace mission were a more disparate mob than the CIA contingent in Vietnam, if that is possible. The man in charge of it all, officially the Chief Military Observer, was Chilean Lieutenant General Louis Gonzala Gazzara, who, when in dress uniform, 'resembled a circus bandmaster', Len said. Len soon found the other men rather childishly called the General 'Louis Banana' behind his back. At their first meeting Gazzara told Len to behave himself as the general had spies everywhere. As a caricature of a wannabe banana-republic dictator, Gazzara seemed to have jumped off a page of Evelyn Waugh's *Scoop*.

The others truly represented the 'nations' in the UN name but not so much the 'united'. Len's Canadian officer-in-charge was forever drunkenly baiting an Italian captain, saying that the Canadians whipped the Italians at El Alamein in World War II (of course Len was having none of that as he knew there were no Canadian units in the Western Desert in 1942). 'Poor old Pietro did his best, admitting that the Italian Army didn't do too well, but the navy performed better (obviously he had not heard of the battles of Matapan and Taranto),' Len wrote. Pietro was an otherwise popular comrade, chiefly for his ability to produce vast quantities of spaghetti. A German member of the team probably stayed quiet during the drunken arguments over past battles. Len wondered how much had changed given he wore a World War II-style uniform—complete with Iron Cross. Then there was a Swedish major, who Len said was, 'Recently divorced, with his new wife, a doctor, on the mission . . . he was a rather unhappy soul because, in Sweden, a divorced man had to pay half his income to his ex, regardless of the rights or wrongs (in this case, I suspect the wrongs).' Len also wrote about a drunken Norwegian, a self-important Danish brigadier and a kindly Finn who loaned Len warm clothes after his luggage was lost in transit. He needed them—his first post was a desperately cold mountain hut about two hours' drive from Rawalpindi. It was often below freezing but Len marvelled at the mountain country—Kashmir was not known as the 'Switzerland of the east' for nothing.

But all the natural beauty in the world could not make up for the cold, isolation and—most of all—lack of action. 'All I wanted was to get out of this forsaken place and back to the peace and warmth of Vietnam,' Len wrote early in his stay, when he was still without his own warm clothes. 'How to do it? I know! I'll upset [Gazzara] and he'll send me home!' Before leaving for Kashmir Len was told not to rock the boat under any circumstances. So he decided to rock the boat. 'My first task was almost my last. I was sent out to look for a suspected and unreported post a couple of miles from the HQ. So I set off with the driver, found the position, which was visible from the road, climbed up, took details of the defensive layout and was back by lunchtime.' He presented his sketch to the drunken Canadian, who said, 'The Italians had looked for it for three days and came back to report that it didn't exist.' Len replied, 'What do you mean it doesn't exist? You can see it from the road and here is a sketch of the layout.' Rock the boat? 'I had almost capsized it! It turned out that the UN had no record of it despite the fact that the post had been there for 25 years! I almost achieved my wish of being sent home before my first week. The OIC [officer in command] seemed to take it as a personal insult!' Not enough of an insult to be sent back to Vietnam, sadly.

Len's boss tried to exact his revenge by ordering Len to wear his campaign ribbons; a smart row of ribbons gave the wearer more authority when dealing with the locals. 'You'll get a lot of mileage out of them,' he said. Len said he did not wear ribbons in the field and certainly did not need to get mileage out of them. The others wrought every last inch out of their decorations, without justification in many cases. The Swedish major's only ribbon was a 'pretty red one which I found was a sports medal'. The Italian captain wore two blue ribbons. 'Considering the fact that he had been put in prison at the end of World War II for being a Blackshirt, I wondered what they were.' Of course the German had his Iron Cross but all their ribbons combined might have come to a quarter of Len's medals from his three wars.

Len's duties were fairly mundane; transmitting radio reports at appointed times, checking the opposing sides' posts, and writing reports—including an account of the Phoenix program for the heads in Vietnam. He continued to pine for Vietnam, but consoled himself by diving straight into the wonders of this mysterious land. He toured extensively throughout the Kashmir region, visited Pakistan and India, and drove across the Khyber Pass into Afghanistan. He stood agape at six-year-old boys weaving carpets in the Rawalpindi markets. He said some of them 'went blind after a few years—talk about slave labour'. When in Delhi he stayed at the Oberoi International, a preferred dining destination of the local upper class; 'the ladies in beautiful saris, looking remarkably sexy despite displaying a minimum of flesh'. The diary is full of mentions of the local women. For instance, 'Jaipur in Rajasthan is noted for the colourful dress of the women—their robes are interwoven with pieces of glass and the Pink Palace was the place where the Rajah's wives and mistresses could peer out at the passing parade through an elaborate screen overlooking the main street.' As well as, 'The outstanding thing about both women and men was their white teeth and, in the case of the women, their glittering eyes, almost as if they put belladonna in them to enhance the effect.' Then there were the 'high-ranking officers' wives . . . beautifully clad in saris with gleaming white teeth and flashing eyes'. He also took great interest in recording his visits to ancient forts, palaces and mosques. He was certainly making the best of his lot. Wherever he went his UN companions complained about the Indian food—what did they expect? Len was generally happy with the local fare. There was an exception, though. He was forever moaning about the Kashmiris' staple meat—goat. 'However goat is cooked, it still tastes like goat.'

Halfway through his year-long tour Len was posted to a mountain station above the Kashmir Valley. He needed medical approval to serve at extreme altitude—some mountains rose well over 3000 metres on this part of the demarcation line—so drove a day and a half to see an Indian doctor, who barely looked up from his tennis match to declare Len fit. Len turned around and started on the return journey. When he arrived at his new post the local brigadier, a Sikh with a 'red band in his turban and his scraggy beard secured by a hairnet', shared wise counsel on living at the 2600-metre elevation. 'Tomorrow walk just to the edge of camp,' the brigadier said. 'Next day, twice as far and again. Take at least a week.' Len followed the advice to the letter. His Swedish companion did not, and was soon on his way home with a heart complaint. Len took less notice when the brigadier gave a lecture on marriage and family planning. The mountain posting agreed with Len. He roamed far and wide—by air, in jeeps and often on foot during long hikes through the ranges—for months, checking on dozens of positions.

The most contentious ground was a 3800-metre peak occupied by the Pakistanis but claimed by the Indians to be in the neutral zone. Len was called in to settle the matter. After negotiations that Len said nearly triggered World War III, he sided with the Indians, so took their soldiers up the hill and into the Pakistani positions. The Indians were far from grateful, arguing they needed to improve the positions to provide greater shelter in the coming winter. Len refused. He took them up in a snowstorm and there they stayed in roofless sangars. Gazzara was angry. 'I could send you home,' he said. Len was unapologetic. 'I'm ready to go. I'm not here to make friends. I'm here to do a job and if you're not satisfied . . . ' At the end of Len's tour the General said he'd be happy to have him back. 'That Captain Opie, I don't know whether he's an old young man or a young old man.' At almost 46, he was more old than young but that wasn't going to stop him heading back to Vietnam.

CHAPTER 17

RETURN TO VIETNAM

'If I'd have been a Vietcong you'd be dead.'
Len Opie

Wanting to return to Vietnam was one thing; getting there was quite another. Of course Len did as Len always did—he drew upon his network of friends in high places. Len immediately wrote to Major General Arthur MacDonald, the army's adjutant-general, asking for a Vietnam posting. According to Len, MacDonald said it might take a while; in the meantime he would have to bide his time as an instructor at Canungra, training the trainers of the Training Team. Upon his arrival he was made to take a test covering the most basic aspects of infantry fighting—and failed. It appeared he had forgotten more about the army than the other instructors. But as his appointment had come from high up, Canungra's officers were stuck with their curious old instructor. 'They had to put up with me,' Len said. 'It was made clear to me from day one that I was not welcome, but that was their problem.' Len was an odd man out from the start. Of course he was never in the habit of wearing his ribbons in the field, and so it was in camp. He also preferred wearing the infantry corps badge, rather than the regiment badge worn by men who had seen action. So the young soldiers, including Duntroon officer candidates, wondered who the hell he was. 'He's been in the army for 107 years and he's never been in the regiment,' is how Len's friend and comrade Mick Mummery summarised the attitude at Canungra. 'But their jaws dropped when he'd arrive at dinner wearing his ribbons.'

Despite his usual clashes with various antagonists, Len settled easily back into the Canungra life. Little wonder—he had been coming here on and off for 27 years. Once again it was made easier by the many familiar faces in the camp, including camp commandant Colonel Edwin 'Ted' Griff, an old Korean comrade who was generally pally with Len save for a clash over Len's decision to fail five students. Griff said the powers-that-be accepted no more than two failures. 'If our word isn't good enough, what are we doing here?' Len replied, pointing out that one of the failures was an overweight and short-sighted comrade of theirs from Korea, Warrant Officer II Francis 'Specs' Raffen. Len decided Raffen was unfit for service but was overruled. 'Poor old Specs' went to Vietnam where, overloaded with equipment on a march, he died of heat exhaustion. The official cause of death was 'illness'. Another of the men failed by Len shot himself, probably accidentally. 'Of the other three, at least two were sent home early for reasons I never found out, but it did go to prove that our estimate bore out our forecasts,' Len said.

After three months at Canungra word came through that MacDonald's efforts to secure a Vietnam posting for Len had borne fruit. He would leave in April. In his short time at the Jungle Training School Len had taught many more men the art of war. He made an impression that lasted a lifetime. Corporal Ivor Alexander said Len taught them lessons not found in any handbook (which was just as well given Len had failed the official test) such as how to deal with Montagnards. 'You don't get anywhere yelling at troops from other countries,' Len told the men. 'I would describe it as quiet leadership,' Alexander said. 'He was fair dinkum. The authenticity of the bloke. There didn't seem to be anything staged about him. He was a bloke who was a bit self-effacing. But he should've been a general. I'll never forget Len. I never saw him again.' Intriguingly, Alexander said Len was suffering from a recurrence of his malaria at the time, but there is no mention of this in Len's diary at the corresponding time. 'He was a bit stooped. His colour was grey. His voice was lowered. Of course he wouldn't go off duty. He was that sort of bloke.' That Len made such an impression on Alexander is impressive given the corporal had already completed two tours of Vietnam. 'I think people like him you could count on perhaps two hands.' Major General John Hartley went one step further, 'I haven't seen anyone else in the military in the niche that he was.'

Len landed in Saigon, at last, in mid-April 1970. This time there was no milling around without a specific role; he was immediately sent to Quang Tri near the North/South demarcation line—a forward area if there was such a thing in this war without borders. There he would serve as senior advisor to South Vietnam's 2nd Battalion, 1st ARVN Regiment. His chopper flight up to his posting had a VIP passenger, Foreign Affairs Minister Billy McMahon. Len referred to him as 'HE' in his diary, presumably for His Excellency. 'He looked for all the world like a possum with his mane of white hair flowing in the breeze,' Len said. McMahon inspected the troops and Len offered to make a speech but was 'put in a corner' while another officer did the honours.

Another speech half a world away a few days later had greater import. President Nixon announced the US would recall 150,000 troops from Vietnam within twelve months. 'There has been an overall decline in enemy force levels in South Vietnam since December,' Nixon told the US nation in his televised address. 'As the enemy force levels have declined and as the South Vietnamese have assumed more of the burden of battle, American casualties have declined.' Yes, the US was winding down its commitment, but Nixon denied it was losing the war. 'The enemy has failed to win the war in Vietnam because of three basic errors in their strategy. They thought they could win a military victory. They have failed to do so. They thought they could win politically in South Vietnam. They have failed to do so. They thought they could win politically in the United States. This proved to be their most fatal miscalculation.' Tell that to the many hundreds of thousands protesting at the Moratorium rallies and marches in the previous months; protests mirrored in Australia.

The west was losing its taste for war, but the killing would go on for a few years yet. Nixon even mentioned the war of terror, albeit by its weasel word—'pacification'. 'Progress in training and equipping South Vietnamese forces has substantially exceeded our original expectations last June. Very significant advances have also been made in pacification. Although we recognize that problems remain, these are encouraging trends.' A new buzzword entered the lexicon: Vietnamisation. It meant the Yanks were pulling out gradually and giving Vietnam back to the Vietnamese.

The South Vietnamese training program might have exceeded expectations, but Len and his Training Team colleagues remained in high demand. In his first week back he caught up with a host of old mates, acquaintances and the occasional adversary, as anyone able to convened at Australia House in Danang for Anzac Day. Leslie 'Ossie' Osborn (from Len's first section in Korea), Ernest 'Ossie' Ostara (nicknames must have been in short supply), Frank Moffitt and Tony Mogridge were among those assembled. Mogridge said the titles 'advisor' and 'head of training' were something of a misnomer. Like Len, Mogridge was senior advisor with a Vietnamese battalion. 'Well, you'd spend more time in the field than out of it,' Mogridge said when asked to paint a picture of Len's role in 1970. 'You'd fly into an area where you knew the enemy would be. Often what was called a hot LZ. Then we'd go out and search.' The patrols were typically 10–20 days long and there was contact virtually on a daily basis, ranging from sniping to 'fair dinkum full-scale battles with artillery support'. It was deadly work, Mogridge said. 'Especially for blokes six inches taller than the blokes you were with. Although Len was so skinny if he turned sideways they couldn't hit him.'

Len was about to spend a lot of time dodging bullets. And the battalion HQ was no safe harbour: a week before Len's arrival the enemy penetrated the perimeter. They were driven out after a shootout during which a GI threw a North Vietnamese Army (NVA) soldier into a shipping container, tossed in a live grenade, and locked the door.

Len could sniff out the enemy. In New Guinea and Borneo the Japanese smelt of sour rice. 'In Vietnam it was *nuk mam* [*nuoc mam*], that's fish sauce,' he said. 'You could always smell the NVA or VC from a distance. They could smell the Americans by their aftershave or their cigarette smoke or cigar smoke, which was even worse.'

As soon as he arrived back at Quang Tri after Anzac Day Len was ordered out on an operation. He went up in a tiny chopper for a quick recce before the patrol set off that night. 'About dawn the next day we were awakened by the sounds of a firefight on a ridge to our south and we felt sorry for the poor people being attacked. Wasted sympathy! Because next morning same time, it was our turn. It was the custom to send out one company ahead of us . . . to give early warning. But this time it didn't work because we came under attack around 0400. We were awakened by a massive explosion on our perimeter. I might mention that nobody dug in—everyone slept in hammocks. We were camped among a lot of felled tree stumps and the first thing I saw when I poked my head up was the CO doing likewise, so all I could think of to say was *Chau Tieu Ta* (Good morning Major). I think he replied likewise but by that time there was so much noise and confusion.'

It was a full-scale attack. A rocket-propelled grenade whizzed past Len's head and exploded behind him, setting his ears ringing. The enemy was hard to see in the early murk and under heavy cloud, so Len radioed for a flare-dropping chopper. Clearly the sun had risen at the chopper's base as the man on the end of the line said, 'Whaddya mean? It's broad daylight here!' It seems the man thought he was talking to some panic-stricken greenhorn. Len was unimpressed. 'Well it isn't here and I'll be requesting a Dustoff as soon as I can.' Len knew there would be many casualties.

After an hour of fighting the enemy disappeared into the jungle, killing five and wounding 28 of Len's unit. The Dustoff duly arrived and Len scuttled up to the chopper to ask how many wounded the pilot could take. 'Just keep loading them in and I'll let you know when to stop,' the pilot replied. The men started loading and after a while the pilot asked if there were any more. There weren't—he had taken all 28. 'The chopper took off and they tell me that back in Quang Tri it was like MASH,' Len said. Apparently the chopper crew was decorated for setting a new record for the most casualties evacuated in one lift. A few weeks later the same chopper was shot down after the commander volunteered to support a hard-pressed unit. Len sent out a rescue party to bring in the crew, including four wounded, and torch the unsalvageable helicopter.

Len's coolness under fire had been at the fore again but the shootout left him with lingering hearing problems. A day later he went to hospital because he was 'suffering from all those loud bangs'. He was soon back at his post. And he was soon back in the air, reprising his early Vietnam role spotting for bombers and ground-attack planes. On 3 May he acted as forward air controller for two air strikes. First came the helicopter gunships—aerial rocket artillery they were called—packing racks of up to 76 rockets each. When they were done, Len called in the Douglas A-4 Skyhawks to unleash their rockets, missiles and conventional bombs. US airpower seemed to rise in inverse proportion with Uncle Sam's fortunes in the war; Len also recorded strikes by F-4 Corsairs and A-37 Dragonflies—an aptly named jet (its pilots dubbed it the Super Tweet) with a Perspex bubble for a cockpit that resembled a dragonfly's bulbous eyes. The Dragonfly was equipped with a deadly arsenal that belied its maker Cessna's name; it was anything but a plodding, propeller-driven trainer. Its Gatling-type guns spat 3000 rounds a minute. Using the knowledge accumulated over almost 30 years, Len pinpointed the enemy positions then guided the planes in. When it was over, two bunkers lay in smoking ruin.

Len barely had time to draw breath. The next three weeks were a blur of patrols, firefights and chopper strikes. A typical day was a long slog through steamy jungle and a sharp fight ended by calling in the aerial artillery, followed by Dustoffs and hot extractions—airlifts under fire.

Len was usually the one calling for help; he described himself as 'the grandfather with a radio set'. Nights were wet and without comforts; Len slept on the ground while his Vietnamese comrades rigged up hammocks, seemingly blithely unconcerned about the danger. Sleep was a relative word; it was usually raining and always dangerous. Enemy sappers attacked Len's command post at 3 am on 17 May, killing six of his men and wounding 25. Most of the wounded were evacuated in one airlift after Len and the men used TNT captured from the sappers to blast a landing zone out of the jungle. Twenty-nine enemy corpses were counted, and Len recorded that, as well as the TNT, his men captured seven AK-47s and 50 rocket-propelled grenade rounds. Len called in aerial rocket artillery to cover their extraction, which was completed—under mortar fire—by noon.

The incessant fighting continued to take a toll on his ears. 'I am stone deaf after all the excitement,' he wrote. He sought further treatment in hospital where he saw a seriously wounded American being treated in a novel way. 'At one stage the doctor lifted a skin flap on his upper arm, packed a field dressing under the flap and bandaged the whole thing up. Every time the doctor asked [the wounded man's] companion anything, the reply was: "Classified!" So I imagine he was hit over in Laos.' Len had a series of hearing tests and eventually was told to stay out of the field for a month. Which was a fortunate coincidence, as about this time he was posted to Phuoc Tuy and another accursed acronym—a MATT unit. The Mobile Assistance Training Teams were small, new formations of Australian specialists charged with conducting training in the field. Len was appointed to command the largest, MATT 3, which would advise the 302nd Regional Force (RF) Battalion at its base in Baria. '[Opie] had earned a reputation for initiative and daring during his earlier tours in Vietnam, primarily in connection with PRUs and other CIA-sponsored activities,' the team's historian wrote. Len's reaction is intriguing. 'It must have been too much sun, but I accepted the job—if only I had the vision to see the future, it was with the 302 RF Battalion in Phuoc Tuy Province . . . one of my worst experiences.'

It was bad from the outset. The 302nd's commanding officer proved to be an elusive fellow and when Len finally tracked him down they immediately clashed. The team's historian, in an account clearly based on information supplied by Len, wrote of the CO, '[He] acted as though he was oblivious of the MATT and rarely gave it information or coop- eration. He lived in Baria with his wife and family, as his frequent and unannounced absences testified. Seldom did the commander keep appointments, and after attending conferences was reluctant to pass on information to Opie. Strongly entrenched in the province with influential friends (Len described it as having 'friends at court'), the commander easily resisted moves by the deputy senior adviser of the province to have him removed . . . When operating near Baria, the commanding officer normally absented himself from the battalion during the day, returning around last light.' This was not going to end well. Len claimed the CO tried to kill him. 'I was up in 7RAR's helicop- ter and I noticed the unit's 81 mm mortar being set up,' Len wrote in mid-June. 'Actually I had asked the pilot to take me around to check on some of the company locations, which I knew were not where the CO claimed they were, so he tried to shoot us down to discourage me, but as I said to the pilot: "He has never hit anything yet, so I wouldn't be too worried." Not so the pilot! He realised that he was out of flight time and had to leave—pronto!' The war in Vietnam had descended to this.

Len and the CO maintained a working relationship on a foundation of keeping out of each other's way. As it turned out the MATT teams spent more time in the field than at their bases, so it was easier for Len to avoid a CO who was seldom with the unit in any case. Len was in the thick of the action in what was a busy time. Consider a 20 June operation, when a patrol found and blew up a bunker, whereupon Len called in an air strike after seeing enemy soldiers nearby. While he was busy radioing details for the attack choppers, a mine exploded, killing five and wounding thirteen. He spent the next hour overseeing three Dustoffs and organising the extraction. On the way out his chopper was diverted to secure a beach. All very Robert Duvall, sans the surfing and the smell of napalm in the morning. One of the Hueys took enemy fire but Len made it back to base by nightfall, unscathed.

But eighteen casualties from one mine? Well, the M16 mine was a vicious beast—a jumping jack that exploded at waist height and was lethal at 25 metres and able to wound anyone within 200 metres. Worse than that, it was Australian-owned. It had been stolen from the largest open air ordnance depot in the world. Early in 1967 the Australians laid an 11-kilometre minefield from the Horseshoe fire base near Dat Do to the Phuoc Tuy coast. The trouble was they then left it unguarded. The enemy lifted thousands of mines and soon the M16s were killing and maiming more Australians than NVA and Vietcong bullets put together.

Three days later Len and his men swept an area of jungle after a firefight the previous night. No VC bodies were found, but there were blood trails. This was common in Vietnam, as Len explained. 'These were the results of enemy dragging their wounded or dead away after the contacts for two reasons—to enable the enemy to bury their dead or hand them back to their relations . . . To this end, before an action, VC/NVA would wind a length of rope around one leg so that, in the event of the person becoming a casualty he/she could be happy in the knowledge that their body would be retrieved for later burial.'

A patrol a few days later was uneventful, save for the unrelenting rain. Len had discarded his nondescript CIA-issue garb for jungle greens—described as a Tiger suit—and often the black pyjama-style clothes worn by the Vietcong. It was apt that the next operation was to Long Son, a large island populated by disciples of the Ong Tran religion who always wore black robes. Len liked to blend in where he could. On one operation he went ahead of the rest of the patrol, which duly filed past an old man sitting cross-legged under a paddy hat. It was Len, teaching them a lesson about concealment. 'If I'd have been a Vietcong you'd be dead,' he told them.

The local soldiers' indifference was a problem that was never really overcome. Len wrote of a cordon search in Dat Do that petered out because of 'poor coordination and a lack of interest'. And this, despite the presence of high-ranking observers keen to see the 302nd in action. Len recorded that the operation's results amounted to one Vietcong captured and one Vietcong woman killing herself with a grenade. An attempted ambush by another local unit ended with one soldier killed in action, two others wounded and an interpreter 'likely to lose a leg . . . an example of amateurs trying to do a professional's job', Len said. The team's historian wrote that the local troops conducted ambushes as if they were on a picnic. This casual attitude, combined with a lack of good officers and equipment shortages, 'appeared to set the MATTs an impossible task', McNeill wrote. In his monthly dispatch to head-quarters for September, Len reported one company was incapable of action. 'Discipline non-existent,' Len wrote, and the other companies were little better. Few of the officers were of any quality and the worst was 'lazy and a playboy'. Another 'fell off his Honda and has not been seen since'. He summed up by saying the 'battalion has not justified its existence'.

Back at AATTV headquarters, Major Ken Phillips wrote it was worth considering withdrawing Len and his team, given the 302nd Battalion was 'sun-baking on the beach'. Len himself wrote that 'parties on the beach are the order of the night . . . Vietnamisation as it applies to 302 Battalion is futile while the present command exists. The CO is the only person who is obeyed.' In one company there was a 'steady increase in drunkenness' and the only reason sentries remained at their posts was because Len checked on them each night. His predica-ment was noted in Canberra when, after reading an AATTV report, the Deputy Chief of the General Staff, Major General Stuart Graham, scribbled, 'When you feel you have a problem, you may derive some comfort from the plight of Captain Opie.'

If all this wasn't enough, distinguishing friend from foe was diffi-cult even within the battalion. Once when a grenade went off in the camp, Len marched in to investigate. 'Mr Tu threw a grenade at his friend because he is a Hoi Chanh,' the company commander explained.

(Hoi Chanh is the name given to a Vietcong persuaded to switch to the South's cause.) 'So?' said Len. 'Well, Mr Tu is a VC,' the company commander said. Mr Tu was arrested.

Len indulged his aerial fixation on a visit to the Horseshoe base in early August. Borrowing the local CO's possum helicopter (every Australian battalion commander in Vietnam was a Korean veteran, so most were well known to Len) for a sweep over the Long Hai mountains, he surprised a Vietnamese man doing his laundry—complete with a pair of black Vietcong pyjamas drying on a rock. 'Unfortunately I left in such a hurry that I did not have a weapon,' Len said. It was the man's lucky day.

In September a highly rated young captain arrived to serve under Len with a view to eventually replacing him as commander of MATT 3. John Hartley had served a tour as a platoon commander and had met Len at Canungra. The future major general recognised a warrior when he saw one. 'He was different and was very well worth listening to because he saw things from a slightly different perspective,' Hartley said. They became friends. 'I valued his judgement and I liked him personally. I suspect I was one of the few people who socialised with him. He wasn't influenced by social graces, wealth or rank. He was a very private man. If you were a friend it was fine, but it took a long time to get to know him.' Hartley said Len was a sensitive soul but often kept that side of his personality hidden under the tough-guy veneer. Almost as if he had to live up to the legend. Hartley also remembered how Len sometimes lacked tact. 'He could be quite openly critical of people. We had lots of idiots and he was quick to point them out.' Hartley cited two examples of Len's plain-speaking. On the day Hartley arrived, a senior soldier in Len's Vietnamese battalion accidentally shot himself in the head. Hartley asked if he should recall the chopper that had delivered him to the base. Len replied, 'Nah, let him go. The silly old fella only has himself to blame.' The soldier died, but Hartley said there was probably no saving him anyway. On another occasion Len remarked to Hartley that a Vietnamese radio operator nearby 'didn't know what he was talking about . . . he said it in English but the soldier would have known the meaning from his tone and arm gestures'. Despite incidents such as these, Hartley said Len, through his bravery, had won the respect of the Vietnamese troops. This was some achievement given the difficulties the role presented—commanding a rag-tag unit of part-time soldiers. 'By that time the Vietnamese army was being increasingly deployed in Cambodia and Laos,' Hartley said. So in order to keep the situation at home under control, the regional battalion was based around their own villages. 'It was quite a different structure. With it came new challenges. Part of the challenge was that you had to deal with a unit that was formed from sub-units that hadn't operated well in the past. Len was selected to head that. He was specially selected.'

Hartley told of how Len was not one to kowtow to his seniors. During an operation on the Long Hai Peninsula he had some fun with a colonel who arrived from headquarters to watch the show. Len led him away from the main body of troops sweeping the coastal road—captain and colonel would conduct a two-man advance along the beach. The staff officer objected, whereupon Len did a 'stocktake' of their weapons and 'came up with my M16 [rifle] plus a .45 pistol and a radio set . . . I did mention that Charlie could come out of the hills and grab us . . . which did not impress the colonel [who] envisaged an urgent need to be back in Baria'. Len pointed in the direction of the closest column of friendly soldiers and suggested the colonel meet up with them. 'As he was about to set off at a gallop, I pointed out some wreckage on the road and told him that it was the remnants of a French column that had been blown up years before, and that there just might be some unexploded ordnance along the path.' The colonel decided to stay with Len but 'took off' as soon as they were safely back with the main force. According to Len, when the colonel arrived at headquarters he told the Team's CO, 'That Opie is mad—he nearly got me killed!'

Len seemingly had a licence to roam wherever and whenever he liked. When not on operations with his Vietnamese battalion, he visited a host of villages, outposts and Cambodian refugee camps. He noted that the US army had resettled Cambodian farmers on the coast and the fishermen inland. In November a company of the battalion was posted to a former US camp at the Vietnamese refugee village Ap Suoi Nghe. Len went with them, and set about making himself comfortable. Rather than writing to his friends and family back home, he was in the habit of making audio tapes, and decided an old watchtower on the camp perimeter would do as a recording studio. Corporal Rob Thornton explains what happened next: 'He told me to burn out the rubbish pits behind his tower as it was stinking the place out. He said not to worry about the old ammo in the pit as he had checked it out, so I tipped in five gallons of diesel and got a nice blaze going. He came out to have a look and said "yes, that'll do", so we strolled back up the bund towards the tower. At that moment we were blown flat by a huge blast, and I cringed as burning jeep tyres, lumps of twisted metal and three years' worth of faeces landed on and around us. We stood up, both covered in Yank shit, and he just looked at me and said with a wry smile "did you do that on purpose?" I was too stunned to reply. Len had a very dry sense of humour, and he seemed almost impossible to rattle.'

Indeed he was, whether it be exploding latrine pits or other subterranean calamities. Arriving back from a patrol one day, Len came upon a commotion—two boys had fallen into a well. Worse than that, the buffalo they had been riding had fallen in as well. One boy appeared to be dead, crushed under the buffalo. The other was seriously injured. How to get them out? The district chief 'partly solved the problem by shooting the wretched animal', Len said, which was duly hoisted out of the well. The injured boy was lifted out—carefully, as both his legs were broken—leaving the rescuers to come back in the morning to retrieve the other boy's corpse. 'Using a bent stick and a rope I managed to drag the body to the surface and I was lowered down to recover him,' Len said. 'We put the lad's body in the back of the Landrover and headed back to the hamlet with dad sitting up front, until we reached the turnoff to the hamlet when dad called a stop. He retired to the back holding his son and began to wail and moan until we reached the centre of the hamlet where he handed the body to the family. After the ceremony I suggested we all go back to our compound for a cup of tea [where] the Vietnamese insisted that I shower before partaking. To keep the peace, I did go for a shower—to find when I came out that my black pyjamas and my bush hat were missing. On enquiring I learned that not only were my clothes missing but also the rope I had used to recover the body. They had all been taken back to the well and thrown in, apparently as a Vietnamese ritual. Well, the morning tea finally got under way, after I had found a new set of greens, but I must say, the atmosphere was somewhat fraught, especially as my only bush hat was gone.'

Rob Thornton served as a medic in MATT 3 but quickly learned Len expected more from him than training the RF troops in first aid. Soon after he arrived Len sent him on a RF patrol with a warning that 'if you lose any don't bother coming back'. Thornton didn't lose any that day, or on any of the countless patrols he led after that. 'Len Opie didn't care what corps you came from—in action you were expected to perform as a skilled Aussie infanteer first, no matter what you were trained in.'

Len eventually trusted Thornton to be his driver—a high honour indeed as Len was wary on the road and demanded his driver go no faster than 30 miles per hour; even when a sniper was taking pot shots at their jeep Len growled at Thornton to slow down. He also taught Thornton the lesson of making do with what you had. On one occasion when they were short of food, Thornton shot a couple of wild peacocks for a curry with sweet potatoes Len had picked from a minefield. 'I can't remember anything that tasted as good as that curry,' Thornton said.

After serving longer in Vietnam than almost any other Australian soldier, not to mention his previous wars, Len was a jungle fighter and leader of the highest order. But the closing pages of his diary show signs of a growing frustration with others' failings. The grumbles about fellow soldiers' skiving off or simply failing to meet the high expectations Len set for himself, and failures of command and organisation, are dotted through the diary. This might also partly explain why the diary entries tail off into shorter, staccato missives. The 18th of December was an exception and is reproduced here:

Up at 0600. At 0800 to PZ and see Major Phillips and C of S.
Same helicopter pilot that we had a JTC, now a Group Captain.
Take off at 0904, to Long Son Island by 0917.
1 Company and WO Lyddieth to LZ YS273583. Move south. Find and blow 1 by 81 mm mortar bomb rigged as a booby trap. 1 bunker sighted.
Call in helicopter to lift out equipment, one was a 25 lb HE shell.
1700 contact with 627 Company (our blocking force) with 6 VC.
1 Company withdrew to allow gunships to work over area.
5 VC (NVA?) sighted and gunships directed to new target.
Possible enemy base camp; search till last light. Eating utensils, 2 by 60 mm mortar bombs found. That night, nothing to report (NTR).

The Boxing Day entry was more typical.

0230 PRU engage 20 VC YS373615, result; one KIA, one by B40 and documents, pictures captured.

But that was an essay when compared with the record of his eight days of home leave in early December. As usual, he listed the plane type—Boeing 707—for the flight home and the fact he was again treated to a lovely steak (food is mentioned so often in the diary it is a wonder Len remained so thin throughout his life), but the pages are blank until the flight back the following week. In Len's diary, if not in his life, the war and home did not overlap. As his niece Jill Marton said, 'He was two different people.'

Len went home for good in April. The story of his final few months in Vietnam is dominated by one big fight. Hartley assumed command of MATT 3 the very day the 302nd's 1 Company went on a search-and-destroy mission in the Long Hais. It all started well enough, with the artillery softening up the enemy positions as planned. The troops boarded the APCs and made their way without incident to the drop-off point. Their mission was to climb a valley to seize a series of peaks, although no one was sure of the enemy's location or strength, as usual. Up they went, with Len, Hartley and other team members climbing with the troops. They soon came upon a large, recently vacated bunker, and twenty minutes later came under AK-47 and rocket-propelled grenade fire. The South Vietnamese returned fire with their M16s, M60 machine guns, rocket launchers and 60 millimetre mortars. Artillery was called in, 105 millimetre howitzers, and the exchange continued for the five or so hours until dark.

Bushranger gunships attacked in the morning and the advance resumed, and soon the company was on its first objective, which the Vietcong had abandoned without much of a fight. 'Small-arms fire continued all day and artillery was employed on the offending area,' Len wrote in his report of the action. Len wanted the local commander to show more verve and attack the enemy, but the action was unfolding as planned, albeit at a torpid pace. Calamity called in the morning.

Concerned by the slow going, Hartley boarded a chopper to head to the front line. Before he went he received an assurance there were no enemy troops on a timbered hill on a flank. As the helicopter eased to within 20 metres of touching down, all hell broke loose. Withering fire rained down from the supposedly unoccupied hill. Hartley was shot through the chest and the chopper's gunner was wounded. The pilot pulled his wounded bird up and out, setting down the stricken chopper 200 metres away. Hartley's command was finished, three days after taking over from Len. He was in hospital for eight months and had to learn to walk again. Bushrangers strafed the offending hill but the damage was done. The 302nd traded shots with its largely unseen enemy over the next three days before pulling out. When they did, seven men were killed or wounded by a mine when they carelessly ambled into a known minefield.

Len was livid, writing in his report, 'I feel that 1 Company of 302nd Battalion was badly led and misemployed during the whole of the operation.' Len had repeatedly urged the commander to attack the enemy. 'Not once during the operation [did he] commit his troops to engage the enemy in a mobile firefight nor attempt to close with and destroy the enemy, even at times when we were sure of their locations. Consequently it was not known what damage, if any, was effected upon the enemy.' Furthermore, camp defences at night were a 'farce', and 'haphazard shooting made any fire we returned ineffective'. The sorry affair was illustrated by how the local troops had little inclination or idea of how to fire their M72 rocket launchers—so Len and his MATT men did the firing for them. This, after months of training in using launchers. At the end of it all, the battalion had sustained sixteen casualties, including the two killed and five wounded by the mine. 'The Vietnamese show no anxiety to get their mine detectors repaired,' Len wrote. And with that he signed off. Len's last shot in anger was very likely from a M72 rocket launcher—a very different weapon to the .303 he lugged around New Guinea in 1943.

When his tour expired the next month, he was ready to go. 'I'd had it by that time. And the job I was doing wasn't the same as in '68. If I'd have stayed there with the same job in '68 I would have been happy to have stayed on for another couple of years. Things had changed there and I didn't really want to stay there. Vietnamisation wasn't working very well and the Americans . . . initially they were pretty gung ho but then they got into drugs and that sort of thing. The American officers were scared to go around the compounds because in each of the bunkers where the sentries were supposed to be, people were smoking [dope].'

After eight and a half years of battle, the warrior, now aged 47, was laid low. But he never stopped fighting.

CHAPTER 18

MAN OF SPARTA

'Nobody ever really wins a war.'
Len Opie

Len served another three years in the army. When he left, it was kicking and screaming. There was no room for ancient full-time CMF majors (he received his last promotion in December 1974) in the modern, downsized army of the Labor government, so Len was out. Len was so angry he hexed Gough Whitlam, who defied the curse to outlive Len. 'He was the quintessential combat soldier but difficult to place in the peacetime army, especially as an officer where broader managerial skills were called for,' Major General Peter Phillips said. In the end Len lasted longer than the Whitlam government; he was added to the retired list on his 52nd birthday—twelve days after Whitlam's dismissal. Len pined for the army the rest of his life. 'He seemed ill at ease out of combat dress,' Phillips said. Asked in 2004 if he found the transition to civilian life easy, Len replied, 'No, not really because the army's a home, you know. I go over every year for two days to Holsworthy [military camp]. It's like putting on an old coat, it's like being home again.' One of the things he missed most was the privileges of rank. 'I got sleepers on the train.'

Almost twenty years after he was shot in Vietnam, Major General Hartley received a letter. It was from Len, asking to be sent to Iran to sort out the latest conflict in the Middle East. That he was in his mid-sixties didn't bother Len one bit. 'I had to let him down very gently,' Hartley said. 'That was his life. The military was his background. He was interested in the history. He was interested in the operational side of it.' The plea was no one-off. Eighty-year-old Len wanted to take on the Russians. 'I'd like to go to another war,' he said in 2004. 'I'd fight the Russians. I offered to go to Afghanistan. I've been to Afghanistan when I was in Kashmir and I've dealt with the mujahideen and I've worked in snow up to 18,000 feet and I've been in two winters in Korea and a winter in Kashmir and I'm used to high altitudes and altitude sickness and all that.' Len even offered to pay his own way but General Peter Cosgrove didn't reply to his letter. Len suspected it was intercepted by an underling, especially when Cosgrove sent him a Christmas card that year. '[Instead] I got a reply from some colonel saying "we have access to all the expertise we require, thanks very much"', Len said. 'That was after I'd written to the prime minister and the minister for defence, the head of the army and everybody else. You know, I'm a dinosaur. They're not interested anymore. They don't want to hear anymore.' While he was at it he asked to be sent to Perth to train the SAS.

What riled him most was how some people in power seemed ignorant of the fundamentals of war. He was livid when a defence minister was quoted saying tanks protected infantry, when anyone with a basic working knowledge of tactics knew it was the other way around. He wrote letter after letter to the newspapers correcting mistakes and arguing against decisions such as when the army bought heavy US tanks—named after General Abrams—in the mid-2000s. Niece Lee Waye said he was 'terribly upset' about how the west waged the Iraq War. Asked if he would ever hang up his hat and forget about the army, he replied, 'Well I believe in the Patron Saint of Lost Causes, you know, you never give up.'

'He tolerated the other life—he wanted to go back again,' niece Jill Marton said. The 'other life' was working in a map shop in Pirie St, Adelaide. (He had closed the bookshop many years earlier. According to Andy Thomas, 'My father said that on principle he refused to sell "gentlemen's magazines", and that is why the business did not fare well.') The map shop seemed a good fit, but it didn't quite offer the same thrills as combat. 'I had trouble working with civilians,' Len said. 'They acted as if I was still in the army and I said "if I was still in the army you'd be running around a lot faster than you are". So I gave them the choice. If they didn't like it, they could leave.'

As was often the case with Len, even a beige job behind a map-shop counter came with an intriguing back story. One of his good friends and old comrades firmly believes it was a front for the CIA. The source was frisked by a man at the front door one day, until Len waved his mate in. Why would Len work for the CIA? Well, the answer forms even as the question is asked—because he wanted to stay involved. It sounds fantastic but as we have learned, anything was possible with Len. What a delicious thought; mild-mannered Len helping grey nomads find a map for their next road trip while the spooks do whatever spooks do out the back.

Vietnam veteran Bob Kearney chuckles quietly when he thinks of the great warrior helping little old women find the right map. 'I thought, if only they knew,' Kearney said. 'I always felt he killed more Chinamen than cholera.' Kearney said Len sat in an exalted place in South Australia's veterans' community in the years after the Vietnam War. The legend grew as the years passed. 'He had a presence about him,' Kearney said. 'I can't think of anything bad to say about Len except that he was a pretty harsh judge . . . he was a good judge of character. He had a good bullshit barometer, you know. He didn't drink and he didn't smoke and he didn't like swearing. [But] he fitted in with everyone. He was a soldier through and through. He would have made someone a very interesting grandfather.'

He certainly was an interesting godfather to Andy Thomas, albeit in absentia given Len was often away at war and Thomas was off being an astronaut. 'I would sometimes ask my father about him, and I would be told that he was in the military and stationed in some exotic place, such as the Middle East,' Thomas said.

And he certainly was an interesting uncle to Lee, Carolyn and Jill. After Len's parents and sisters died they and their families became his family. He spent Christmases with them and always gave the best presents. No diving under the table when the crackers popped either. 'I love the smell of napalm in the morning,' he would say, proving that you don't have to be a dad to crack dad jokes. Jill thought Uncle Len found civvy street quite challenging. 'He was accepted because he was the brave person he was,' Lee countered. 'He wasn't actually frightened of anything as I recall.' Jill added, 'That's because he didn't worry about dying.' Speaking of fear, Jill also said, 'I was scared of Uncle Len. I was scared of him to the day he died.'

Len spoke his mind to the end of his army days. At Canungra he sat through a long lecture about an earlier campaign, before standing—diary in hand—to growl at the lecturing officer, 'When are you going to tell the truth!' There are numerous stories about generals leaving politicians and VIPs to their canapés to make a beeline for Len. 'He could speak to two-, three-, four-star generals, maybe because he taught most of them,' Colonel Peter Byrne said. Kapyong veteran Reg Anock told a similar tale: 'When we were over at Puckapunyal there were brigadiers and generals and the next minute Len was over there talking to them like they were ordinary fellas.' Len was revered in official army channels but as the years passed inevitably there was someone who did not know his name. Such as the functionary who rejected his application for the Infantry Combat Badge, a medal that came close to what the diggers call the EBM—Every Bastards Medal. Any infantry soldier who served in 'warlike operations' could wear one. 'When Len applied for an Infantry Combat Badge many years ago his application was rejected though I can't recall the reason,' Barry Caligari said. 'When Len mentioned this interesting decision all hell broke loose up the command chain. He received personal apologies from the Chief of the General Staff . . . and the Military Secretary, Brigadier John Hartley.' How Hartley must have chuckled at his Vietnam comrade being rejected for a common service medal. Len kept the CGS's written apology. 'I cannot think of anyone more deserving and apologise for the administrative oversight which has obviously occurred.' Lieutenant General John Coates signed off by saying the medal was enclosed.

Len ended up with nineteen medals. 'There's not too many diggers that can claim nineteen medals . . . when Len's got all his medals on you've got a row from here to here,' Korean veteran Reg Anock said, stretching his arms as if describing the one that got away. The medals stretched off his chest into thin air, and when he chose to wear his ribbons he looked like a caricature of a US general.

'I don't know if I was a good soldier,' said Len, 'I only tried to be one. I used to say, when I was training people for Korea: "If you want to hate somebody, hate me." You know, you've got to focus your hate or desire on something so why not me, it doesn't worry me. And afterwards if you come back and say "well in spite of Opie I survived" then that's the thanks that I got. And I've never had anybody come after me from any of the wars I've been in looking for me, and I've known that to happen with some people.' His views on war resonate to this day. When asked in 2004 what, if anything, war proved, he said, 'Well, we're right and they're wrong and you hope that the other side will make more mistakes than you do. That's really what it amounts to. You don't win a war, you only lose a war. Nobody ever really wins a war.'

Len was a fixture on the Adelaide returned-service circuit for the rest of his life. He joined the RSL after World War II but resigned in a fit of pique after returning from Vietnam. He was upset at the RSL's lack of response to a graffiti attack on the National War Memorial on Adelaide's North Terrace. He also disliked one of the state presidents. But he rejoined in 2004. He once walked out of a service for Vietnam vets when those officiating refused to recite the Ode of Remembrance; their argument being the 'we that are left grow old' part did not apply to them as they would also die young, from alcoholism, Agent Orange exposure, or the effects of their post-traumatic stress. Len didn't believe in PTSD. Load of rot, he said. He was a regular, however, at Royal Australian Regiment functions and official battle commemorations, where he was a hallowed guest. He remained teetotal, but that didn't stop him telling some of the best stories as the banter flowed at the bar. 'At veterans' gatherings Len would just be one of the crowd, drinking his lemon squash,' Brigadier Laurie Lewis said. 'But it was always special to receive Len's nod of acknowledgement and be invited to join him. I will always remember his steely, light-blue eyes, which had a way of fixing you and letting you know he was evaluating what you were saying.'

'He was like a ghost,' Bob Kearney said. 'He's got those eyes that look straight through you.'

The army remained his chief interest but he kept making his models and playing with his trains. In 2004 he received an award on the occasion of his 60th year as a member of the National Model Railroad Association. He was a willing volunteer at the Army Museum of South Australia; his modelling skills can be seen in the museum's Gallipoli diorama. He read extensively—war histories mostly—and his unit in Mitcham, in Adelaide's inner south, and holiday houses on the south coast were full of books, maps, models and the occasional deadly weapon. He dabbled in other hobbies; an attempt at becoming a boatie was a bit of a fiasco—he soon learned he was a natural land lubber so he sold his boat. Before that, Ross Johnson and Gretta McDonough were invited down to Goolwa for a day on the water. 'He soon realised you couldn't just step on a boat,' Ross said. Gretta hated it: 'I was terrified.'

The last of Len's dogs, Sally, was a loving little ball of fluff who liked little better than warming a stranger's lap while Len regaled the visitor with war stories over weak cups of tea and a biscuit. When he died Len left money to the RSPCA, Animal Welfare League and the Guide Dogs. 'He was very affectionate as he got older,' Lee said. When his long-time companion in later life, Heather Woods, died, Len cried. 'Len could be emotional about things, he was sad. He was very sad this day. He was tearful.'

As we have heard, Don Beard said Len was his happiest in the Vietnam days 'unlike what he eventually became'. Beard is referring to how Len's annoyances grew into minor obsessions in later life. He set his own bar high and expected others to follow suit. When they inevitably did not, he became upset. Hence the letters to the editor, to the army, to the prime minister . . . 'As the years went on after Vietnam he became a bit critical, which was really not him,' Beard said. 'Towards the end he became a bit bitter about senior officers and about military decisions that were made that he thought were not good enough. He sort of felt that he wasn't being recognised adequately, although he was a wonderful soldier. He didn't want to be lauded, but he felt that he should have been recognised.' A 1984 letter to Special Minister of State Mick Young, is a good example of Len's growing bitterness. The new Labor government had brought in an Australian medals system and Len was furious. 'I am writing to express my disgust at the decision to abandon the British Honours and Awards,' Len thundered. 'For those who have never served in operations and been bound by the bonds of tradition, the depth of feeling engendered by this decision cannot be understated.' He also waged long paper wars with military bureaucrats who denied him medals to which he knew he was entitled. It was not about Len blowing his own trumpet—rather he merely sought justice.

His three wars had left their mark on Len physically. In 1995 he was acknowledged by the Veterans' Affairs Department as having the following disabilities: 'Osteoarthritis left knee and left hip; spondylosis; basal cell carcinoma of the right mid-back and all malignant neoplasia; solar keratoses; shrapnel wound under right eye; tinnitus with resultant nervous condition; hiatus hernia with reflux oesophagitis; conjunctivitis; migraine; sensorineural deafness [and] frostbitten toes.' Yes, the Korean cold was still biting, more than 40 years after the war. A grateful nation looked after their old warrior well—treatment for any of the above was covered by the department. Surgery and radiation treatment for prostate cancer was apparently successful but he was in pain a lot of the time. He would show up unannounced at former Training Team doctor Peter Byrne's consulting rooms and would arrange for a cup of tea to be made while he waited. 'He had multiple medical problems but never told anyone about them,' Byrne said.

In 2008 Beard and Len came across each other at a Government House function. Beard said he looked washed out; anaemic. It was leukaemia. About this time he told the author he needed a hand with his memoirs as he was 'on the way out'. He said it casually, without emotion. Lee was there when the doctor gave him the news. 'He was very brave when he was crook,' Lee said. 'I sat there and the doctor explained and Len sat there and asked relative questions such as "how long?", and that was it.' One of his last social outings was Gretta McDonough's 90th birthday. He was clearly in great pain, but soldiered on without complaint. 'He looked awful,' Ross Johnson said. 'It was terrible. I felt bad because eventually he took a cab home.'

He was very ill indeed when he accepted the army's invitation to farewell the Afghanistan-bound 7RAR in Darwin. He and team comrade George Mansford formally and informally addressed the departing troops. 'It was a memorable visit to see yet another young generation of the regiment preparing for war,' Mansford said. 'We stayed with the battalion for what was to be a very demanding 48 hours. Clearly age was showing but Len was very much in his element and he never faltered. I recall his address on soldiering. His theme was all about duty regardless of the consequences and that death was part of the game. He certainly made an impact on the young warriors.' Don't take Mansford's word for it. 'His visit made a huge impact on the team prior to deploying into what was a new mission,' 7RAR's Commanding Officer Lieutenant-Colonel David McCammon said.

Len Opie died in Adelaide on 22 September 2008, aged 84. The troops in Afghanistan immediately named a post for him. 'I have no doubt that such a grand old warrior could not have asked for a better final phase of life than to be with yet another generation of warriors preparing for war,' Mansford said. 'It was certainly a very fitting end for one of Australia's best.' The soldiers sent Mansford photos of the post, showing how it was scarred with shrapnel. 'Even in death he still stands beside a new generation of Australian soldiers confronting the enemy. Len Opie would have liked that.'

Carolyn said he 'never boasted about war . . . it wasn't until his funeral that I realised'. Jill only realised Uncle Len was a war hero when she visited the Australian War Memorial. 'He was everywhere.' They were thrilled that a wing of an RSL aged-care home was named in his honour. The man himself would have been just as thrilled when the National Model Railroad Association struck an award in his name. In 2013 the Army Museum of South Australia—where Len was a volunteer— opened a permanent Len Opie exhibit focusing on the Korean War. 'Shortly before his death he said in an almost self-deprecating way that his military service was a hobby, not a business,' Colonel Bill Denny told the exhibit opening. 'Well, all I can say is, some hobby. And indeed, some man.'

Len would have liked his funeral. It had all the trimmings: gun carriage, riderless horse, rifle volley . . . the lot. There was more brass and ribbon at Adelaide's Centennial Park that day than even Len could have imagined. Keith Payne VC said Len was a 'warrior soldier', but also a gentleman and a quiet achiever. Brigadier Laurie Lewis gave the eulogy: 'Len Opie was a man of Sparta. It irks me when I read or see in the media some of our leading sportspersons and others referred to as heroes. Len put his life on the line on more than one occasion for his mates and his country. Len Opie was a true hero.' Lewis said Len's philosophy as a true infantry soldier was to 'close with and kill' the enemy. 'He was a wonderful man and a gallant soldier. I know, with a great certainty, that Len Opie will never be forgotten by his mates.'

'The biggest wreath of all was from the troops in Afghanistan,' Lee said. And so to the next generation of soldiers. A service was held in Tarin Kowt and 3RAR sent a 'message from the troops' to Len's kith and kin: 'Major Opie is an example and inspiration to us all. [His] actions and deeds make us not only proud of what he has done, but also help us to hold our heads high with pride as we try to live up to his example, as we attempt to follow his footsteps. Major Opie will be sorely missed now he has moved on from our extended family. Our thoughts are with you all on this day. May He Rest In Eternal Peace.'

LEN OPIE'S MEDALS

The full set, as listed and displayed at the Army Museum of South Australia, is:

DCM, 1939–45 Star
Pacific Star, War Medal 1939–45
Australian Service Medal
Australian Active Service Medal 1945–75 (Clasp Korea, Vietnam)
Korea Medal
United Nations Service Medal (Clasp Korea)
Vietnam Medal, Australian Service Medal (Clasp Kashmir, South-West Pacific)
Reserve Force Decoration
National Medal (Clasp Further Service)
Australian Defence Medal, Efficiency Decoration (Clasp Australia)
Vietnam People's Medal (Clasp 1960)
United Nations Medal (Ribbon India and Pakistan)
Netherlands Cross
USA Bronze Star
USA Air Medal
Republic of Vietnam Gallantry Medal, with Palm.

On his right breast he wore three unit citations:

US Presidential Citation, Korea
US Meritorious Unit Commendation, Vietnam
Cross of Gallantry with Palm Unit Commendation, Vietnam.

ACKNOWLEDGEMENTS

P.G. Wodehouse disliked acknowledging individuals without whom 'this book would never have been written'. He considered such acknowledgements 'weak-minded'. Well in this case the cliché is true in the most literal sense. For the book is formed around Len's diaries, faithfully and painstakingly transcribed by his comrade-at-arms, Vic Pennington. Vic also cast his net wide to drag in accounts from fellow Australian Army Training Team Vietnam veterans. I owe so much to so many people but the chief debt, after Vic, lies with Len himself, who asked me to help get his memoirs published and/or write his biography. He died before we could map out our path, which seemed to be the end of the matter. Which is where we come to another outstanding debt; Peter Brune, in his usual no-nonsense way, said I owed it to Len to write his biography, so here we are.

The Army Museum of South Australia's Paul Longstaff gave me his time even when swamped with myriad unpaid research projects. To everyone at the museum: my most sincere thanks.

The ex-service community is bonded by strong links and the network whirred into action whenever I needed help. There are too many to list here but Rod Graham, Steve Larkins, Robert Kearney, Moose Dunlop, Chris Roe, Peter Lloyd, Peter Lutley, Laurie Lewis, Mick Mummery, John Hartley, Peter Phillips, Jim Hughes, Barry Caligari and Peter Scott were all kind and generous. I am also grateful to all the diggers who gave their time so willingly. Their contributions are themselves a tribute to Len. They are listed in the bibliography.

When I issued a desperate call for help with a map of the Hill 614 stunt, Fred Fairhead not only gave me a scratch lesson on field map reading—teaching me that the 'law for the use of topographical maps in warlike circumstances states the operational objective is at the centre of where four maps are joined'—he drew the map that appears in Chapter 6 of this book. The other maps are the work of the redoubtable— and might I venture, peerless—Keith Mitchell, who, as he did with *Arthur Blackburn, VC*, prepared excellent maps in double-quick time.

Lee Waye, Carolyn Harry and Jill Marton have been generous with their time and in imparting expansive anecdotes of their uncle.

When narrative problems were encountered, they were usually no match for the formidable Saturday morning coffee crew of authors and scholars Nigel Starck, Alan Brissenden, Peter Morton and Bernard Whimpress.

I am deeply grateful to my editors at Allen & Unwin, Rebecca Kaiser, Angela Handley, Foong Ling Kong and Chris Kunz. Thank you for your professionalism, support, flexibility—and most of all your patience. Melanie Reid has also demonstrated remarkable patience, even more than all of you who have wondered when the Len anecdotes would finally come together in a book.

NOTES

Chapter 1   A warrior in training

Len's childhood details are sourced from interviews with his nieces Lee Waye, Carolyn Harry and Jill Marton, childhood friend Jack Cox, and Andy Thomas, son of schoolfriend Adrian.

The rabbit anecdote was told to the author during an interview for *The Australian*.

'Len, he used to be keen.'—Merv Fox in an interview with the author.

The story of Kingsbury and his highly decorated section can be read in Russell, *The Second Fourteenth Battalion*.

For more about Honner, see Brune, *Ralph Honner*.

MacArthur's strategy and plan can be found in Long, *The Six Years War*, and from Dexter, *Australia in the War of 1939–45*, Vol. VI, *The New Guinea Offensives* (the official history).

Details of the plane crash, including the inquiry, can be found in the 2/33rd Battalion's unit diary, AWM52.

Chapter 2   Up the Ramu

The Lae campaign is detailed in Dexter, *Australia in the War of 1939–45*, as is the action at Kaiapit and the drive up the Markham/Ramu valleys.

The action in which Honner, the 2/14th CO, was wounded is detailed in Brune, *Ralph Honner*.

Details of the 2/14th's advance up the Markham/Ramu are taken from Russell, *The Second Fourteenth Battalion* and Uren, *A Thousand Men at War*.

The Pallier's Hill fight is mostly sourced from Russell, *The Second Fourteenth Battalion*.

Chapter 3   Balikpapan

The Balikpapan strategy is addressed in great detail in Dexter, *Australia in the War of 1939–45*, and in Long, *The Six Years War*.

The men's confidence in their supporting firepower from all three arms of the military is a common thread of the 2/14th, 2/16th and 2/10th unit histories.

The 'ruined oil refinery' remark appears in several sources, including Feuer, *Australian Commandos*, where it is attributed to a Colonel Courtney, probably the 2/5th Field Regiment's William Courtney.

Len's grief at Clark's death resurfaced more than 50 years later, when Roger Burzacott—whose father Louis was killed at Balikpapan—showed Len a photo of Clark's grave.

Details of the advance to Manggar are taken from the 2/14th Battalion unit diary, AWM52, and Russell, *The Second Fourteenth Battalion*.

The account of the soldier 'correspondent', Sergeant Lawrie, is published in Russell, *The Second Fourteenth Battalion*.

Laurie Lewis was interviewed by the author.

Chapter 4   Korea

For the Korean War volunteers' motivation to enlist, see Gallaway, *The Last Call of the Bugle*.

Allan Bennett was interviewed by the author.

'Some told lies about their experience in the infantry.'—Jack Gallaway in an interview with the author.

For the origins and early stages of the war, see O'Neill, *Australia in the Korean War 1950–53*, Vol. II, *Combat Operations* (the official history).

Charlie Green's remarkable life is recorded in a biography written by his widow, Olwyn, from where the account of how the battalion's new commander shaped the unit is taken: Green, *The Name's Still Charlie*.

Gwyther's 'lust for killing' remark is taken from a *Sunday Mail* article, 29 August 1953.

Wilson's *Age* interview is sourced from Forbes, *The Korean War*.

The C119 accident is described in Gallaway, *The Last Call of the Bugle*.

Forbes said the fine was five pounds, while Gallaway said they were 'heavily fined': Forbes, *The Korean War*; Gallaway, *The Last Call of the Bugle*.

MacArthur's assurances to Truman that the Chinese would not intervene were made at their meeting at Wake Island in October 1950, which has been recorded by the Miller Center, University of Virginia—'Harry S. Truman: Foreign Affairs', <http://miller-center.org/president/biography/truman-foreign-affairs>.

'Russkis, Russkis!' is sourced from Bartlett, *With the Australians in Korea*.

Gwyther's account of the tank action is taken from the *Sunday Mail* interview.

'All the fighting had to be done with infantry weapons . . . ' is included in Bartlett, *With the Australians in Korea*.

Harris's quote is from his memoir, *Only One River to Cross*.

Gordon's dispatch is included in Dapin (ed.), *The Penguin Book of Australian War Writing*.

'Give us a smoke will you?' is included in Harris, *Only One River to Cross*.

'Remember Len Opie?' is included in Green, *The Name's Still Charlie*.

'As big as a block of flats' is sourced from Green, *The Name's Still Charlie*, and resembled the 'taxation building' is attributed to Pte Geoff Butler in Bartlett, *With the Australians in Korea*.

' . . . pop a bullet out in a flash'—Reg Bandy in an interview with the author.

'After that they can send them by the divisions . . . ' is quoted by multiple sources, including in Gallaway, *The Last Call of the Bugle*.

Croll's remarkable story is told by O'Neill, *Australia in the Korean War 1950–53*.

Gallaway's version of the foxhole encounter was told to the author.

'Well we've made it Arch' is published in Green, *The Name's Still Charlie*.

Chapter 5 The Third World War has started

Laurie Lewis was interviewed by the author.

The strategic picture at the time of the Chinese intervention can be read in O'Neill, *Australia in the Korean War 1950–53*, Hastings, *The Korean War*, and Gallaway, *The Last Call of the Bugle*.

'The Third World War has started!' is from Coad's 'The Land Campaign in Korea', and included in Bartlett, *With the Australians in Korea*.

The 'theorist' was 11 Platoon's Roy Musgrave—Gallaway, *The Last Call of the Bugle*.

'It was an all-Australian day'—Ferguson quoted in Bartlett, *With the Australians in Korea*.

Gallaway's account of Walsh's removal is included in *The Last Call of the Bugle*. He expanded upon it in an interview with the author.

'When we came to put a section together . . .'—O'Dowd in Bartlett, *With the Australians in Korea*.

'Look at me, I'm a white man.'—Reg Anock in an interview with the author.

'Fancy getting a photo with a black bastard like you?'—Reg Bandy in an interview with the author.

'2 MILLION' is sourced from Hastings, *The Korean War*.

'He was a breath of fresh air . . .'—Colonel John Michaelis quoted in Hastings, *The Korean War*.

Donald Beard was interviewed by the author.

Chapter 6 Hills are for heroes

Saunders made the remark after watching the attack with his troops, including Allan Bennett, who told the author, as did Reg Bandy.

Ridgway's 'crumbling' strategy is described in Gallaway, *The Last Call of the Bugle*.

'It was like fighting the Nips in the islands.'—Hughes quoted in Bartlett, *With the Australians in Korea*.

Robertson's quotes are from Andrew Rule's *Sydney Morning Herald* article, 6 April 2004.

Robertson's photo is in the Len Opie collection, Army Museum of South Australia.

Hughes' quotes were published in *The Advertiser*, 2 March 1951.

Gallaway was interviewed by the author.

Bandy was interviewed by the author.

Muggleton was interviewed by the author.

Brown's assessment is from his book, *Stalemate in Korea*.

'If that man doesn't get a high medal . . .'—Peter Byrne in an interview with the author.

' . . . belting the enemy, accepting a few drop shorts in the process . . .'—O'Dowd quoted in Gallaway, *The Last Call of the Bugle*.

Chapter 7 Kapyong

Allan Bennett was interviewed by the author.

Further details of the Kapyong battle are sourced from Breen, *The Battle of Kapyong*, O'Neill, *Australia in the Korean War 1950–53*, Bartlett, *With the Australians in Korea*, and Gallaway, *The Last Call of the Bugle*.

'We don't know whatever happened to that beer . . .'—Donald Beard in an interview with the author.

'I had heard it before . . .'—Saunders quoted in Bartlett, *With the Australians in Korea*.

' . . . old men, women, children . . . '—O'Dowd, Australians at War interview, <www. australiansatwarfilmarchive.gov.au>.

' . . . those who did not were shot'—Sergeant From paraphrased in Gallaway, *The Last Call of the Bugle*.

Gallaway's letter to Len is from the Len Opie collection, Army Museum of South Australia.

' . . . little probing movements . . .'—O'Dowd, Australians at War interview.

'It ended up in a lot of hand-to-hand fighting . . . '—Reg Bandy in an interview with the author.

' . . . sharp, neat action' is Gallaway's description of the fight in *The Last Call of the Bugle*.

'They were greatly outnumbered . . .'—O'Dowd, Australians at War interview.

Harris's quote is published in Gallaway, *The Last Call of the Bugle*.

'Certainly some who did would have survived . . . '—O'Dowd quoted in Gallaway, *The Last Call of the Bugle*.

' . . . putting dressings on, stopping bleeding . . . '—Beard, Australians at War interview, <www.australiansatwarfilmarchive.gov.au>.

' . . . which highly amazed the Australians and helped relieve the tension.'—Salvation Army Major Edwin Robertson quoted in Bartlett, *With the Australians in Korea*.

Richardson's article was published in *The Argus*, 11 October 1954.

' . . . like apples off the end of a branch.'—O'Dowd, Australians at War interview.

'Smith's pit "bore the brunt of each enemy attack" . . . '— O'Neill, *Australia in the Korean War 1950–53*.

O'Dowd's response to Laughlin's prisoners is from his book, *In Valiant Company*.

'Don Company got it all day . . .'—O'Dowd, Australians at War interview.

'His fingers were all burned off . . .'—Dunque quoted in Breen, *The Battle of Kapyong*.

'I immediately called control . . . '—Hatfield quoted in Gallaway, *The Last Call of the Bugle*.

' . . . the most determined we had experienced . . .'—Gravener quoted in Bartlett, *With the Australians in Korea*.

'The last platoon out was, of course, 11 Platoon . . . '—Gravener quoted in Gallaway, *The Last Call of the Bugle*.

'The Chinese followed immediately of course . . . '—O'Dowd, Australians at War interview.

' . . . I imagine there were 600 others like me . . . ' Saunders quoted in Bartlett, *With the Australians in Korea*.

'I feel bloody awful skipper . . .'—unnamed soldier quoted in Gallaway, *The Last Call of the Bugle*.

'They had, without artillery support . . .'—O'Dowd, Australians at War interview.

'The critical judgement, which enabled 3RAR to win at Kapyong . . .'—Gallaway, letter, the Army Museum of South Australia collection.

Chapter 8   Kill or be killed

'Len Opie was a cold-eyed killer . . .'—Morrison's assessment was told to Lewis.

'We look up a map . . .'—Reg Bandy in an interview with the author.

'Our only casualties were two men killed on mines . . .'—3RAR unit diary, AWM85.

Chapter 9   Maryang San

Hassett's quote is published in Bartlett, *With the Australians in Korea*, and confirmed by Hassett on <koreawaronline.com>.

Further details of the battle are sourced from Breen (ed.), *The Battle of Maryang San*, and from O'Neill, *Australia in the Korean War 1950–53*, and Bartlett, *With the Australians in Korea*.

' . . . a new forward UN defence line . . .'— Bartlett, *With the Australians in Korea*.

'You won't get it . . .'—unnamed US Battalion commanding officer in O'Neill, *Australia in the Korean War 1950–53*.

'Run the ridges . . .'—Hassett in O'Neill, *Australia in the Korean War 1950–53*.

'We'd move forward and go so far . . .'—Shelton, Australians at War interview, <www.australiansatwarfilmarchive.gov.au>.

'The big rotation.'—Hughes in an interview with the author.

'We started at four in the morning . . .'—Langdon in an interview with the author.

'I am lost sir, I don't know where I am . . .'—Nicholls quoted in Breen, *The Battle of Maryang San*.

'Not very happily we set off . . .'—Young quoted in Bartlett, *With the Australians in Korea*.

'They opened up and it was on.'—Langdon interviewed by the author.

'OK, we're short of stretcher bearers . . .'—Johnson in an interview with the author.

'Upwards and onwards went Leary's men . . .'—Richardson's article appeared in *The Argus*, 12 October 1954.

'Smack in the guts.'—Young quoted in Bartlett, *With the Australians in Korea*.

'A Chinese company ceased to exist.'—Keys in <koreanwaronline.com>.

'Running along the top, shooting down into the trenches . . .'—Hassett quoted in Breen, *The Battle of Maryang San*.

'Company strength was now less than 50 . . .'—Len Opie quoted in Breen, *The Battle of Maryang San*.

'Each platoon had a backbone of people who had served in World War II.'—Hughes in an interview with the author.

'In Korea, no Victoria Crosses were given to Australians.'—Keith Langdon in an interview with the author.

'There are a number of reasons why Maryang San was so successful . . . '—Hassett in
<koreanwaronline.com>.

' . . . a post-World War II classic.'—Coates in Breen, *The Battle of Maryang San.*

Chapter 10 Private, temporary corporal . . .

'WO On Apathy Over Korea.'—*The Advertiser*, 31 October 1951.

The Barrier Miner, 2 November 1951.

The News, 30 October 1951.

Chapter 11 Eyes like a cat and no nerves at all

'Meeting Len Opie . . . '—*The Courier-Mail*, 10 February 1953.

'Out you get Jim . . . '—Jim Hughes in an interview with the author.

'A "terrific bloke" who would "go out on patrols on his own" . . . '—Keith Langdon in an
interview with the author.

'His reason for going out by himself . . . '—Mick Mummery in an interview with the author.

' . . . had a reputation for being very effective after dark.'—Peter Byrne in an interview
with the author.

'He was different and was very well worth listening to . . . '—John Hartley in an interview
with the author.

'You'd talk to Len about his one man patrols in Korea . . . '—Tony Mogridge in an interview with the author.

'Two sergeant-majors'—Brown, *Stalemate in Korea.*

'Troops Found Korean Service Was Boring.'—*The Sydney Morning Herald*, 21 July
1953.

'Troops bored by Korean War inactivity.'—*The Advertiser*, 21 July 1953.

Chapter 12 Belles and bullies

'I didn't worry about girls . . . '—Len Opie, Australians at War Film Archive.

Lee Waye, Carolyn Harry and Jill Marton were interviewed by the author.

Ross Johnson and Gretta McDonough were interviewed by the author.

'When Ellie saw Len's car drive in our back driveway, she raced out our front door and
drove herself off.'—Anne Johnson in an email to the author.

'We asked why he went to so many wars . . . '—Brian Kilford in an interview with the
author.

'He rarely raised his voice . . . '—Rob Thornton in an email to the author (via Vic
Pennington).

'It is with much regret that . . . '—from the Len Opie collection, Army Museum of South
Australia.

Chapter 13 Vietnam

'The Vietcong were thoroughly on top . . . '—Jackson quoted in MacNeill, *The Team.*

'There was constant emphasis on fitness . . . '—Mike Wells in an email to the author (via
Vic Pennington).

'The pilot would set the coordinates . . . '—Bob Guest quoted in Len's diaries.

'The National Police Field Force's role was to "maintain control throughout areas cleared by the regular forces" . . . '; 'a picturesque town . . . '; 'wise to carry a carbine . . . '—MacNeill, *The Team*.

Laurie Lewis included the 'salty' story in his eulogy for Len. He and Mick Mummery also told the story to the author.

' . . . brash, abrasive, statistics-crazy . . . '—William Colby quoted in a *Guardian* obituary for Komer, 14 April 2000.

Chapter 14   On the trail

Payne quoted in *The Advertiser*, 3 October 2008.

' . . . a supersonic Phantom was not much use against a Vietcong soldier on a bicycle in the jungle'—Hans Roser in Ham, *Vietnam*.

'Len was sent to organise them . . . '—Donald Beard in an interview with the author.

'The Vietnamese—north and south—have no time for the Montagnards at all . . . '—Patrick Beale in an interview with the author.

Chapter 15   'Sneaky work'

For further reading on Phoenix, see the CIA's Centre for the Study of Intelligence <https://cia.gov/library/center-for-the-study-of-intelligence/csi-publications/csi-studies/studies/vol51no2/a-retrospective-on-counterinsurgency-operations.html>, this paper from the RAND Corporation <www.rand.org/content/dam/rand/pubs/occasional_papers/2009/RAND_OP258.pdf>, and the website of former CIA agent Ralph McGehee <http://serendipity.li/cia/operation_phoenix.htm>. MacNeill, *The Team*, and Ham, *Vietnam*, also summarise Phoenix as it related to the Australian experience in Vietnam.

'I was well aware of it.'—Patrick Beale in an interview with the author.

'The sea was only 50 metres away on a great stretch of beach . . . '—Rob Thornton in an email (via Vic Pennington).

'Captain Opie reduced the length of training . . . '—US recommendation for Len's Bronze Star from the Opie collection, the Army Museum of South Australia.

'At that stage he was a very happy man . . . '—Donald Beard in an interview with the author.

Chapter 16   Kashmir interlude

Hartley's quote comes from an interview with the author.

'Observers had to be fit and tough.'—<www.awm.gov.au/exhibitions/peacekeeping/observers/kashmir.asp>

Chapter 17   Return to Vietnam

'He's been in the army for 107 years . . . '—Mick Mummery in an interview with the author.

'I would describe it as quiet leadership.'—Ivor Alexander in an interview with the author.

The Nixon speech can be read at <www.presidency.ucsb.edu/ws/?pid=2476>.

'Well you'd spend more time in the field than out of it.'—Tony Mogridge in an interview with the author.

For more about the mine debacle, see Lockhart, *The Minefield*.

'... sun-baking on the beach'—from AATTV monthly reports, AWM95.

'When you feel you have a problem, you may derive some comfort from the plight of Captain Opie.'—, MacNeill, *The Team*.

'Mr Tu threw a grenade ...'—from AATTV monthly reports, AWM95.

'He was different and was very well worth listening to ...'—John Hartley in an interview with the author.

'He told me to burn out the rubbish pits behind his tower ...'—Rob Thornton in an email (via Vic Pennington).

Chapter 18 Man of Sparta

'He was the quintessential combat soldier but difficult to place in the peace-time army ...' —Phillips in an interview with the author.

'I had to let him down very gently.'—John Hartley in an interview with the author.

'My father said that on principle he refused to sell "gentlemen's magazines" ...'—Andy Thomas in an email to the author.

'I always felt he killed more Chinamen than cholera.'—Bob Kearney in an interview with the author.

'When are you going to tell the truth!'—Reg Bandy in an interview with the author.

'He could speak to two-, three-, four-star generals, maybe because he taught most of them.'—Peter Byrne in an interview with the author.

'When we were over at Puckapunyal there were brigadiers and generals and the next minute ...'—Reg Anock in an interview with the author.

'When Len applied for an Infantry Combat Badge many years ago his application was rejected though I can't recall the reason ...'—Caligari email to the author.

'I cannot think of anyone more deserving and apologise for the administrative oversight which has obviously occurred.'—Coates letter from the Opie collection, Army Museum of South Australia.

'At veterans' gatherings Len would just be one of the crowd ...'—extract from Laurie Lewis's Len Opie eulogy.

'He soon realised you couldn't just step on a boat.'—Ross Johnson and Gretta McDonough in an interview with the author.

'I am writing to express my disgust at the decision to abandon the British Honours and Awards.'—letter from Len Opie, the Opie collection, Army Museum of South Australia.

'Osteoarthritis left knee and left hip; spondylosis; basal cell carcinoma of the right mid-back and all malignant neoplasia ...'—from the Opie collection, Army Museum of South Australia.

'He had multiple medical problems but never told anyone about them.'—Peter Byrne in an interview with the author.

'It was a memorable visit to see yet another young generation of the regiment preparing for war.'—George Mansford in an email to the author.

BIBLIOGRAPHY

This book is primarily based on Len Opie's diaries, as faithfully transcribed by Vic Pennington. The other main sources are Len's interviews for the Australians at War Film Archive, his interview with Colonel David Chinn, and interviews conducted by the author.

Primary sources
AWM52 (2/14 Battalion unit diary)
AWM52 (2/33 Battalion unit diary, including court of inquiry into Port Moresby plane crash disaster)
AWM85 (3RAR Korean War unit diaries)
AWM95 (AATTV monthly reports)
AWM honours and awards
Len Opie collection, Army Museum of South Australia
Len Opie's diaries (unpublished family collection, as transcribed by Vic Pennington)

INTERVIEWS
The Australians at War Film Archive, interview with Len Opie, 23 January 2004, Department of Veterans' Affairs (www.australiansatwarfilmarchive.gov.au/aawfa/interviews/998.aspx)— Donald Beard, Jack Gallaway, Jim Hughes, Tom Muggleton, Ben O'Dowd and Jeffrey 'Jim' Shelton interviews are from the same series
William Colby interview, 1981, <http://openvault.wgbh.org/catalog/vietnam-4e3224-interview-with-william-egan-colby-1981>
Len Opie interview by Colonel David Chinn MBE (Rtd) on 24 August 2001—AWM S02654
Brigadier Jeffrey 'Jim' Shelton (officer commanding A Company 3RAR 1951–1952) interview by Colonel David Chinn MBE (Rtd) on 22 June 2001—AWM S02291

INTERVIEWS BY THE AUTHOR
Ivor Alexander
Reg Anock
Reg Bandy
Patrick Beale

Donald Beard
Allan Bennett
John Bennett
Roger Burzacott
Peter Byrne
Jack Cox
Merv Fox
Jack Gallaway
Carolyn Harry
John Hartley
Jim Hughes
Jim Johnson
Ross Johnson
Bob Kearney
Brian Kilford
Keith Langdon
Laurie Lewis
Gretta McDonough
Michael McDonough
Jill Marton
Tony Mogridge
Tom Muggleton
Mick Mummery
Len Opie
Peter Phillips
Hartley Symons
Andy Thomas
Lee Waye

CORRESPONDENCE WITH THE AUTHOR

Barry Caligari
Anne Johnson
George Mansford
David McCammon
Wolf Seith
Andy Thomas
Rob Thornton (via Vic Pennington)
Mike Wells (via Vic Pennington)

Secondary sources

BOOKS

Ahern, Thomas L., *Vietnam Declassified: The CIA and counterinsurgency*, Lexington: University of Kentucky, 2009

Allchin, Frank, *Purple and Blue: The history of the 2/10th Battalion, AIF*, Adelaide: 10th Battalion AIF Association 1958

Bartlett, Norman (ed.), *With the Australians in Korea*, Canberra: Australian War Memorial, 1954

Breen, Bob (ed.), *The Battle of Kapyong: 3rd Battalion, the Royal Australian Regiment, Korea 23–24 April 1951*, Sydney: Headquarters Training Command, 1992

—— (ed.), *The Battle of Maryang San: 3rd Battalion, the Royal Australian Regiment, Korea 2–8 October 1951*, Sydney: Headquarters Training Command, 1994

Brown, Colin H., *Stalemate in Korea: And how we coped, 1952–1953*, Sydney: Australian Military History Publications, 1997

Brune, Peter, *Ralph Honner: Kokoda hero*, Sydney: Allen & Unwin, 2007

Currey, Cecil B., *Edward Lansdale: The unquiet American*, Boston: Houghton Mifflin, 1988

Dapin, Mark (ed.), *The Penguin Book of Australian War Writing*, Melbourne: Penguin, 2011

Davies, Bruce, and McKay, Gary, *The Men Who Persevered*, Sydney: Allen & Unwin, 2005

Dexter, David, *Australia in the War of 1939–45*, Series 1, Army, Vol. VI, *The New Guinea Offensives*, Canberra: Australian War Memorial, 1961

Fairhead, Fred, *A Duty Done: A summary of operations by the Royal Australian Regiment in the Vietnam War 1965–1972*, Adelaide: Royal Australian Regiment Association of SA, 2014

Feuer, A.B., *Australian Commandos: Their secret war against the Japanese in World War II*, Mechanicsburg, Pennsylvania: Stackpole Books, 2005

Forbes, Cameron, *The Korean War: Australia in the giant's playground*, Sydney: Pan Macmillan, 2010

Gallaway, Jack, *The Last Call of the Bugle*, Brisbane: University of Queensland Press, 1999

Grant, Zalin, *Facing the Phoenix*, New York: WW Norton & Company, 1991

Green, Olwyn, *The Name's Still Charlie: Lieutenant-Colonel Charles Green DSO*, Sydney: Australian Military History Publications, 2010

Ham, Paul, *Vietnam: The Australian war*, Sydney: Harper Collins, 2007

Harris, A.M., *Only One River to Cross: An Australian soldier behind enemy lines in Korea*, Loftus: Australian Military History Publications, 2004

Hastings, Max, *The Korean War*, London: Pan Books, 2010

Horner, David, *Duty First: The Royal Australian Regiment in war and peace*, Sydney: Allen & Unwin, 1990

Lockhart, Greg, *The Minefield: An Australian tragedy in Vietnam*, Sydney: Allen & Unwin, 2007

Long, Gavin, *Australia in the War of 1939–45*, Series 1, Army, Vol. VII, *The Final Campaigns*, Canberra: Australian War Memorial, 1963

—— *The Six Years War: A concise history of Australia in the 1939–45 war*, Canberra: Australian War Memorial and Australian Government Publishing Service, 1973

MacNeill, Ian, *The Team: Australian Army advisers in Vietnam, 1962–1972*, Brisbane: University of Queensland Press and Canberra: Australian War Memorial, 1984

O'Dowd, Ben, *In Valiant Company*, Brisbane: University of Queensland Press, 2000

O'Neill, Robert, *Australia in the Korean War 1950–53*, Vol. II, *Combat Operations*, Canberra: Australian War Memorial and Australian Government Publishing Service, 1985

Pears, Maurie, *Battlefield Korea*, Army History Unit and Australian Military History Publications, Sydney, 2007

Pennington, Vic, *The Team in Vietnam: The lighter side*, Adelaide: Wakefield Press, 1992

Russell, W.B., *The Second Fourteenth Battalion: A history of an Australian infantry battalion in the Second World War*, Sydney: Angus & Robertson, 1948

Thompson, Peter and Macklin, Robert, *Keep Off the Skyline: The story of Ron Cashman and the Diggers in Korea*, Milton, Qld: John Wiley & Sons, 2004

Uren, Malcolm, *A Thousand Men at War: The story of the 2/16th Battalion, A.I.F.*, London: Heinemann, 1959

JOURNAL ARTICLES

Coad, Major-General B.A., 'The Land Campaign in Korea', *Journal of the Royal United Service Institution*, vol. XCVII, February 1952

A Retrospective on Counterinsurgency Operations: The Tay Ninh Provincial Reconnaissance Unit and Its Role in the Phoenix Program, 1969–70 (Centre for the Study of Intelligence—CIA)

NEWSPAPERS/MAGAZINES

The Advertiser (2 March 1951; 31 October 1951; 21 July 1953; 24 March 1954; 3 October 2008)

The Argus (11 October 1954; 12 October 1954)

The Australian (25 April 2008)

The Australian Women's Weekly (28 February 1962)

The Barrier Miner (2 November 1951)

The Courier-Mail (10 February 1953)

The Guardian (14 April 2000)

The News (24 April 1951; 30 October 1951)

The Sunday Mail (29 August 1953)

The Sydney Morning Herald (21 July 1953; 6 April 2004)

PRINCIPAL WEBSITES

<cia.gov/library/center-for-the-study-of-intelligence/csi-publications/csi-studies/studies/vol51no2/a-retrospective-on-counterinsurgency-operations.html>

<Koreanwaronline.com>

<pacificwrecks.com/aircraft/b-24/42–40682.html>

<rand.org/content/dam/rand/pubs/occasional_papers/2009/RAND_OP258.pdf>

<serendipity.li/cia/operation_phoenix.htm>

INDEX